Seek Jesus intently
Seek Sobriety intently

Seek abstinance
Seek Humility
Seek Honesty
Seek Wisdom
Seek patience
Seek Love
Seek peace
Seek innocence
Seek discipline
Seek Balance
Seek Truth
Seek Sobriety
Seek adventure
Seek fellowship

The Beautiful Dream

PEGGY SIMS

God bless you!
Peggy Sims

DEDICATION

I dedicate this book to You, Jesus. You are my Life, my Hope and my Salvation. You gave me *The Beautiful Dream*, and I am forever grateful! Because of it, I cannot be satisfied with anything less than drawing closer to You. Thank You for giving me this *dream gift* to treasure as I make my way closer to our Father's heart. And thank You for sending Holy Spirit to me, who is constantly making this dream come to life through Your Word. I dedicate this book to You, Jesus, my King, my Warrior and the Lover of my soul. It is my song of praise, honor, thanks and love. I give it to You for everything I have is Yours. Use it as You desire. I love You, Jesus, because You have loved me so extravagantly — *and You always will!*

APPRECIATION

To my wonderful husband and best friend, Mark—There is only One I love more, and I know you are happy about that! I respect and honor you for your faithfulness to God and your amazing love for our wonderful family. Your love for God's children is beautiful and is expressed so well through the many gifts God has blessed you with. I love that about you! Thank you for encouraging me through every step of my journey with Jesus. You have cheered me on as I have endeavored to use my words for God's glory. I appreciate your help with the Greek and Hebrew words mentioned in the book. Thank you for loving me as Christ loves His Bride *and* for bringing much needed humor into my life! I love you so very much!

Thank you to those in the Body of Christ who have encouraged me in so many different ways through the years. The weak, the strong, the funny, the serious, the wild, the stoic, the athletic, the academic, the quiet, the boisterous, and everyone in between—all of you have such a special place in my heart because you love well. As I write this, I can see your faces playing in my mind like a video. I wouldn't be able to name everyone here because there are so many. You have helped lift me up to a higher place in my walk with Jesus. I love y'all! You're amazing and appreciate you so much!

CONTENTS

The chapters are not long and contain quite a bit of scripture. You may want to try reading aloud while listening to your favorite Christian soaking instrumental music. I hope you'll take your time reading and let God's Spirit give you personal revelation from His Word. Be seated and enjoy Jesus' company!

INTRODUCTION

The Bakery

1960's Asuncion, Paraguay

Mama and I had been to the open market and filled her big baskets with all sorts of vegetables and fruits. I was around five years old and too young for school, so Mama let me tag along. On the way home she let me know that we were going to stop off at the *Check Bakery*.

She parked the car beside the road, and we walked on the cleanly swept dirt yard toward a small one-story stucco house. The big shady trees all around were inviting. I turned toward the yard thinking, "I would like to play out here!" But Mama called me to follow her inside. As we opened the door, the aroma of fresh baked bread overwhelmed me!

We stepped inside, and right away I noticed the floor looked just like the checkers board game we had at home—only the floor was made of large black and white tiles. "That's why it's called the *Check Bakery*," I thought to myself. The floor was clean but worn out, just like the old house. I noticed some flour dust on the floor in the room opposite to the entrance. I imagined *that* was the kitchen where the bread was being baked.

The front room was dark and mostly lit by the tall windows. Mama turned to the left and walked over to greet the baker, but my eyes distracted me from listening to the kind exchange of Spanish words. Between Mama and the baker was a display of pastries that lit up my senses like blinking lights on a Christmas tree! Mama rarely took me along when she went to market, and

I'm sure this was one reason why!

There were all sorts of tea cookies of every different flavor and color: Macaroons, pastries with jam nestled in the center, palmiers, cream horns and so much more, just trapped behind the glass. I had never seen anything like it in my very young life!

I tried to get her attention to show her all of the pastries, but she just ignored me. I tugged on her dress and whispered to her respectfully, pointing my finger at one of the delicacies. She obviously didn't hear me, so I raised my voice a little louder, interrupting her conversation with the baker. Mama leaned down and kindly but sternly said, "No, Peggy," and finished paying for her purchase. I couldn't understand why Mama was only getting two loaves of bread when there were all of those beautiful, sweet things she could buy!

After getting into the car, she pulled one of the fresh hot loaves from the paper bag and handed it to me. The steam billowed out as I tore a huge chunk off one end. My cravings were satisfied as I began to explore the difference in the soft middle and the crispy nutty taste of the top crust. In that moment I forgot about the pastries, and our family of six enjoyed the delicious bread for several days. But it was never better than fresh out of the *Check Bakery* oven! I entered first grade and don't remember going back into the bakery for several years.

As missionary families did many years ago, we took a year of furlough in the USA to visit family and to stay familiar with American culture. My parents spoke in churches to encourage congregations to support missions. We kids often had to dress up in the historic cultural Paraguayan attire to support the cause. After a year, we would return to Paraguay for four more years, and this pattern would repeat again and again. So this story picks up *several* years later when I was much older.

On the way home from school one afternoon, Mama told us kids that she was going to swing by the new *Check Bakery*. I was amazed! It was in a new location. The bakery had a beautiful walkway from the sidewalk leading to the front door. The green grass on either side of the walkway was perfectly manicured and thriving in the tropical sunshine. The flowers gracing the house were like something in a storybook. The stucco building was brand new and freshly painted with a shady inviting porch in front.

As we entered, the aroma brought back sweet memories, and *there* was the same checkered black and white tiled floor — *only shiny and new!* The front room was smaller than the old one but full of light, not only from the windows, but from the bright fluorescent lights overhead and in the new curved glass display. Even though I was several years older, the sweets were just as beautiful and tempting as before!

The baker's wife cheerfully greeted Mama, remembering her well. The others were called from the kitchen to the front to say hello and briefly catch up. Mama introduced me to them because I had grown up *a lot* since they had seen me last. As I listened to their conversation, I noticed several things I had missed many years earlier. The people who ran the bakery were all from the same family! They spoke with an unusual accent, and they were fair-skinned and blonde, unlike most Paraguayans!

Suddenly I put two and two together and continued to look and listen for further clues. As we walked toward the car with our loaves of fresh hot bread I asked my mother, "Are they Czechoslovakian?" She answered, "Yes." With a little embarrassment I chuckled, "Oh. I always thought you called it the *Check Bakery* because of the floor!"

We got in the car and all of us kids devoured an entire delicious hot loaf of bread! That sweet bakery probably had a different name altogether, but I choose to remember it by our nick-name and the checkered floor. The smell of freshly baked bread, sugary-crunchy palmiers and eye-catching cream horns always will remind me of the *Czech Bakery!*

In a way, this childhood story of mine reflects my spiritual growth with God. There were many things I didn't understand when I first met Jesus, but I loved Him! As I matured spiritually, I began to *pay attention* to the Holy Spirit. Just opening my spiritual eyes and ears helped me understand the Lord and His family so much better.

I feel honored as the Lord reveals truth to me at a deeper level of relationship with Him. Those moments invite me to desire another encounter with Jesus. And so often I hear the Lord calling me to simply sit with Him and eat the Bread of the Gospel — the greatest of all revelations that grows sweeter with every experience. It is the personal revelation of His Love being unveiled in my heart. Just as the *Check Bakery* changed to the *Czech Bakery* for me in one moment of time, the Holy Spirit can reveal God's Word in an instant and change your heart forever!

See Notes: #1 The Bakery

I

The Beautiful Dream

Scene One

I was standing alone in a dark place, looking straight ahead. There were no stars and no moon. All I could see were wavy strings of white floating vapor against a dark backdrop in the distance. They formed what looked like a ridge of mountains. But really, it was only a void – nothing beautiful to look at. My soul felt numb.

Someone was approaching me from behind on my right side. I didn't see him, but I sensed his presence coming toward me. Strangely, I wasn't afraid. As he came closer, I turned my head to the right and looked into his face and then his eyes. I felt lovingly drawn to him, even though I didn't know who he was.

His face was handsome to me – of olive skin tone and clean-shaven. Though he had chiseled masculine features, his countenance was softly inviting. He had dark, medium length hair that was straight and layered, and his dark black eyes looked back into mine.

With the kindness of a true gentleman he asked me to dance with him – even though he spoke no words from his mouth. I quickly agreed, and then suddenly felt uncomfortable with the thought that he might discover my flaws. As he approached me I thought to myself, "I don't know how to dance!" All I knew about dancing was that I should follow his lead.

Standing behind me, he placed his arms loosely around me with his hands on the front part of my waist. I placed my hands over his. He kept his head near my right ear.

As soon as he touched me I felt intense love like I've never felt in my whole life! His love permeated my being and all my cares were gone — *all of them!* I was instantly in love! He danced the most simple but beautiful dance with me — deeply romantic but purely innocent. We took slow steps swaying to the left and to the right. He even dipped me gently to the left and to the right. All too soon, the dance was over.

Then he stood beside me. Still saying no words, he asked to see me again and I eagerly agreed. I asked him when I would see Him again. He said he would return to me, but when he answered, the day and time was unclear.

Scene Two

I saw my husband, Mark, and myself sitting together on sand-toned concrete bleachers, the big squared chunky kind. It was daytime and there were no other people there. The scene was zoomed in on the area where we were seated so that I couldn't see how high or wide the bleachers were.

I was telling Mark all about the amazing man I had danced with and how much I loved him. The immense love and joy I felt when I danced with the man was still just as strong! Mark was so happy for me as I told him with great enthusiasm how the man's love had completely transformed me. He wanted to hear all about it!

Scene Three

The man who danced with me was leading me into a room of his house. He was to my right as we walked, and I was still full of ecstasy! The opening into this room was wide, slightly arched, with curved edges and no doors. There was a table in the room, so I assumed it was a dining room, however, there was nothing on the table to define its purpose. There was no decor in the house. It was clean, white, and bright with possibly a faint sky-blue hue.

As we walked toward the room, I wanted to ask him when we could be alone again. I loved him so much! But I sensed this wasn't the right time, so with joyful anticipation, I kept silent. It seemed that he was escorting me into a very important meeting with his family, but I was not anxious about it at all. Love and acceptance were in the atmosphere, and I knew I was right where I was supposed to be. I felt so special!

As we entered the room, we approached an oblong table. It had rounded corners and seated eight. He led me around the left end of the table to the first chair on the other side. I stood behind my chair like everyone else. My chair was across the table from *him*, next to one end of the table. The mother stood at the other end of the table. I turned my head to the left to look at her because she seemed to be in charge at that moment. She was rather large and she wore a solid pink dress like the one my mother wore to her grandchildren's weddings.

Absent-mindedly, I gazed upward and to my left at the blank white ceiling. I was still daydreaming about the man I loved — even though he was right there across the table from me. I was still wondering when I could be alone with him again! He was so amazing!

All of a sudden I glanced back down and realized that everyone was seated except me! I felt so embarrassed and ashamed. I didn't know what to do. Right then, the mother stood back up and everyone at the table followed her lead. They stood as well. Then I heard the mother say kindly to everyone, "Be seated." At that moment, I woke up from the dream.

2

Awake

On February 21, 2013, I awoke from this dream feeling like a teenager in love. But then I suddenly became alarmed! The man I had dreamed about was *not my husband!* I danced with the man in the dream, and *I was so in love with him!* I began to ask God to forgive me for having the dream. But right away I remembered scene two, where my husband, Mark, was thrilled about my love-relationship with the man.

At that moment, I knew this dream was from God and I had danced with Jesus, God's Son! I can't express the overwhelming awe I felt! Jesus came in such an intimate way to reveal His love for me. That morning, I was flooded with tears of joy and anticipation. The dream contained secrets for me to discover. So, I asked the Lord for an interpretation and the dream has been unfolding to me ever since.

Around two weeks later, I was sitting at our kitchen table having some alone time with God and I asked the Father a question. "Father, why was I seated to your left?" I heard Him quickly respond, "Because I want you close to my heart." I welled up with tears and was awestruck by His answer! His love was so strong that I had to stop everything and just let Him love me.

To this day I picture my Heavenly Father seated to my right assuring me of His love and faithfulness, the Holy Spirit at the other end of the Table assuring me that I am dearly loved and accepted, and Jesus across from me where I can look into His wonderful face! All my Brothers and Sisters in Christ from all over the world are there too! Our God is so amazing! I don't know how He does it, but I believe each of His children have been offered the same seating arrangement. Father God loves us so much that He wants us *seated very close – next to His heart!*

The Common Thread

The thread woven so deeply throughout this dream is God's immense love. If I had the ability to convince you of anything through this dream, it would be that God loves you with a pure and unending love unlike any earthly love, and that He is worth pursuing with *all* of your heart!

Why Did God Give Me This Dream?

I fell in love with Jesus when I was eleven years old and knew that He loved me. I had made it my habit to pray, read His Word, worship, serve and stay away from sin. I wrote songs to Jesus, sang them in public and told my classmates about Jesus because I loved Jesus so much. I had a good relationship with Jesus and served Him the best way I knew how. But for most of my life I felt very insecure. My striving to do things to prove my worth revealed that I didn't have a true revelation of my identity, value and inheritance as God's child.

Not long before I had this dream, I was struck by a very painful physical attack all over my body. I realize now that it was a spiritual attack from the devil on my soul that eventually affected my body. I loved the Lord and didn't want to misrepresent Him so I *pushed on* despite the pain. I knew Jesus would heal me but didn't know how He was going to do it. The physical pain I experienced took me by surprise and I was finding it hard to receive the healing I needed from God. I began to focus on the love of God.

Pressing into His goodness I prayed, "*Jesus, I just want to be close to You! I'll do whatever You say, even if it is embarrassing.*" This amazing dream was His response to my desperate prayer! It was an invitation to seek Him with my whole heart and to know His supernatural healing love at a higher level!

But several years after the dream, I realized that I didn't know how to *be seated with God* as well as I had believed. Without asking the Lord I tried a special diet and various natural therapies to try and ease the physical pain. If the Lord orders the diet or the therapy it will help you physically, emotionally, spiritually, mentally and in every way. But I never sincerely asked Holy Spirit waiting for His response, so I was *not following* the Spirit. The more I *put my hope and trust* in these other things the more anxious I became.

I finally realized that *The Beautiful Dream* was God wooing me to Himself alone. I also learned through the dips of my mistakes that He would catch me because I really did love Him. I just needed to learn to *follow His lead!*

With all other options off the table, I have been pursuing the Lord with all my heart, soul, mind and strength. *The Beautiful Dream* gave me a foundation of truth for victory. Though it is taking me a while to battle through the lies of the enemy, repent of them and renew my mind in God's Word, every victory has brought me closer into God's love, wholeness and hope for fulfilling His plan for my life. My mountain is being moved like a series of landslides crumbling into the sea. But by faith, it is moving!

Saying *yes* to Jesus is a daily choice, an honor and an adventure. *Following His lead* has been like taking the clumsiest woman in the world and *teaching her to dance.* But Jesus doesn't give up because this clumsy dancer is His Bride and she will forever be in His arms of love! I felt Jesus' love in the dream and it literally felt like Heaven. In the dream, I never felt like crying—even for joy. That's because Jesus wiped away every tear. There is nothing on earth that compares to Him! Jesus is the King who rescued us by His love and He alone is worth living and dying for!

Why Did I Write This Book?

The dream itself was so vivid and filled with *God's life-giving power* that I knew this was a gift that needed to be shared with God's children. As I began to *search God's Word* through the clues in this dream, the Lord showed me things I had not really *seen* before. I do not claim to come close to understanding all Truth. The closer I get to Jesus, the more I realize that His love is wider, longer, higher and deeper than I can imagine! *The Beautiful Dream* was not supposed to be kept a secret. So I give it away as God's loving prophetic message to you.

Many Christians are living their lives from the earthly realm hoping God who lives in the heavenly realms will take notice and do something for them. Scripture tells us that *Jesus has already provided everything for us* through His death on the cross. He has taken us to the Father and *seated us with God* in the heavenly realms so we can live out our lives on earth by the power of the Holy Spirit.

Your life story may be very different from mine. But the message in this dream is the same for all of us — male, female, young or old. As you read, may the light of God's Word and His phenomenal love flood you with desire for an even more intimate and honest relationship with God. Jesus loves you more than you can imagine! He invites you to *dance, dine and reign* with Him in this life and forever!

3

A Short Interpretation

Scene One
Jesus comes to you and offers to rescue you from the kingdom of darkness as only He can do. All Jesus asks is a sincere *yes* to His invitation to becoming one with Him and *follow His lead*. The moment He touches you, Jesus supernaturally cleanses you from all evil, fear and shame. God's Holy Spirit comes inside you, fills you with *indescribable love* and *eternal life*. You are *born again* and become God's child.

God freely gives you forgiveness of sin, healing, protection, provision, deliverance, righteousness and His loving character for eternity through His Spirit. You love Jesus *so much* that you want to be close to Him, follow Him and obey Him.

Scene Two
You are seated with someone *on earth* telling them about Jesus. His life inside you is like a seed in your heart. Telling someone about your encounter with Jesus is the first fruit of your spiritual tree!

God's love in you is overflowing and blessing others! Jesus has changed the way you view God, yourself and everyone. You realize that those who know Jesus are also in love with Him. They have also been set free! Their hearts and faces are free of fear and shame and they love the Lord like you do. Jesus is the foundation and source of your life but you still need to grow. You need to go *higher up the steps of faith and love* in Christ Jesus.

Scene Three

Jesus takes us to the *heavenly realms* to be seated next to our Father. Our eternity has begun in the Spirit as we live on earth! We were *born again* to have an *actual intimate loving relationship* with God. Many believers pay a lot of attention to living in the earthly realm but very little attention to living in the Spirit.

When a believer only lives from the earthly realm, their spiritual tree will begin to wither. They have not understood who they are in Christ. Following the Spirit happens while we are seated with God in the heavenly realms where the atmosphere is extravagant love.

Christians who don't realize that Jesus has taken them to the heavenly realms are easily affected by earthly circumstances. They can be pulled downward by trusting in the lies of the enemy. What other people think is more important to them than what God thinks. They have exchanged the truth that sets them free for lies that bind them up. *Fear* and *shame* creep back in — the very things Jesus freed us from! They have not been *paying attention* to God by being seated with Him.

We stay connected to God by being seated with God in the Spirit. His perfect love drives out everything that doesn't belong in Heaven. I'm not saying that the earth is Heaven. I'm saying that through the Spirit, *Heaven has come to us* even in a dark and chaotic world!

God placed a desire to succeed inside every human, but separation from God distorted that gift. When Jesus places us back into God's presence, He restores our purpose. We have been asked to *be seated* above the chaos where God can speak to us, heal us and empower us to fulfill our destiny in His strength, not in our own. *But we have to want to be close to Jesus so much that we will do whatever He says, no matter the cost!* We can live in the atmosphere of God's love and grace if we'll be seated in the heavenly realms and follow God's lead.

God's Love

God's romantic love was so overpowering in every scene of the dream. *God's saving grace feels like extravagant love!* His love is now my driving force to know Jesus more intimately. I don't just want the feeling. I want *Jesus* and what *He* desires! What He desires for us is always very good!

Come close to God, and God will come close to you.

James 4:8a NLT

According to some scholars, the writers of the New Testament came up with a new word in the Greek language for God's love. That is because they had *experienced God's supernatural love so fully* and there was absolutely no word to describe it. The word written in English is *Agape*, pronounced: *ah-GAH-peh*. The writers sometimes used this special word. Other times they wrote "the love of God" or *implied it* in the passage of scripture. I think it is safe to say that when the Word of God refers to love that comes *from God*, whether in the Old or New Testament, it is the same *supernatural Agape love* that drenched me in *The Beautiful Dream*! It feels like Heaven!

And I pray that you, being rooted and established in love, may have power, together with all the Lord's holy people, to grasp how wide and long and high and deep is the love of Christ, and to know this love that surpasses knowledge — that you may be filled to the measure of all the fullness of God.

Ephesians 3b:17-19 NIV

Paul, who wrote the book of Ephesians in the Bible, had experienced this *full measure of God's love* that I experienced in the dream! We can all experience God's Agape Love, seated with Him at His Table! God has freed us from fear and shame!

God is love.   *1 John 4:8b NIV*

From this point forward in the book, I will capitalize the word Love or use the word *Agape* when referring to God's Love. This *Agape Love* drives out all evil bringing complete wholeness —

spirit, soul and body. I also capitalized Family, Church, Brothers and Sisters when referring to those seated with God in the heavenly realms. There are a few other capitalized words like Heaven and the Blood. I get a little carried away magnifying the Lord and His Kingdom! But it also helps keep the reading simple instead of explaining every time.

This book is the unfolding of *The Beautiful Dream* for God's children. This book is more than just the interpretation God gave to me personally. I have taken the dream and asked the Spirit for relevant truth in the Word of God that I believe many born again Christians need today. They are not new revelations, but maybe they are explained from a new perspective — through the lens of *The Beautiful Dream*.

Wherever you are in your relationship with Jesus, I believe this book will encourage you to let God Love you more fully so that you can live fearlessly and courageously for His glory. I hope you will experience *a new beginning* in your intimate relationship with God because that is what God wants.

As you read *The Beautiful Dream,* I pray that you will step into a new realm with God — the realm of His supernatural, powerful and transformational Love. May you experience the *light* of the Father's Presence, devour the *Bread of Life* and taste for yourself the *sweet delicacies* of the Holy Spirit! And if you do, you will be overwhelmed by the goodness of our God, the extravagant Love He has for you and the fellowship we have with Him and one another, *seated together at His Table in the heavenly realms!*

You have been given a place of honor at God's Table — next to the Father's heart, across from Jesus, and lead by the beautiful and powerful Holy Spirit. More than ever before, Holy Spirit is now saying to the Bride of Christ, *"Be Seated."*

4

God Came to Us

For this is how God loved the world: He gave his one and only Son, so that everyone who believes in him will not perish but have eternal life. God sent his Son into the world not to judge the world, but to save the world through him. There is no judgment against anyone who believes in him. But anyone who does not believe in him has already been judged for not believing in God's one and only Son.

John 3:16-18 NLT

In *The Beautiful Dream*, Jesus came to me—not the other way around. His eyes were black because He saw me in darkness and came to set me free. God has always made the first move. He has shown His Love to everyone in the beauty of creation and in so many other ways.

He causes His sun to rise on the evil and the good, and sends rain on the righteous and the unrighteous.

Matthew 5:45b NASB

The Father Loved us before we ever knew Him and sent His Son, Jesus, to take the punishment for our sin! God wanted us close to Him again. His motivation was His amazing Love!

We love, because he first loved us.   *1 John 4:19 NASB*

It doesn't matter what you have done, good or bad, where you came from, how much money you have or what you look like. God doesn't Love you any less or any more than any other person on earth. He Loves us all very uniquely and perfectly. Jesus invites every person to *receive and experience* His transforming Agape Love.

The first two people on earth, Adam and Eve, walked and talked with God in His pure Agape Love. God had given them purpose, destiny, responsibilities and perfect satisfaction in the assignments He delegated to them. They never lacked the strength, wisdom or joy to rule the earth as God had asked them to do. They lived in God's presence on earth!

But one day they listened to Satan and disobeyed God. Their spirits became separated from God. Sin cut them off from God's presence, but He didn't stop Loving them! Because of their sin, mankind *inherited a sinful nature and a sentence of death.* This meant that every person's body would eventually die. But worse than that, it meant that when they died physically, they would continue to be spiritually separated from God for eternity in hell, where there is no Agape Love at all. But God *Loved us so much*, He had *a plan* to bring us back into His arms!

When we were utterly helpless, Christ came at just the right time and died for us sinners. Now, most people would not be willing to die for an upright person, though someone might perhaps be willing to die for a person who is especially good. But God showed his great love for us by sending Christ to die for us while we were still sinners.

Romans 5:6-8 NLT

The one and only *true* God is holy and faithful. He will never sin. The Bible tells us that God is *three persons in One*: Father, Son (Jesus), and Holy Spirit. God is always in unity. Unlike us, God sees and understands *everything*, therefore, He alone is Judge.

The sentence for mankind's sin is *death*—the absence of God's presence. In hell there is nothing good, because *everything good* we experience here on earth has been given to us from God. Even the Love we experience before we meet Jesus has been loaned to us by God to draw us to Himself. He gives us a taste of His Love so we will desire a relationship with Him. But total separation from God is everything evil we can imagine — excruciating pain, hatred and terror forever. The God who Loves us offers to change our horrible sentence!

For the wages of sin is death, but the free gift of God is eternal life in Christ Jesus our Lord.

Romans 6:23 NASB

In the dream, Jesus *came* and *gave* me eternal life. All I did was say *yes* and His dance set me totally free. We can't *earn* the gift. In this world, if someone owes money, they *work* to pay off the debt. If they commit a crime, they *do jail-time* to *earn their release*. But the Kingdom of God is different.

We are all infected and impure with sin. When we display our righteous deeds, they are nothing but filthy rags.

Isaiah 64:6 NLT

The sentence of death we inherited cannot be reversed by doing good works or by being punished in this life. Only the *blood-sacrifice* of a perfect, sinless person can take our sin-debt away. That sinless person is Jesus, God's Son!

... and without shedding of blood there is no forgiveness.

Hebrews 9:22b NASB

God Loved us so much that He sent His only Son, Jesus, to earth as a baby, to be born from a virgin named Mary. Jesus did not inherit a sinful nature because the Holy Spirit placed Jesus in Mary's womb. Jesus was born in human form like us, grew up around sinful people and was tempted to sin just like us — but He always chose not to sin.

Look! The virgin will conceive a child! She will give birth to a son, and they will call him Immanuel, which means "God is with us."

Matthew 1:23 NLT

Jesus, *Immanuel*, came to us! When He was 30 years old, He began to teach about God, heal the sick, and drive demons out of people setting them free! After three years of ministry, the religious leaders of His day were *so jealous of Jesus* that they had Him beaten and nailed to a cross. Jesus never fought back because He knew that His death was going to *bring us life!* After Jesus died, God raised Him from the dead!

... They killed him by hanging him on a cross, but God raised him from the dead on the third day and caused him to be seen... All the prophets testify about him that everyone who believes in him receives forgiveness of sins through his name.
                                                    Acts 10:39-40,43 NIV

Our eternal death sentence has been *paid in full by Jesus!* Those who receive Jesus *instantly* receive God's mercy and free gift of grace. We are made holy by believing that Jesus came and died to pay for our sin. Jesus paid for *all* of our sin! But even more, God's Holy Spirit comes inside us so that we *personally know God* and can *follow Him* every day of our lives!

The one who is the true light, who gives light to everyone, was coming into the world. He came into the very world he created, but the world didn't recognize him. He came to his own people, and even they rejected him. But to all who believed him and accepted him, he gave the right to become children of God. They are reborn—not with a physical birth resulting from human passion or plan, but a birth that comes from God.
                                                    John 1:9-13 NLT

Whoever believes in Jesus as the Savior is *immediately forgiven of all their sin* and becomes God's child. They are *born again*—born of God's Spirit! The Holy Spirit comes inside us to guide us for the rest of our lives on earth. One day, we will be with God in Heaven. But until then, we must be seated with God in the heavenly realms—so we can follow God's lead. This is *the Gospel*, the *Good News* of Jesus Christ!

He will come with his mighty angels, in flaming fire, bringing judgment on those who don't know God and on those who refuse to obey the Good News of our Lord Jesus. They will be punished with eternal destruction, forever separated from the Lord and from his glorious power. When he comes on that day, he will receive glory from his holy people—praise from all who believe. And this includes you, for you believed what we told you about him.

2 *Thessalonians 1:7b-10 NLT*

Those who *reject* God's offer of eternal life and *refuse to follow Jesus* into the Kingdom of God are choosing for themselves eternal separation from God in hell. But there is no reason for anyone to reject their Creator and Savior! Jesus Loves us so much that *He came to save us!* There is only one way to be saved—through Jesus, and everyone is invited to live in His Agape Love at God's Table!

There is salvation in no one else! God has given no other name under heaven by which we must be saved.

Acts 4:12 NLT

The Greek word, *sozo*, in the Bible means *saved*. It doesn't only mean saved from hell. It also means healed, protected, rescued, provided for and so much more. It means *everything is made right!* In *The Beautiful Dream*, Jesus came to me and asked me to dance with Him. I said *yes*, and Jesus *saved* me! *All evil left* and Jesus filled me with *supernatural life* that felt like perfect Love.

Salvation is not a process, it's *instantaneous*. But like tree, we have to stay connected to the root and drink from the life-filled water that comes from the root system. The seed that gave us life was Jesus, and our root system is God. He *came to us* and gave us life. Now we stay connected to God because He is the source of life! Jesus makes connecting with God possible by seating us with Him in the heavenly realms. That's where we learn to live in the Spirit by paying attention to Him. That is where we can stay in the atmosphere of His extravagant Love!

The Lord is not slow about His promise, as some count slowness, but is patient toward you, not willing for any to perish, but for all to come to repentance.

2 Peter 3:9 NASB

Jesus is going to come back to earth again one day. But this time He will not come as a baby, but as King. And He will take those who follow Him to His Kingdom in Heaven.

In scene one, I was staring into a dark spiritual scene. Jesus came to me and recreated my whole life—He saved me! We were all in darkness and couldn't go to God—so *God came to us* through Jesus and set us free!

In scene two, God's Love was so powerful in me that I had to tell someone! But God had even more in store for me. He has so much more for all of us who want to remain in Him!

In scene three, because I *danced* with Jesus and *followed His lead*, Jesus took me to the Father where there was no darkness—*only light!* We can *be seated* spiritually with God because of Jesus. God wants to teach us, protect us, provide for us, heal us, rescue us, and do miraculous things through us for His glory.

Jesus has come to you. He invites you to be forgiven, *free of guilt and shame,* and to become a temple of God's Holy Spirit. You can have a real relationship with God and experience the freeing power of His Love every day of your life! He will reveal your God-given destiny and empower you to fulfill it! I hope you will say *yes* to Jesus. His *dance* is full of grace *and* supernatural Agape Love!

Declaration

JESUS CAME TO ME!

5

Turning to Jesus

The view I saw in the first scene of *The Beautiful Dream* was quite dark with only a few wavy white horizontal strands of light. I sensed someone approaching from behind me on the right side. The moment I *turned my face* away from the darkness and looked into His face, *I knew something good was about to happen.*

The Love of Jesus had already begun to draw my heart to Him. So when He asked me to dance with Him, I did not refuse. *I said yes,* and the *instant* He touched me *I was transformed!* All darkness and shame left me. Nothing else mattered from that point on— just Jesus!

Turning away from darkness to say *yes* to Jesus is called *repentance.* Repentance in the Bible means *changing the way we think.* We do this by *agreeing with Jesus* and *following His lead* instead of going our own way. When we do, He becomes our Savior *and* King! Our whole life will change!

From that time Jesus began to preach and say, "Repent, for the kingdom of heaven is at hand."
Matthew 4:17 NASB

Even we Christians can find ourselves in a dark place, holding on to only a few strands of light. When that happens, we have forgotten who we are in Christ and who God truly is! We have misunderstood the Gospel. We need to *change the way we think!*

Some Christians try to live in the kingdom of darkness *and* the Kingdom of Light. But the ways of this world and the ways of God are *polar opposites*. Satan, the ruler of darkness, will drive you like a taskmaster to *do more, do better and succeed*. And when you don't succeed Satan calls you a failure. But the King of the Kingdom of Heaven is a gentleman, *inviting you into His dance of Love*. When you repent of sin and say *yes* to His Love, He forgives you and makes you holy — set apart for Himself! You aren't a slave to sin and shame! You belong to Jesus!

No one can serve two masters; for either he will hate the one and love the other, or he will be devoted to one and despise the other. You cannot serve God and wealth.

Matthew 6:24 NASB

Repentance doesn't *try Jesus out* or just *believe some of the things* He has said in the Bible. When we turn to Jesus, He rescues us and makes us *one* with Him!

Those who love their life in this world will lose it. Those who care nothing for their life in this world will keep it for eternity. Anyone who wants to serve me must follow me, because my servants must be where I am. And the Father will honor anyone who serves me.

John 12:25-26 NLT

Repentance is letting go of your own desires and *giving your whole heart to Jesus*, choosing to *be where God is*, in the heavenly realms, instead of being grounded in the world. This is done by *faith* — not because you have every question answered. Repentance is *trusting Jesus* with your entire life.

Do not lay up for yourselves treasures on earth, where moth and rust destroy and where thieves break in and steal, but lay up for yourselves treasures in heaven, where neither moth nor rust destroys and where thieves do not break in and steal. For where your treasure is, there your heart will be also.

Matthew 6:19-21 NKJV

Repentance is turning your gaze away from the earthly realm and being seated face to face with Jesus in the heavenly realms. The Lord will help you *think differently*, and change your priorities. Even though you are completely *saved* by God's grace, your mind, will and emotions will need to grow in God's truth. You lived by certain *patterns of the world*, but now you will be *transformed* daily by living from a different realm!

Peter replied, "Each of you must repent of your sins and turn to God, and be baptized in the name of Jesus Christ for the forgiveness of your sins. Then you will receive the gift of the Holy Spirit. This promise is to you, to your children, and to those far away—all who have been called by the Lord our God."

Acts 2:38-39 NLT

God Loves you so much! He wants to bless you with the power of the Holy Spirit. He will give you supernatural power to live in Agape Love and help you with every decision you make.

Those whom I love, I rebuke and discipline; therefore be zealous and repent.

Revelation 3:19 NASB

In the scripture above, Jesus was talking to Christians. In fact, He was telling about *the end times* that we are living in right now. Many believers will be *deceived* by the devil and tempted to *drop out of the dance with Jesus.* Jesus warns us to stay close to Him through the Holy Spirit so that our Agape Love *for Him and our new Family* stays strong.

If you give your life to Jesus, He will never leave you! He won't break His covenant with you. But if you decide to rebel against Him, it is possible for you to leave Him. Turning away from Jesus can harden your heart, so you don't spiritually see or hear clearly. It is so difficult to find your way back home when you are spiritually blind and deaf. *But with God all things are possible!* So, keep your heart and mind tender and close to God.

When the Spirit reveals actions or attitudes that aren't from God, be humble, *repent* and ask His forgiveness. *He is faithful to forgive!* But don't live your life *fearing* that you might not be saved! If you keep telling God you are so sorry about the same things He has already forgiven you of, you may be having trouble believing in God's grace. Start *thanking Him* that you are forgiven and enjoy the freedom Jesus paid for you to have!

John the Baptist (John who baptized) was very harsh with the Jewish religious leaders because at that time in history they claimed to Love God, but their hearts were full of evil pride. Instead of being compassionate and helping people in need, they were dishonest and cruel. Their lives showed that they had turned away from their Loving God.

But when he [John] saw many Pharisees and Sadducees coming to watch him baptize, he denounced them. "You brood of snakes!" he exclaimed. "Who warned you to flee the coming wrath? Prove by the way you live that you have repented of your sins and turned to God. Don't just say to each other, 'We're safe, for we are descendants of Abraham.' That means nothing, for I tell you, God can create children of Abraham from these very stones. Even now the ax of God's judgment is poised, ready to sever the roots of the trees. Yes, every tree that does not produce good fruit will be chopped down and thrown into the fire."

Matthew 3:7-10 NLT

The religious leaders thought of themselves as *better than everyone else.* They were not *connected* to the presence of God. They knew scripture but they didn't allow God's presence on the Word to change their hearts. Knowing the Bible and knowing the One who spoke it into being are two very different things. Those who *turn to Jesus* have experienced His Love. They realize that we are all very special in His eyes!

After this, Jesus went out and saw a tax collector by the name of Levi sitting at his tax booth. "Follow me," Jesus said to him, and Levi got up, left everything and followed him. Then Levi held a great banquet for Jesus at his house, and a large crowd of tax collectors and others were eating with them. But the Pharisees and the teachers of the law who belonged to their sect complained to his disciples, "Why do you eat and drink with tax collectors and sinners?" Jesus answered them, "It is not the healthy who need a doctor, but the sick. I have not come to call the righteous, but sinners to repentance."

Luke 5:27-32 NIV

The prideful don't *think* they need to repent. They need to change the way they think! But God specializes in the humble ones who *know they need a Savior*—just like a desperately sick person who stops everything to go to a doctor! When you *turn around* and say *yes* to Jesus, *God will not shame you!* Jesus will give you a brand new life in Him!

Therefore repent and turn back so that your sins may be wiped out, so that times of refreshing may come from the presence of the Lord...

Acts 3:19-20a NET

Demonic forces will try to keep you from *turning to Jesus* and letting go of your past life. They don't want you to experience the Love, truth and freedom Jesus has for you. Jesus is *all-powerful* over every demonic power. He will strengthen you as you say *yes* to Him and *no* to the devil!

If you repent of your sin and say *yes* to Jesus you have been made right with God. Your past, present and future sin has been forgiven because you believe that *Jesus atoned* (made amends) *for your sin on the cross.* Your soul (mind, will and emotions) needs to learn to *be seated in this truth.*

As believers in Jesus Christ, we will need to *renew our minds.* That's part of growing in God. As the Lord reveals His Word through the Spirit, we will *change the way we think* and become more like Him. It's impossible to know everything we need to know at the beginning of our relationship with God. God is very pleased as we mature in Him and get closer to His light.

God is not as interested in us gaining knowledge as He is growing our relationship with Him and remaining in His Love. When we're seated in the heavenly realms, both *knowledge* and *relationship* will come at the same time. Being seated with God keeps us in His Love and helps us resist sin.

Joshua told the people, "Purify yourselves, because tomorrow the LORD will perform miracles among you."

Joshua 3:5 GNT

But if for some reason you do sin, you can *repent*, asking God for forgiveness. If you're sincere, He will forgive you. But thinking you are still the same person you were *before* you received God's grace will give you an excuse to sin. You aren't a "sinner" anymore! You are a new creation in Christ!

Thinking from the earthly realm will make you see yourself and other believers *struggling to become clean*. That's not true. We have already been made clean through our faith in Jesus! If you are seated with God at His Table in the heavenly realms, you will see God's children through His eyes—completely *cleansed* by the Blood of Jesus! Hallelujah! What Jesus did for us was not ordinary. It was powerful enough to drive all our sin away and fill us with His Love!

If you have never met Jesus, He is right there with you asking you for this dance. Turn your heart and mind around and look into His face. Accept His invitation of supernatural Agape Love and simply follow His lead! Jesus will escort you to be seated with your Father in the heavenly realms and Holy Spirit will guide you by His light for the rest of your life!

Declaration

I HAVE DECIDED TO FOLLOW JESUS!

6

Will You Dance with Me?

In *The Beautiful Dream*, Jesus asked me to dance! What does that mean? It is a picture of God *offering* to rescue us and set us free from our own sin and from Satan's plan to destroy our lives.

So, why does Jesus have to *ask* to rescue us? Well, think about it. It would *not* have been a very loving dance if He had *forced* me to dance with Him, right? Salvation is an extravagant *gift* of Love that must be received by *choice*. Only by saying *yes* to Jesus can we enter into a life-giving relationship with God, who Loves us beyond comprehension.

From the beginning, God wanted mankind to *choose* His heart of Love. Adam and Eve enjoyed paradise — walking and talking with God every day in the beautiful Garden of Eden. There was no evil to disrupt their lives!

And they were both naked, the man and his wife, and were not ashamed.

Genesis 2:25 NKJV

God was their Father and authority, but He gave Adam and Eve the joy and responsibility of *ruling* or *managing* the earth. He gave them every plant as food, *except one*, and its fruit was forbidden. They never considered disobeying God until Satan came along and tempted them using lies. They began to question the Love God had for them. Satan is still *deceiving* people today, lying to them and blinding their minds so that they don't *choose* Jesus.

35

If the Good News we preach is hidden behind a veil, it is hidden only from people who are perishing. Satan, who is the god of this world, has blinded the minds of those who don't believe. They are unable to see the glorious light of the Good News. They don't understand this message about the glory of Christ, who is the exact likeness of God.

2 Corinthians 4:3-4 NLT

Adam and Eve were deceived and *chose* to disobey God. In a sense, they had *chosen to dance with Satan.* The moment they ate the forbidden fruit, something terrible happened.

Then the eyes of both of them were opened, and they knew that they were naked; and they sewed fig leaves together and made themselves coverings.

Genesis 3:7 NKJV

For the first time, they felt *fear* and *shame.* God didn't stop Loving them though! He came "looking" for them and "found" them hiding.

Then the LORD God called to Adam and said to him, "Where are you?" So he said, "I heard Your voice in the garden, and I was afraid because I was naked; and I hid myself."

Genesis 3:9-10 NKJV

Full of compassion, God killed an animal and made leather clothing from the skins so they would be *covered.* The animal that died that day represented the sacrifice that Jesus would make many years later for the sin of the whole world. Adam and Eve *chose* God's Love and forgiveness by *choosing* His covering for their guilt.

Jesus said to him, "I am the [only] Way [to God] and the [real] Truth and the [real] Life; no one comes to the Father but through Me.

John 14:6 AMP

Adam and Eve *chose* to let God cover their *fear* and *shame*. They didn't understand that thousands of years later, Jesus would come to die for their sin. But because they *accepted God's mercy*, the blood of Jesus covered their sin *in advance*. Humanity inherited a sinful nature, but God has always offered every person His covering of mercy and grace.

In *The Beautiful Dream*, I *chose* to dance with Jesus but I was *afraid* He would not like me if He noticed my faults. I was *ashamed* of myself. But instead of rejecting me, *He covered* all my fear and shame, filling me with Himself.

In scene three, I was distracted. *Fear* and *shame* caught me off guard. Holy Spirit gave me *another opportunity to believe* that *Jesus had already covered my guilt*. Without *the gift of choice,* we would be like robots, not have the ability to give and receive Love. But when we *choose Jesus*, we get to have a real relationship with our Loving God!

The Bible teaches us to take our old way of thinking captive and renew our minds in the truth. When you said *yes* to Jesus, He saved you spiritually and brought you into His Spirit. But your soul (mind, will and emotions), and your body might fight against the new person you are in Christ. Now that we have the power of the Holy Spirit, we have to *rule* over our soul and body by choosing to believe in God's Love over how we feel. This is like dancing with Jesus! God is so patient and understanding. He knows we aren't always paying attention, but it's time to wake up. We only have one life, and it's in this life that we must *choose to follow God*, the creator of life.

Today I have given you the choice between life and death, between blessings and curses. Now I call on heaven and earth to witness the choice you make. Oh, that you would choose life, so that you and your descendants might live! You can make this choice by loving the LORD your God, obeying him, and committing yourself firmly to him. This is the key to your life.
Deuteronomy 30:19-20a NLT

In the dream, I had a *choice* and I chose life! I chose Jesus! From what I experienced in *The Beautiful Dream*, eternity with Jesus in Heaven is going to be amazing! But Jesus is telling us something extra-ordinary through this dream. Freedom from sin, sickness and oppression is our reality the moment we *choose* Jesus. For that heavenly reality to become a reality on earth, we have to choose to *be seated with God at His Table* in the Spirit.

Many believers live with *fear* and *shame* even after Jesus *covered* their guilt with His Blood. They don't see fear or shame as choices, but they really are. Fear and shame are the result of a guilty conscience. If Jesus forgave us of all sin and removed our guilt, why do we still struggle with fear and shame? We must remember the *dance!* *Fear* and *shame* can affect us spiritually, emotionally, mentally and physically. *Choose life and blessings!*

You were taught, with regard to your former way of life, to put off your old self, which is being corrupted by its deceitful desires; to be made new in the attitude of your minds' and to put on the new self, created to be like God in true righteousness and holiness.

Ephesians 4:22-24 NIV

At the moment you *choose Jesus*, you become *a new creation!* Most of us have been taught that complete freedom is not attainable in this life. This dream is telling us that *all freedom has already been purchased for us on the cross and given to us by Jesus the moment we say yes!*

You don't have to *try* to respect others. Because of Jesus, you *are* a respectful person. Your soul (your mind, will and emotions) may not believe it yet, but that's who you are in Christ. So you have to *rule over the old patterns in your mind* and yield to the Spirit's truth. *Choose* to believe the truth.

Jesus said to the people who believed in him, "You are truly my disciples if you remain faithful to my teachings. And you will know the truth, and the truth will set you free."

John 8:31-32 NLT

The more you get to know Jesus and let Him reveal His Word to you, the more you will be set free! Jesus never sinned but He was beaten and falsely accused. *He understands* pain and *He cares.* That's why He died and rose again for us—so we can be free from Satan's power.

Now the Lord is the Spirit, and where the Spirit of the Lord is, there is freedom. And we all, who with unveiled faces contemplate the Lord's glory, are being transformed into his image with ever-increasing glory, which comes from the Lord, who is the Spirit.

2 Corinthians 3:17-18 NIV

Choosing to stay connected with the Lord's Spirit is *choosing* to experience His freedom and glory. That freedom and glory is what I felt and received in *The Beautiful Dream!* God's glory is all that He is: His Love, life, judgment, mercy, authority, grace, peace, joy, power, healing, deliverance, holiness—*His presence!*

Most of the time we encounter the Lord's glory in small doses. But when we do, we are *being transformed into God's image.* We do this by having alone times with God, worshiping Him, seeking His Word and obeying Him. Even at work or play we can connect with God's presence. We also touch God when we spend time with other believers in worship and even in social settings. We grow spiritually when we *choose* to live by the Spirit for life, seated in the heavenly realms with God.

A *decision* to give up, to doubt, to fear, to be ashamed, or to sin will get in the way of us *receiving* what Jesus has for us. Jesus told us *we would have trials and troubles,* but He said we could overcome them by choosing to draw close to God and resisting the devil!

So submit to [the authority of] God. Resist the devil [stand firm against him] and he will flee from you.

James 4:7 AMP

Submitting to God is *choosing* to change what you have believed to believing in God's truth. It is connecting with God's Spirit by *being seated at His Table.* Then you can resist the devil with the authority God has given us over the enemy! Choose God and you have chosen life!

So Jesus called a child to come and stand in front of them, and said, "I assure you that unless you change and become like children, you will never enter the Kingdom of heaven. The greatest in the Kingdom of heaven is the one who humbles himself and becomes like this child. And whoever welcomes in my name one such child as this, welcomes me.
Matthew 18:2-5 GNT

When I said *yes* in the dream, I worried about not knowing how to dance. Jesus is not looking for someone prideful who thinks they can be strong and victorious on their own. God is looking for people who *know they need His gift of grace* — people who will trust the Father like a little boy or girl and are willing to learn and grow up in Him. When we *choose humility,* we are submitting to His authority as King, but He surprises us with unimaginable Agape Love and power!

Jesus' dance is not difficult. It's slow and full of God's romance — free of fear and shame. Saying *yes* to the *dance* means committing to a beautiful life-long relationship with the Son of God — the King who adores you and will never let you down. I pray you will discard your old life of fear and shame and *choose to follow Jesus* with all of your heart! God Loves you and He wants the best for you!

Declaration

I CHOOSE LIFE AND BLESSINGS!

7

God's Kingdom of Light

At just the right time Christ will be revealed from heaven by the blessed and only almighty God, the King of all kings and Lord of all lords. He alone can never die, and he lives in light so brilliant that no human can approach him. No human eye has ever seen him, nor ever will. All honor and power to him forever! Amen.

1 Timothy 6:15-16 NLT

God is so holy that no sinful human can come close to His pure light and live. But because God's Love and mercy is also holy, He provided a way for us to be forgiven and come back into His Holy presence! Jesus came to earth in sinless human form to pay the ultimate price for our sin—His life's blood. The night before Jesus died for our sin, He went to the Mount of Olives to pray. Angels came and strengthened Jesus, but He was in such anguish that sweat fell from Him like drops of blood. Then He was betrayed, taken to court and falsely accused.

The whip tore Jesus' back, and a crown of thorns ripped His beautiful head. The cross the Messiah carried gouged His skin with splinters. Huge nails were driven between the bones of His hands and feet, fastening Him to the wooden beams. After Jesus died His side was pierced with a sword. The Blood that flowed from His body paid the price to forgive, heal and deliver us from evil. Jesus' resurrection made it possible for Him to give us resurrection life and take us to the Father! Now we *live in the Light*—in Jesus Christ, our King!

Once more Jesus addressed the crowd. He said, "I am the Light of the world. He who follows Me will not walk in the darkness, but will have the Light of life."

John 8:12 AMP

In *The Beautiful Dream*, I followed Jesus as He led me in the dance of salvation. He placed His Spirit inside me who *drove out all darkness.* Because I *followed Him* and Loved Him back, He led me into His Kingdom filled only with light!

In order *to be seated* there and engage with the King of all kings and Lord of all lords, we must do so *on His terms. His truth* is the source of all light. Every believer will experience this truth in its complete reality the day we go to Heaven. But because we live in God's Kingdom now, *we can* learn to reject any physical, mental, spiritual or emotional lie from the kingdom of darkness. *Our faith rests in Jesus* as we are seated in God's light!

We also pray that you will be strengthened with all his glorious power so you will have all the endurance and patience you need. May you be filled with joy, always thanking the Father. He has enabled you to share in the inheritance that belongs to his people, who live in the light. For he has rescued us from the kingdom of darkness and transferred us into the Kingdom of his dear Son, who purchased our freedom and forgave our sins.

Colossians 1:11-14 NLT

Jesus didn't purchase partial freedom for mankind. He purchased freedom out of *all* darkness. The moment we say *yes* to Jesus, God rescues us from the kingdom of darkness. Then He transfers us into the Kingdom of Jesus, *the Light!* That's where we are seated in the Spirit. We are forgiven *and* free! Do you see the picture?

Saul, who was a Jewish leader, a Pharisee, had been persecuting anyone who believed that Jesus was the crucified and risen Messiah. After Jesus rose from the dead, He came to visit Saul in His supernatural glory. Jesus Loved Saul even though he was responsible for the deaths and cruel treatment of many Christians!

As he was approaching Damascus on this mission, a light from heaven suddenly shone down around him. He fell to the ground and heard a voice saying to him, "Saul! Saul! Why are you persecuting me?" "Who are you, lord?" Saul asked. And the voice replied, "I am Jesus, the one you are persecuting! Now get up and go into the city, and you will be told what you must do." The men with Saul stood speechless, for they heard the sound of someone's voice but saw no one! Saul picked himself up off the ground, but when he opened his eyes he was blind.

So his companions led him by the hand to Damascus. He remained there blind for three days and did not eat or drink. Now there was a believer in Damascus named Ananias. The Lord spoke to him in a vision, calling, "Ananias!" "Yes, Lord!" he replied. The Lord said, "Go over to Straight Street, to the house of Judas. When you get there, ask for a man from Tarsus named Saul. He is praying to me right now. I have shown him a vision of a man named Ananias coming in and laying hands on him so he can see again." "But Lord," exclaimed Ananias, "I've heard many people talk about the terrible things this man has done to the believers in Jerusalem! And he is authorized by the leading priests to arrest everyone who calls upon your name." But the Lord said, "Go, for Saul is my chosen instrument to take my message to the Gentiles [non-Jewish people] and to kings, as well as to the people of Israel. And I will show him how much he must suffer for my name's sake."

So Ananias went and found Saul. He laid his hands on him and said, "Brother Saul, the Lord Jesus, who appeared to you on the road, has sent me so that you might regain your sight and be filled with the Holy Spirit." Instantly something like scales fell from Saul's eyes, and he regained his sight. Then he got up and was baptized. Afterward he ate some food and regained his strength.

Acts 9:3-19a NLT

Ananias was clearly seated with God in the heavenly realms! He was able to talk with God, and even against all *natural reasoning*, Ananias, full of God's Love *obeyed* the Lord and ministered *Agape Love* to Saul.

Saul was filled with God's Love and grace. He fell in Love with Jesus. Saul's name was changed to Paul and his entire life was devoted to telling the Good News of Jesus! Saul had been *"doing everything right"* according to his Jewish religious peers, but he was living in darkness, *void of Agape Love*.

The same Light of glory that blinded Saul's eyes for three days entered his heart and he could finally *see clearly – physically and spiritually!* He met Jesus! His whole life changed because Jesus, the Light, forgave him and came into his heart!

The Holy Spirit asked Ananias to *stand up* for Paul, just like my Brothers and Sisters stood up for me in *The Beautiful Dream*. And because Ananias was full of God's Agape Love, he obeyed from his heart. Paul was *spiritually born again, his eyes were healed* and he became one of the greatest apostles of the first believers. In fact, the Lord called Paul to preach to non-Jewish people because he was able to *see* that *everyone can be saved* by faith in Jesus — not by keeping Jewish laws.

For God, who said, "Let light shine out of darkness," made his light shine in our hearts to give us the light of the knowledge of God's glory displayed in the face of Christ. But we have this treasure in jars of clay to show that this all-surpassing power is from God and not from us.

2 Corinthians 4:6-7 NIV

Paul wrote the scripture above and was describing the Holy Spirit's light deposited in each person who says *yes* to Jesus. Those who stay in the *Agape Love* of the Spirit and are *seated with God* will shine like lanterns made of clay! They will drive out darkness and fill the earth with the light of Jesus!

This is the message we have heard from Him and announce to you, that God is Light, and in Him there is no darkness at all. If we say that we have fellowship with Him and yet walk in the darkness, we lie and do not practice the truth; but if we walk in the Light as He Himself is in the Light, we have fellowship with one another, and the blood of Jesus His Son cleanses us from all sin.

1 John 1:5-7 NASB

Jesus asked Saul, "Why are you persecuting me?" Persecuting a believer is persecuting Jesus. That's because Jesus lives inside every believer through the Holy Spirit.

If we are seated with God in the heavenly realms we are beaming with light! Jesus calls us *out of darkness* into His light. Those who live out the truth will not dance with darkness because they have been given a seat at God's Table in the Kingdom of Light! If they notice sin in their own life, they want Holy Spirit to expose it so that they can repent, be forgiven, healed and grow. They stand up for their Brothers and Sisters giving them another chance to be seated as well. They Love everyone, but will not participate in the world's sin. They aren't being legalistic. They just want to *be seated in the Light* — in Jesus! They hope others will come to *the Light* as well!

This is the verdict: Light has come into the world, but people loved darkness instead of light because their deeds were evil. Everyone who does evil hates the light, and will not come into the light for fear that their deeds will be exposed. But whoever lives by the truth comes into the light, so that it may be seen plainly that what they have done has been done in the sight of God.

John 3:19-21 NIV

Many don't know they can be rescued from darkness. We have the honor of carrying Jesus, the Light, to the world!

You are the light of the world. A town built on a hill cannot be hidden. Neither do people light a lamp and put it under a bowl. Instead they put it on its stand, and it gives light to everyone in the house. In the same way, let your light shine before others, that they may see your good deeds and glorify your Father in heaven.

Matthew 5:14-16 NIV

We carry God's Spirit of light! When we are *seated* with God, we are *like a city on a hill at night*. At His Table of light we can see from God's perspective. We do good deeds from hearts full of God's Love — *not out of obligation*. Many things that seemed so important to us before no longer are. As God's light touches our hearts, He reveals *who we really are!* We are the Father's royal children, dearly Loved, cleansed by the Blood of Jesus and fully equipped to destroy the works of the kingdom of darkness!

Jesus, the Son of God, humbled Himself and became *the approachable light of God* in human form! The Light of the World died on the cross so we could be *free from darkness*. That's how much He Loves us and that's how valuable we are to God! He rose again so we could be filled with His Spirit and spiritually *rise to be seated with God* at His Table in His Kingdom of Light!

If you have never met Jesus, it is no mistake that you are reading this book. God Loves you and wants to rescue you from the kingdom of darkness and bring you into His Kingdom of Light. I believe you are about to encounter Jesus in a real and life-changing way!

See Notes: #2 Saying Yes to Jesus

Declaration

I LIVE IN THE LIGHT!

8

Know God

Jesus spoke with His disciples about how He was going to die and be raised to life again. Jesus then prayed the most beautiful prayer for all who say *yes* to Him and follow His lead. The prayer is packed with revelation about our relationship with the Father, Son and Holy Spirit. In this prayer Jesus discloses that the Father's Love is in us and that Jesus Himself is in us. This is the first part of the prayer. It reveals important truth about His generous Love-gift of eternal salvation — *knowing God.*

After saying all these things, Jesus looked up to and said, "Father, the hour has come. Glorify your Son so he can give glory back to you. For you have given him authority over everyone. He gives eternal life to each one you have given him. And this is the way to have eternal life — to know you, the only true God, and Jesus Christ, the one you sent to earth. I brought glory to you here on earth by completing the work you gave me to do. Now, Father, bring me into the glory we shared before the world began."

John 17:1-5 NLT

Eternal life is *"knowing the only true God and Jesus Christ."* The dance in *The Beautiful Dream* represents our salvation experience with Jesus. It wasn't a casual hello. Though our salvation experience certainly is a legal transaction in the spiritual realm, it is so much more! The dance was an intimate, Love-drenched, unforgettable encounter that left me completely enamored with Jesus! The Table represents our ongoing relationship with God the Father, Son and Holy Spirit — our salvation!

"My Father has entrusted everything to me. No one truly knows the Son except the Father, and no one truly knows the Father except the Son and those to whom the Son chooses to reveal him." Then Jesus said, "Come to me, all of you who are weary and carry heavy burdens, and I will give you rest. Take my yoke upon you. Let me teach you, because I am humble and gentle at heart, and you will find rest for your souls. For my yoke is easy to bear, and the burden I give you is light."

Matthew 11:27-30 NLT

A yoke secures two animals together at their necks for the purpose of getting them to work together. It can be a wooden device on the necks of two oxen also attached to a plow. One ox is usually dominant, but a good team of oxen work together in unity. They work together like dancers. One leads and the other follows, but their unity is as if they are one force.

Every person is *spiritually yoked.* The question is, "Who or what are you yoked to?" You cannot be *yoked* to Jesus *and* to other things, ideas, religions, people, etc. Know Jesus so well that you are yoked to Him! No matter what your circumstances are He won't lead you in the wrong direction. *Jesus* will give your soul (mind, will and emotions) peace. When it's time to pull the plow, He will do the heavy lifting and you will simply follow His lead. You'll walk together as one and you will get to know God's goodness in the worst *and* the best times of your life.

Did you know that people can *say* the right words, *do* all sorts of good works and even *do miracles* in Jesus' name but in the end, not *know God?* Knowing *about* God is not the same as knowing Him. Doing Christian things doesn't make you a believer. We must get to know Him personally while we're living here on earth because our eternity with Jesus begins right now.

"Not everyone who calls out to me, 'Lord! Lord!' will enter the Kingdom of Heaven. Only those who actually do the will of my Father in heaven will enter. On judgment day many will say to me, 'Lord! Lord! We prophesied in your name and cast out

demons in your name and performed many miracles in your name.' But I will reply, 'I never knew you. Get away from me, you who break God's laws.'"

Matthew 7:21-23 NLT

God has things for us to do, but if we don't *know Him intimately* and yield to Holy Spirit's Love, our works are worthless in eternity! To know God is to *know His Love*. Any deeds done outside of relationship with the God of Agape Love are dead, prideful religious works.

If I could speak all the languages of earth and of angels, but didn't love others, I would only be a noisy gong or a clanging cymbal. If I had the gift of prophecy, and if I understood all of God's secret plans and possessed all knowledge, and if I had such faith that I could move mountains, but didn't love others, I would be nothing. If I gave everything I have to the poor and even sacrificed my body, I could boast about it; but if I didn't love others, I would have gained nothing.

1 Corinthians 13:1-3 NLT

Throughout *The Beautiful Dream*, I felt the overwhelming Love of God! I wanted to *be with Jesus* and to *know Him*. We get to *know Jesus* intimately when we are *seated* with God and our Brothers and Sisters in the heavenly realms.

Scene three was my chance to *know God*, but I was missing it by daydreaming *about* Jesus. God wanted me to move deeper in my relationship with Jesus. Salvation is never stagnant, and Jesus is my salvation. If Jesus is seated with God and I am in Him, then I must be seated with God as well. That's how I can know God. Let the Love you have for Jesus drive you *to know God more and more!* Otherwise, you will be dancing your own dance alone, or staring at the ceiling going nowhere.

This is what the LORD says: "Let no wise man boast of his wisdom, nor let the mighty man boast of his might, nor a rich man boast of his riches; but let the one who boasts boast of this, that he understands and knows Me, that I am the LORD who exercises mercy, justice, and righteousness on the earth; for I delight in these things," declares the LORD.

Jeremiah 9:23-24 NASB

Worldly pride keeps us from knowing Him. The world says you are important if you have nice clothes, look a certain way, hold a certain title, are really smart about something, do good deeds or hold power over people. These things aren't necessarily bad unless you are following them instead of the Lord. Feeling insecure because you don't have these things or feeling secure because you do *are both pride* because your trust is in worldly wisdom, power, deeds or riches.

Trust in the Lord. Learn how He speaks to you and follow His lead. Don't act impulsively out of religious fear and shame. Stay in the Love of God. Open your whole heart to Him and be willing to do whatever He says. If you do, you will know Him!

King Jesus owns the entire universe and *His Kingdom will last forever.* So don't make it your goal to build your own kingdom on this earth. Submit to the Kingdom that will last forever! Your relationship with the King will cost you everything in this life but you will have gained eternal life in Christ. *Knowing your Loving Savior* is not an option but it is a beautiful requirement you will never regret!

I once thought these things were valuable, but now I consider them worthless because of what Christ has done. Yes, everything else is worthless when compared with the infinite value of knowing Christ Jesus my Lord.

For his sake I have discarded everything else, counting it all as garbage, so that I could gain Christ and become one with him. I no longer count on my own righteousness through obeying the law; rather, I become righteous through faith in Christ. For God's way of making us right with himself depends on faith.

I want to know Christ and experience the mighty power that raised him from the dead. I want to suffer with him, sharing in

his death, so that one way or another I will experience the
resurrection from the dead!

Philippians 3:7-11 NLT

Having faith in Jesus is *knowing Him*, not just the first day you met Him but intimately for the rest of your life. Through Jesus' Blood, God sees you as perfect, even with all your flaws and mistakes. That's because in the heavenly realms you are already perfect and ready for Heaven. But think about this: God Loved you even while you were still a sinner! His Love is amazing! As you *get to know Him better*, it will seem like His Love grows. But really, God's Word and His Spirit are *unveiling* His Love to you. God's Love doesn't change. He just *reveals Himself a little at a time* to those who *seek* His presence!

"For this is the covenant which I will make with the house of Israel after those days," declares the LORD: "I will put My law within them and write it on their heart; and I will be their God, and they shall be My people. They will not teach again, each one his neighbor and each one his brother, saying, 'Know the LORD,' for they will all know Me, from the least of them to the greatest of them," declares the LORD, "for I will forgive their wrongdoing, and their sin I will no longer remember."

Jeremiah 31:33-34 NASB

Since the early Church began over 2,000 years ago, many religious leaders throughout history have kept their congregations from the truth. They wouldn't allow the common person to have a copy of the Bible, which led them to believe that only certain men of *high religious status* could hear from God. Whole nations and tribes were oppressed, suppressed, and even enslaved by wicked leaders who called themselves Christians but elevated themselves as gods. Those so-called Christian leaders had Bibles, but they didn't know God. They actually persecuted anyone who was found with a Bible. Thankfully, because of some brave Brothers and Sisters in Christ, the Bible is now available to many nations!

The Word is now saturating the earth! Holy Spirit will teach us, lead us and counsel us through God's Word. We must be patient with ourselves and others as we break out of unbelief and press on to know the Lord of Love. God knows our hearts and He is patient with us when we sincerely *pursue Him!*

Now therefore, O kings, act wisely; be instructed and take warning, O leaders (judges, rulers) of the earth. Worship the LORD *and serve Him with reverence [with awe-inspired fear and submissive wonder; rejoice [yet do so] with trembling. Kiss (pay respect to) the Son, so that He does not become angry, and you perish in the way, for His wrath may soon be kindled and set aflame. How blessed [fortunate, prosperous, and favored by God] are all those who take refuge in Him!*

Psalm 2:10-12 AMP

What an honor it is to be asked of God to kiss the Lord's Son with our undivided devotion! Jesus gave up *everything* and suffered so we could *know God intimately!* The Lord is the joy of our salvation, our personal Counselor, our Prince of Peace, Healer, Protector and Provider. He is Creator, Judge, the Most High God, Mighty God and our Everlasting Father!

God is Holy, Love, Compassionate and Faithful! He was there when time was created and He will be the One who decides when every clock stops ticking. God knows everything, possesses all power and authority, and He is present everywhere! What a blessing and privilege to be seated with God and *to know Him personally!*

So let's learn, let's press on to know the LORD. *His appearance is as sure as the dawn; and He will come to us like the rain, as the spring rain waters the earth.*

Hosea 6:3 NASB

Declaration

I KNOW THE LORD INTIMATELY!

9

Not Ashamed of Jesus

One day as Jesus was walking along the shore of the Sea of Galilee, he saw two brothers—Simon, also called Peter, and Andrew—throwing a net into the water, for they fished for a living. Jesus called out to them, "Come, follow me, and I will show you how to fish for people!" And they left their nets at once and followed him.

Matthew 4:18-20 NLT

When you follow Jesus, He will show you how to fish for people! In scene two, I saw Mark and myself sitting on concrete bleachers. *I was so happy* I couldn't stop describing Jesus' Love and all that He had done for me. There was *no hesitation, no shame and no doubt* in the way I shared my Love for the Lord. It is only natural for us to share good news, right? This is the heart-cry of our Father—that we share the Good News of His Son!

If you openly declare that Jesus is Lord and believe in your heart that God raised him from the dead, you will be saved. For it is by believing in your heart that you are made right with God, and it is by openly declaring your faith that you are saved.

Romans 10:9-10 NLT

Sharing your faith because you truly Love Jesus causes the seed that Jesus placed inside you to grow. The desire to share your faith is the first sign that you are drinking Living Water!

The Lord doesn't want us to see sharing our faith like a *law* — that if we tell someone about Jesus we will be saved. We aren't saved by our works! The main theme of *The Beautiful Dream* was the Agape Love of God. The Lord's Love deposited in us is *so powerful* we naturally want to tell someone else!

The Bible tells us that *our own Love for God and others* can grow cold. The devil will also try to keep us from telling people about Jesus. But if we are seated next to our Father at His Table, we will be passionate about those He longs to have seated next to His heart.

Many around the world are being persecuted, imprisoned and even killed because they told people about Jesus. That's because their relationship with God is *authentic* and *spiritually hot*. They are not *ashamed of Jesus*.

After He was resurrected from the dead, Jesus asked His disciples to wait in Jerusalem until the promised Holy Spirit came on them.

...but you will receive power when the Holy Spirit has come upon you; and you shall be My witnesses both in Jerusalem and in all Judea, and Samaria, and as far as the remotest part of the earth.

Acts 1:8 NASB

The Holy Spirit still empowers us to share the Good News of Jesus with others. But if we don't cherish our relationship with God and keep it fresh, the fire of the Love we once had will grow dim. Holy Spirit wants to give us *fresh fire* with power to Love and be His witnesses.

Tax collectors and other notorious sinners often came to listen to Jesus teach. This made the Pharisees and teachers of religious law complain that he was associating with such sinful people — even eating with them! So Jesus told them this story: "If a man has a hundred sheep and one of them gets lost, what will he do? Won't he leave the ninety-nine others in the wilderness and go to search for the one that is lost until he finds it? And when he has found it, he will joyfully carry it home on his shoulders. When he arrives, he will call together his friends and neighbors, saying, 'Rejoice with me because I have found my lost sheep.' In the same way, there is more joy in heaven over one lost sinner who repents and returns to God than over ninety-nine others who are righteous and haven't strayed away!

Luke 15:1-7 NLT

There is nothing more *valuable* in life than leading someone to Jesus, and nothing more rewarding! The greatest treasures are not material things, fame or power on earth. Eternal treasures are the *people* that can be brought into the arms of Jesus!

"Or what woman, if she has ten silver coins and loses one coin, does not light a lamp and sweep the house and search carefully until she finds it? And when she has found it, she calls together her friends and neighbors, saying, 'Rejoice with me, because I have found the coin which I had lost!' In the same way, I tell you, there is joy in the presence of the angels of God over one sinner who repents."

Luke 15:8-10 NASB

There are people who would *love* to know Jesus. We just have to Love people enough to let the Holy Spirit lead us to them. Some will reject the message, but God wants Jesus shared with *everyone* so that they can have the opportunity to know Jesus and be set free!

For I am not ashamed of this Good News about Christ. It is the power of God at work, saving everyone who believes:

Romans 1:16a NLT

The Holy Spirit gives us His compassion and His *power* to bring people to Jesus! Wherever you live, work, go to school, buy groceries or tools—that's where you can shine the most. If you begin to pray for opportunities, *they will arise*, and *the Spirit will show you* what to do or say. It may start with a sincere, "God bless you," or an act of kindness. God may prompt you to ask a person if they need prayer. Be ready to walk through the open doors with Jesus! The Holy Spirit will lead you.

Instead, you must worship Christ as Lord of your life. And if someone asks about your hope as a believer, always be ready to explain it. But do this in a gentle and respectful way. Keep your conscience clear. Then if people speak against you, they will be ashamed when they see what a good life you live because you belong to Christ. Remember, it is better to suffer for doing good, if that is what God wants, than to suffer for doing wrong! Christ suffered for our sins once for all time. He never sinned, but he died for sinners to bring you safely home to God. He suffered physical death, but he was raised to life in the Spirit.

1 Peter 3:15-18 NLT

You may ask why my husband and I were sitting on empty concrete bleachers in the second scene, and why it was zoomed in so I couldn't see how wide or tall the bleachers were. I believe the Lord is telling us that the number of people we are able to bring into the Father's Love is *greater than we can imagine!* Our Love and joy in the Lord will spill out first to those we know and then creatively spread out to others — like a beautiful fragrant perfume!

But thank God! He has made us his captives and continues to lead us along in Christ's triumphal procession. Now he uses us to spread the knowledge of Christ everywhere, like a sweet perfume. Our lives are a Christ-like fragrance rising up to God. But this fragrance is perceived differently by those who are being saved and by those who are perishing. To those who are perishing, we are a dreadful smell of death and doom. But to those who are being saved, we are a life-giving perfume.

2 Corinthians 2:14-16 NLT

Not telling others about the life-giving power of Jesus Christ is like putting the top on your scented jar candle while it's still burning. The flame will go out, the fragrance will be lost and the inside of the jar will become dirty with soot. If we don't believe Jesus has set us free we probably won't shine. We'll likely stop dancing in Love. We are meant to burn brightly with the fragrance of Christ from the moment God's light enters our hearts until the day we are taken to Heaven.

Our tree *will* bear fruit. Not everyone we talk to will receive the Good News of Jesus, *but some will.* The Spirit equips us to display God's Love through kind words, deeds, signs, wonders, healings and miracles.

And as you go, preach, saying, 'The kingdom of heaven has come near.' Heal the sick, raise the dead, cleanse those with leprosy, cast out demons. Freely you received, freely give.
Matthew 10:7-8 NASB

God has freely poured His forgiveness, healing and deliverance into our hearts through the Holy Spirit so we can freely give it away! We are *generous* like our Father! Even if we don't see all the results of our inheritance yet in the earthly realm, we know they are ours! From that place of faith, we can lead people to Jesus, heal the sick and drive out demons. Oh yes... and even raise the dead! Praise the Lord!

The man who had been freed from the demons begged to go with him. But Jesus sent him home, saying, "No, go back to your family, and tell them everything God has done for you." So he went all through the town proclaiming the great things Jesus had done for him.
Luke 8:38-39 NLT

Telling others about Jesus is just as important *for us* as it is *for others.* As the Holy Spirit leads us to share our faith, we are allowing God's Love to burn in us! While we are still on earth, we can stay close to Jesus, let Him replenish our candle jars and emit the fragrance of His Agape Love. We really do Love Jesus! The Holy Spirit in us is not *bashful* so let's go! It's starting to get really dark in this world and people need the Light!

As long as it is day, we must do the works of him who sent me.

Night is coming, when no one can work. While I am in the world, I am the light of the world.

John 9:4-5 NIV

In the end times, *spiritual darkness will increase* making it hard for believers to share their faith openly. But the light of the Holy Spirit lives inside us — *The Light of the World!* So, while we can, let's *be seated in the Light!* Keep your candle lit with fragrant Agape Love, fill your stadium and fish for people! It may not be *easy* to plant the seeds of the Gospel of Jesus, but one day we will be full of joy when the beautiful harvest of souls starts to come in! Our hearts will be filled with the joy of the Lord!

They weep as they go to plant their seed, but they sing as they return with the harvest.

Psalm 126:6 NLT

Declaration

I AM NOT ASHAMED OF JESUS!

IO

Raised from the Dead

If you turned from your old life and put your faith in the grace of Jesus, *He has washed you clean!* You are not the person you were. Your *old life is dead* and your *new life* with Jesus has begun! Now that's something to be happy about!

Well then, should we keep on sinning so that God can show us more and more of his wonderful grace? Of course not! Since we have died to sin, how can we continue to live in it? Or have you forgotten that when we were joined with Christ Jesus in baptism, we joined him in his death? For we died and were buried with Christ by baptism. And just as Christ was raised from the dead by the glorious power of the Father, now we also may live new lives.

Since we have been united with him in his death, we will also be raised to life as he was. We know that our old sinful selves were crucified with Christ so that sin might lose its power in our lives. We are no longer slaves to sin. For when we died with Christ we were set free from the power of sin. And since we died with Christ, we know we will also live with him. We are sure of this because Christ was raised from the dead, and he will never die again. Death no longer has any power over him. When he died, he died once to break the power of sin. But now that he lives, he lives for the glory of God. So you also should consider yourselves to be dead to the power of sin and alive to God through Christ Jesus.

Do not let sin control the way you live; do not give in to sinful desires. Do not let any part of your body become an instrument of evil to serve sin. Instead, give yourselves completely to God, for you were dead, but now you have new life. So use your whole body as an instrument to do what is right for the glory of God. Sin is no longer your master, for you no longer live under the requirements of the law. Instead, you live under the freedom of God's grace.

Romans 6:1-14 NLT

Satan can't bind you up in chains of sin and yank you around *unless you let him.* The person you used to be *is dead!* In *The Beautiful Dream*, Jesus touched me and the person I was, died. I became a *totally new person filled with Love.* God wants us to *be seated* in this truth. We are not, in any way, who we were before we met Jesus. *We are brand new!*

If we're *fearful* and *ashamed*, it's because we are trusting in our own ability to live perfectly and not break any of God's laws. It will cause us to see others through that lens as well— with a judgment mindset. No one can live perfectly! That's why we are eternally grateful for the mercy and grace of Jesus Christ!

For whoever shall keep the whole law, and yet stumble in one point, he is guilty of all... So speak and so do as those who will be judged by the law of liberty. For judgment is without mercy to the one who has shown no mercy. Mercy triumphs over judgment.

James 2:10 & 12 NKJV

Every person sinned and was destined for hell because of the law of death. But whoever says *yes* to Jesus is filled with God's Spirit of mercy and liberty. Instead of living from an earthly judgmental realm, we live from our chair in the heavenly realms where mercy flows freely!

Jesus tells us to be *baptized in water* because of the powerful death-to-life reality of following Jesus. Water baptism is not just a *symbol*, but also a *spiritual event*. Picture yourself laying down in the water at a river, pond, etc., completely submerged, and then coming back up drenched. Water baptism *announces* that the old you is dead and the new you is *alive in Christ!*

You can *renounce* strongholds and sin by name, receive the blessing from your Father God, and *expect freedom* as you come out of the water! Sometimes, strongholds of the devil can leave if a new believer is in the process of spiritually putting to death their old life. Don't underestimate the power of this beautiful command of Jesus!

In *The Beautiful Dream*, as I danced with Jesus, He *dipped* me gently to the left and to the right. I believe this can symbolize several things, but one of them is the baptism (death) of our old life. It must die so Jesus can live in us and through us. The other *dip* would represent the baptism of the Holy Spirit with fire and the power of God. We have the great honor of dying to our sinful nature on this earth and living for God from a different Kingdom!

All praise to God, the Father of our Lord Jesus Christ. It is by his great mercy that we have been born again, because God raised Jesus Christ from the dead. Now we live with great expectation, and we have a priceless inheritance—an inheritance that is kept in heaven for you, pure and undefiled, beyond the reach of change and decay. And through your faith, God is protecting you by his power until you receive this salvation, which is ready to be revealed on the last day for all to see.

So be truly glad. There is wonderful joy ahead, even though you must endure many trials for a little while. These trials will show that your faith is genuine. It is being tested as fire tests and purifies gold—though your faith is far more precious than mere gold. So when your faith remains strong through many trials, it will bring you much praise and glory and honor on the day when Jesus Christ is revealed to the whole world.

You love him even though you have never seen him. Though you do not see him now, you trust him; and you rejoice with a glorious, inexpressible joy. The reward for trusting him will be the salvation of your souls.

1 Peter 1:3-9 NLT

The greatest reward for *trusting Jesus in this life* is eternal life with Him in Heaven! The *trials* and the *tests* of life prove where our faith lies. Difficult times can expose hidden sin such as doubt, fear, unrighteous anger, etc. Then we can put that sin back on the cross where it belongs. When our faith is tested and we overcome through God's power, we become *stronger and closer to God's glory*. It will be worth every trial in the end!

Jesus said to her, "I am the resurrection and the life; the one who believes in Me will live, even if he dies,

John 11:25 NASB

If you are a child of God and your body dies, Jesus will escort you to Heaven and give you a brand new body! You will be *raised from the dead!* For now, you are spiritually seated with God at His Table. But one day, God's Heavenly Kingdom will become your *new* eternal Home! It's going to be glorious!

He will wipe every tear from their eyes, and there will be no more death or sorrow or crying or pain. All these things are gone forever. And the one sitting on the throne said, "Look, I am making everything new!" And then he said to me, "Write this down, for what I tell you is trustworthy and true."

And he also said, "It is finished! I am the Alpha and the Omega—the Beginning and the End. To all who are thirsty I will give freely from the springs of the water of life. All who are victorious will inherit all these blessings, and I will be their God, and they will be my children. But cowards, unbelievers, the corrupt, murderers, the immoral, those who practice witchcraft, idol worshipers, and all liars—their fate is in the fiery lake of burning sulfur. This is the second death."

Revelation 21:4-8 NLT

Those who put their faith in the grace of God will have no fear of physical death because they have *died to sin* and are *spiritually alive in Jesus*. Their trust has not been in their own power to keep from sinning, but in the cross of Jesus and the Spirit's life-giving power! They will have a smooth transition from *life* on earth to *life* in Heaven!

Jesus said, "There was a certain rich man who was splendidly clothed in purple and fine linen and who lived each day in luxury. At his gate lay a poor man named Lazarus who was covered with sores. As Lazarus lay there longing for scraps from the rich man's table, the dogs would come and lick his open sores.

Finally, the poor man died and was carried by the angels to sit beside Abraham at the heavenly banquet. The rich man also died and was buried, and he went to the place of the dead. There, in torment, he saw Abraham in the far distance with Lazarus at his side. The rich man shouted, 'Father Abraham, have some pity! Send Lazarus over here to dip the tip of his finger in water and cool my tongue. I am in anguish in these flames.'

But Abraham said to him, 'Son, remember that during your lifetime you had everything you wanted, and Lazarus had nothing. So now he is here being comforted, and you are in anguish. And besides, there is a great chasm separating us. No one can cross over to you from here, and no one can cross over to us from there.'

Then the rich man said, 'Please, Father Abraham, at least send him to my father's home. For I have five brothers, and I want him to warn them so they don't end up in this place of torment.' But Abraham said, 'Moses and the prophets have warned them. Your brothers can read what they wrote.' The rich man replied, 'No, Father Abraham! But if someone is sent to them from the dead, then they will repent of their sins and turn to God.' But Abraham said, 'If they won't listen to Moses and the prophets, they won't be persuaded even if someone rises from the dead.'"
Luke 16:19-31 NLT

Our time on earth is short. If we are seated next to the Father's heart, listening to the Holy Spirit, our lives will look much different from those seated in the earthly realm. We'll be able to see through Jesus' eyes of Love and live for a Kingdom we have not yet seen. *Heaven is a real place* and it will be worth every sacrifice the Father asks of us!

Do not let your heart be troubled; believe in God, believe also in Me. In My Father's house are many rooms; if that were not so, I would have told you, because I am going there to prepare a place for you. And if I go and prepare a place for you, I am coming again and will take you to Myself, so that where I am, there you also will be.

John 14:1-3 NASB

Heaven is beautiful beyond words! It has rivers, trees, lakes and a magnificent city with golden streets. It is endlessly more stunning and colorful than anything we've ever seen! There will be no sin, darkness, pain or fear ever again. We will not have to battle against the kingdom of darkness anymore! Hallelujah! Darkness doesn't exist in Heaven! The atmosphere of Heaven will be permeated with the Love of God because God's Spirit will be everywhere! So until then, enjoy living the new life Jesus is giving you and *bury the old!* Be seated in the heavenly realms and begin living your eternal life in Christ right now—*for His glory!* You are seated in the atmosphere of Agape Love and life!

See Notes: #3 Resisting the Devil

Declaration

MY OLD LIFE IS DEAD ~ I'M ALIVE IN CHRIST!

II

TABLE TALK: *The Still Small Voice*

God speaks in so many different ways. If we tried to list them all, we would limit Him. He is so creative and reserves the right to surprise and awe us with His voice. One of the ways is the quiet voice that Elijah heard. Elijah was a prophet who Loved God and did miracles by God's power because he was obedient. But after a great spiritual victory that shamed the gods of the enemy, an evil "Jezebel" demon attacked Elijah and he ran in panic. Even though he was strong, victorious, protected, saved and very Loved by God, Elijah *felt* fatigued, defeated, vulnerable, intimidated, abandoned, lonely and angry. The Lord was with him the whole time but he ran away in fear and hid in a cave.

But the LORD said to him, "What are you doing here, Elijah?"

Elijah replied, "I have zealously served the LORD God Almighty. But the people of Israel have broken their covenant with you, torn down your altars, and killed every one of your prophets. I am the only one left, and now they are trying to kill me, too."

"Go out and stand before me on the mountain," the LORD told him. And as Elijah stood there, the LORD passed by, and a mighty windstorm hit the mountain. It was such a terrible blast that the rocks were torn loose, but the LORD was not in the wind.

After the wind there was an earthquake, but the LORD was not in the earthquake. And after the earthquake there was a fire, but the LORD was not in the fire. And after the fire there was the sound of a gentle whisper. When Elijah heard it, he wrapped his face in his cloak and went out and stood at the entrance of the cave.

1 Kings 19:9b-13 NLT

Elijah, one of the most honored prophets in the Bible, had been *faithful to the Lord.* In his faithfulness, he was attacked by demons to the point that he was ready to give up. But Elijah didn't stop talking with God because he knew God. The Lord was there to help him finish his race. The Lord taught Elijah, and us, not to be terrified when demons attack our thoughts and emotions, but to *be still and listen to God's gentle voice.* In the middle of disaster and calamity, be *seated at God's Table* and wait for Him to speak.

Most of my childhood years were spent near Asuncion, the capital city of Paraguay. Paraguay is the beautiful country in South America where my parents served as missionaries. Once a year, my Christian school would pick a campground away from the "big city" to hold a spiritual retreat. I enjoyed them so much, and some of my best memories as a missionary kid happened at these retreats. I will share one *unforgettable* camp memory with you now.

It was probably my first school retreat because I was so young—around 7 years old. The campground was located on a very shady hill. Summers were so extremely hot that Paraguayans depended on their big, beautiful trees for natural air conditioning.

The old house located at the top of the hill was made of stone. Hammocks were strung up on the porches and wooden lattice-work painted hunter green helped trim the porch. This was not typical Paraguayan architecture and it seemed so special to me at that time. The camp speakers or counselors usually slept in that old house. Behind it was a small water tower connected to a well that supplied the whole camp with water. We enjoyed helping crank the big iron handle until the cold water began spilling out of the top! It didn't seem like work to us. It was an adventure!

The kids slept in plain camp style buildings with bunk beds and lots of screened windows for ventilation. Soon after arriving we ran with our belongings to claim our bunks!

Meals were served at the covered patio attached to the kitchen. It was located down the hill but not too far from the cabins. I drank "bug juice" for the first time at lunch. The camper assigned to make the drink would mix water and a fruit flavored syrup. I was told that one year a bug flew into the juice pitcher and from then on it was called "bug juice." These were the joys that made camp *so thrilling* to us!

We had a devotional in the morning and a service at night. In between were so many fun activities but what we looked forward to the most was swimming! There was a little river at the bottom of the hill where we could cool off in the afternoon and have fun. So when the big old-fashioned school bell was rung, we would dash down the dirt path to the river.

The rules were clear. Only the older kids could swim in the deep part, from the bend of the river on the left, to the end of the clearing where the path was on the right. My age group had to stay in the shallow water near the bank of the river. There was a small, partly-submerged sand bar near the bend of the river that we could play on only to the half-way point. Past that point was off-limits.

The temptation was too much for our little minds. My friend and I ventured out as close to the end of the sandbar as *we decided* was safe. Like a slide on a playground, both of us accidentally slid right into the deep waters! We were pulled into the middle of the river by the strong current. The river was loud with the sounds of many children and teens splashing, playing, and screaming joyfully. Kids were jumping off the rocks and trees on the other side of the river, splashing into the water. The big kids were on shoulders playing "chicken fight." Our little heads were *two of many heads* bobbing and flailing in the happy scene.

I only knew how to dog paddle! We were swept down the river about a third way past the other kids playing wildly in the water when my friend grabbed my shoulders from behind. She pulled herself up using my shoulders, but that pushed me under the water. So I paddled back up for air. As soon as I got a quick breath she pushed me under again!

We were like a moving seesaw going up and down as we floated swiftly beyond our control. I was frustrated with her for pushing me under. When I came up for air, I frantically screamed toward the river's edge, "Help!" but then was pushed back under. No one heard my screams for help because *everyone was screaming!* And no one noticed us drowning because there was so much fun going on around us.

I remember seeing the last of the swimmers and only the river rushing ahead of me. It suddenly looked much wider than before. The dense jungle-like forest draped both sides of the river like curtains closing at the end of a performance. There was no plan, no strategy, and no hope ahead.

I went under again and paddled hard to the surface for air, screaming back toward the shore for the last time. As I did, I saw one of the tall, older boys turn and look at me with alarm on his face. In that split second I knew he was coming to save us!

The next thing I remember, we were safe at the riverbank. I was a little embarrassed but thankful! I didn't think much about it after that day and no one mentioned it. Several years later at our yearly retreat, I said *yes* to Jesus around a campfire, under the beautiful starry Paraguayan sky!

The young man may not have heard my cry for help, but the Lord did and turned his head just in time! Around 50 years later I was talking to the Lord about this traumatic event in my life, allowing Him to speak in whatever way He wanted to. The Holy Spirit is the best counselor!

I got still and pictured Jesus right there in front of me. I thanked Him again for saving my life and for the teenager who came to my rescue. I asked God to forgive me for disobeying the swimming rules. I also asked forgiveness for being upset with my little friend who kept pushing me under — even though I had not remained upset with her after we were saved from drowning. And that's when the Lord *quietly spoke to me*, "You saved her life."

I sobbed with tears and deep emotion as Jesus affirmed me and Loved me so kindly! I had been focused on what I did wrong and so determined to repent for something, hoping to gain some relief that way.

But the Lord never said anything about *guilt.* Jesus made me feel special, perfectly Loved and protected at His Table. He showed me that I never shook her grip off of my shoulders and because of that, my little friend did not drown. I called out for help when she couldn't. God used my strength to save her precious life.

It was as if He never saw the disobedience or mistakes I had made, only the good I had done! My sins had been washed away at age 11 when I gave my whole heart to Jesus. *My sins weren't there anymore and all my shame was gone!* Thank You, Jesus!

The Lord's *gentle whisper* brought *revelation* and *new life* to me as we spoke across the Table to each other that day. A tiny dark closet in my heart was cleared out, renovated, and filled up with His light and Agape Love! Since then, the Lord has revealed more spiritual truth from that event.

My family never shamed me or made me feel afraid of the water. *They just taught me to swim.* And from that point forward, I was one of the happy kids swimming in deep waters! Just like my family didn't shame me, the Lord doesn't shame us. All our sins have been washed away! If our faith is in Jesus, they are nowhere to be found!

You will trample our sins underfoot and send them to the bottom of the sea!

Micah 7:19b GNT

If we follow the Lord intimately, Holy Spirit will show us any sin we need to confess and repent of. But we must not go deep sea fishing for sins! Our sins were crushed on the cross and buried in the tomb! They're gone! Hallelujah! God wants us to learn the ways of the Spirit. He wants us to learn to swim in the heavenly realms and live joyfully at the top of the water.

But first we have to *humble ourselves.* As newborn babes we need guidance, training and a few rules. We will learn to float in shallow waters with our family holding us up. Then we'll be taught different strokes and gain strength as we read the Word, worship and learn to follow Love Himself. Soon we will learn to swim against the constant currents of this world as we face trials and overcome.

At that point in our journey we won't need the rules and boundaries. We will be *following the Spirit* in His righteousness, not drowning in our own pride. But imposing rules upon seasoned swimmers and keeping them at the water's edge produces disappointment, confusion and even fear. God's Spirit is calling us to mature and learn to swim with Him on top of the deep waters where there is refreshing joy and laughter!

Let's enjoy the wonderful life Jesus has purchased for us and *live from the heavenly realms!* But in the middle of our loud and joyful celebrations, the precious drowning ones are crying out desperately for help! We won't hear them unless we keep our eyes and ears open and attentive to the Holy Spirit. He is going to use us to rescue many of them before the great curtain at the end of the ages is finally closed.

12

The Heavenly Realms

In *The Beautiful Dream*, Jesus ushered me into the heavenly realms to be seated with God. God's Kingdom is in Heaven and Heaven is promised to those who will not abandon their relationship with Jesus. But since we are living on earth right now, He has given us access to the Kingdom through *the heavenly realms*—by the Spirit. We don't have to try to get there. If you follow Jesus, He has already taken you there. God brings *His Kingdom to earth* and does His will through us because we are seated in *the heavenly realms*.

Being *born again* is spiritual and supernatural! The *power* of the presence of Jesus literally comes inside us removing all our sin, taking us out of darkness into His light and resurrecting us from spiritual death to life in the Spirit. Our eagerness to tell others about Jesus is evidence that the Word of God, Jesus Himself, has been *planted like a seed* and is *rooting and growing* in our hearts.   Then, Jesus escorts us to be seated at our place at the Table with God in *the heavenly realms*! It is a place of faith that *rests* in the power of the grace of God and not in the wisdom or works of man. This is *the realm of the Spirit*.

As for you, you were dead in your transgressions and sins, in which you used to live when you followed the ways of this world and of the ruler of the kingdom of the air, the spirit who is now at work in those who are disobedient. All of us also lived among them at one time, gratifying the cravings of our flesh and following its desires and thoughts. Like the rest, we were by nature deserving of wrath. But because of his great love for us, God, who is rich in mercy, made us alive with Christ even when we were dead in transgressions — it is by grace you have been saved.

And God raised us up with Christ and seated us with him in the heavenly realms in Christ Jesus, in order that in the coming ages he might show the incomparable riches of his grace, expressed in his kindness to us in Christ Jesus. For it is by grace you have been saved, through faith — and this is not from yourselves, it is the gift of God — not by works, so that no one can boast. For we are God's handiwork, created in Christ Jesus to do good works, which God prepared in advance for us to do.

Ephesians 2:1-10 NIV

God planned for us to live from a different spiritual plane so we could *grow strong in Him* and so He could send us out to share His Love effectively. The *riches* that are ours if we are willing to *engage with God* at His Table are beyond our earthly comprehension. This is part of a powerful prayer Jesus prayed to the Father for us before He went to the cross:

I'm not asking you to take them out of the world, but to keep them safe from the evil one. They do not belong to this world any more than I do. Make them holy by your truth; teach them your word, which is truth. Just as you sent me into the world, I am sending them into the world. And I give myself as a holy sacrifice for them so they can be made holy by your truth.

John 17:15-19 NLT

Jesus has separated us from the world by His holy sacrifice so that we are not like we were before we met Him. God planned for our faith to reside at a higher level. Being seated with God means *believing* that the Father is answering Jesus' prayer and *keeping us safe from the evil one*. We don't belong to this world. That's why we live from the heavenly realms as we carry out the will of our Father on earth.

Therefore, if you have been raised with Christ, keep seeking the things that are above, where Christ is, seated at the right hand of God. Set your minds on the things that are above, not on the things that are on earth. For you have died, and your life is hidden with Christ in God. When Christ, who is our life, is revealed, then you also will be revealed with Him in glory.

Colossians 3:1-4 NASB

The focus of our thought life is being seated with God in the heavenly realms where Love and acceptance permeates the atmosphere. We have died to our earthly life and God is our reality now! In scene three of *The Beautiful Dream*, the Holy Spirit told everyone to *be seated*. I didn't hear Him and I felt *ashamed*. But everyone stood back up for me!

"The most important one [commandment]," answered Jesus, "is this: 'Hear, O Israel: The Lord our God, the Lord is one. Love the Lord your God with all your heart and with all your soul and with all your mind and with all your strength.' The second is this: 'Love your neighbor as yourself.' There is no commandment greater than these."

Mark 12:29-31 NIV

In *the heavenly realms* we have already been made perfect, good looking, talented, healed, delivered, joyful, confident, provided for, protected, Loving and Loveable because of Jesus. But if we don't see that the power of God's grace has given us all these things, we won't see our Brothers and Sisters that way either, and we make God's grace out to be deficient and faulty. We must see one another from God's heavenly perspective.

I'm not saying that we should lie about the suffering we experience on earth—of course not. Neither am I suggesting that God is disappointed in us if we haven't been completely healed and delivered yet. There is no *fear* or *shame* in the heavenly realms—*no condemnation* for any believer! But we don't have to wait until we get to Heaven to pursue freedom from the power of the devil. We can be seated at God's Table and receive from Jesus now.

Jesus was the perfect sacrifice because He never sinned. He is the "spotless Lamb of God," and because of that, we can trust that all of our sins are gone! He has set us apart in His righteousness so the Holy Spirit can live inside us and bring us supernatural life!

Now on the last day, the great day of the feast, Jesus stood and cried out, saying, "If anyone is thirsty, Let him come to Me and drink. The one who believes in Me, as the Scripture said, ' From his innermost being will flow rivers of living water.'" But this He said in reference to the Spirit, whom those who believed in Him were to receive; for the Spirit was not yet given, because Jesus was not yet glorified.

John 7:37-39 NASB

Holy Spirit is a perpetual holy river that brings true life to us from Heaven! We have continual access to the river of life through the Holy Spirit in the heavenly realms.

Then the angel showed me the river of the water of life — water as clear as crystal — pouring out from the throne of God and of the Lamb, flowing down the middle of the city's main street. On each side of the river is the tree of life producing twelve kinds of fruit, yielding its fruit every month of the year. Its leaves are for the healing of the nations.

Revelation 22:1-2 NET

The *river of the water of life*, the Living Water, is in Heaven, but He is also in us! If we aren't *seated* at the Table, getting instructions from Holy Spirit, we may wonder why parts of our lives are withering. We have to drink from Him! We have to learn to connect with God through the Holy Spirit.

But you will receive power when the Holy Spirit has come upon you, and you will be my witnesses in Jerusalem, and in all Judea and Samaria, and to the farthest parts of the earth.

Acts 1:8 NET

This power is the baptism of the Holy Spirit with fire, and it is for every believer. But it's not just for our own benefit. When we spend time with God in the heavenly realms, His power is on us so that God's will is done in and through us bringing *leaves of healing for the nations.* Jesus is in us! It is *Him* at work in us and through us, not our own power. What God offers us when we are seated with God in the heavenly realms is astounding! He receives *all* the glory!

Those who live in the shelter of the Most High will find rest in the shadow of the Almighty. This I declare about the LORD: He alone is my refuge, my place of safety; he is my God, and I trust him. For he will rescue you from every trap and protect you from deadly disease. He will cover you with his feathers. He will shelter you with his wings. His faithful promises are your armor and protection.

Do not be afraid of the terrors of the night, nor the arrow that flies in the day. Do not dread the disease that stalks in darkness, nor the disaster that strikes at midday. Though a thousand fall at your side, though ten thousand are dying around you, these evils will not touch you. Just open your eyes, and see how the wicked are punished.

If you make the LORD your refuge, if you make the Most High your shelter, no evil will conquer you; no plague will come near your home. For he will order his angels to protect you wherever you go. They will hold you up with their hands so you won't even hurt your foot on a stone. You will trample upon lions and cobras; you will crush fierce lions and serpents under your feet!

The LORD says, "I will rescue those who love me. I will protect those who trust in my name. When they call on me, I will answer; I will be with them in trouble. I will rescue and honor them. I will reward them with a long life and give them my salvation."

Psalm 91:1-16 NLT

Rescue, protection and deliverance from all the evil of the enemy are ours! But *we have to believe* that Jesus has taken us to the shelter of the Most High, the heavenly realms, where His

Kingdom comes to earth through us. Because we are in Love with God and follow His lead, He takes care of us. If we stay seated with Him, His Kingdom will come to earth through His children!

Truly I say to you, whatever you bind on earth shall have been bound in heaven; and whatever you loose on earth shall have been loosed in heaven. Again I say to you, that if two of you agree on earth about anything that they may ask, it shall be done for them by My Father who is in heaven. For where two or three have gathered together in My name, I am there in their midst."

Matthew 18:18-20 NASB

When we are *seated together in unity with our Father*, we can ask Him in Jesus' name and it will be done. We can bind and loose things on earth in Jesus' name! But we must grow in God's Love and righteousness so we're no longer *fearful* and *ashamed*. In the atmosphere of His unfailing Love, where we Love God and Love one another wholeheartedly, we can come boldly to the Throne of Grace and receive what He has for us.

There are clues in God's Word about this amazing place in the Spirit: the Mountain of the Lord, the Upper Room, the House of Prayer For All Nations, the Shelter of the Most High, soaring high on wings like eagles, the Promised Land, the Most Holy Place, and on and on! Though they may also have an earthly meaning or in Heaven itself, the Holy Spirit is urging us to *be seated with God now* in the heavenly realms! God has amazing plans for our lives, our communities and our nations. We need to *be seated* together in the unity of Agape Love and *pay close attention!*

Declaration

I'M SEATED WITH GOD IN THE SPIRIT!

13

Be Seated Next to Abba

For all who are led by the Spirit of God are children of God. So you have not received a spirit that makes you fearful slaves. Instead, you received God's Spirit when he adopted you as his own children. Now we call him, "Abba, Father." For his Spirit joins with our spirit to affirm that we are God's children.

Romans 8:14-16 NLT

Jesus called His Heavenly Father *Abba (AH-bah)*, which is Hebrew for *Daddy* or *Papa*. Now that we are God's children, Jesus wants us to have the same intimate and loving relationship with *Abba* as He did! If you know Jesus, you know His Father because Jesus is just like Him, and they are One!

The Son radiates God's own glory and expresses the very character of God, and he sustains everything by the mighty power of his command. When he had cleansed us from our sins, he sat down in the place of honor at the right hand of the majestic God in heaven.

Hebrews 1:3 NLT

Our *adoption* and *inheritance* were bought at a precious price, because our Father Loves us so much! Until you see yourself and all His children as totally cleansed and made perfect in your Abba's eyes, you will be subject to fear. And if you read the words of Jesus and only see a set of rules and regulations, you are probably viewing God the Father as a cruel and unforgiving rule-enforcer. Jesus has taken us to the heavenly realms so we can be seated in the atmosphere of our Father who is Love! Jesus' teachings tell us what it's like to live from the heavenly realms with Abba, and what it looks like if we're not seated with Him. Jesus knows, because He is just like His Abba!

Jesus *is* the radiance of the beauty, holiness, pure Love, light, life, power, majesty, authority, justice, goodness, creativeness, honor, grace, mercy, joy, strength and *all the fullness of Abba's glory!* Jesus was obedient to go to the cross because He Loved His Father and He Loved us. He was humble. Now Jesus is seated in victory! He accomplished what He set out to do—to bring us to our Father, perfectly Loved and accepted because we are perfectly forgiven!

So Jesus explained, "I tell you the truth, the Son can do nothing by himself. He does only what he sees the Father doing. Whatever the Father does, the Son also does. For the Father loves the Son and shows him everything he is doing. In fact, the Father will show him how to do even greater works than healing this man. Then you will truly be astonished. For just as the Father gives life to those he raises from the dead, so the Son gives life to anyone he wants.

In addition, the Father judges no one. Instead, he has given the Son absolute authority to judge, so that everyone will honor the Son, just as they honor the Father. Anyone who does not honor the Son is certainly not honoring the Father who sent him. I tell you the truth, those who listen to my message and believe in God who sent me have eternal life. They will never be condemned for their sins, but they have already passed from death into life.

John 5:19-24 NLT

The Father has set everything up for our success *through Jesus!* When Jesus lived on earth He spent time with the Father in the heavenly realms through the Holy Spirit. That's how He knew what the Father wanted Him to do. And now that Jesus has taken us to the Father in the heavenly realms, we can do what the Father has for us to do. Jesus accomplishes the Father's will through us by the power of the Holy Spirit. However, if we don't experience the Love of the Father for ourselves, it will be tempting to try and *impress Him* with our works. The Father is already impressed with us! We are His children! He Loves us!

Opening his mouth, Peter said: "I most certainly understand now that God is not one to show partiality, but in every nation the one who fears Him and does what is right is acceptable to Him... You know of Jesus of Nazareth, how God anointed Him with the Holy Spirit and with power, and how He went about doing good and healing all who were oppressed by the devil, for God was with Him.

Acts 10:34-35, 38 NASB

Abba Loves everyone! Jesus forgave sins, healed the sick, drove demons out of people, and raised the dead. He was demonstrating the Father's Love. Abba's Love was not just for the people living in Jesus' day, but for us as well. He is the one who instructed and empowered Jesus to set people free and teach them to live by the Holy Spirit. Abba is Agape Love!

Jesus replied, "Have I been with you all this time, Philip, and yet you still don't know who I am? Anyone who has seen me has seen the Father! So why are you asking me to show him to you? Don't you believe that I am in the Father and the Father is in me? The words I speak are not my own, but my Father who lives in me does his work through me.

Just believe that I am in the Father and the Father is in me. Or at least believe because of the work you have seen me do. I tell you the truth, anyone who believes in me will do the same works I have done, and even greater works, because I am going to be with the Father. You can ask for anything in my name, and I will do it, so that the Son can bring glory to the Father. Yes, ask me for anything in my name, and I will do it!

John 14:9-14 NLT

Because we are *in Christ*, we are *in the Father* and He is in us. We can do *the same works Jesus did — even greater!* Wow! That's hard to believe, right? But that's what Jesus said, so we can begin growing our faith in that truth. As we grow in relationship with our Loving Abba, we can grow in the supernatural gifts that Jesus did on earth. Holy Spirit lives in us to carry on the works of Jesus *for the Father's glory!*

A couple of weeks after God gave me *The Beautiful Dream*, I asked the Father why I was seated to His left. He said, *"Because I want you next to my heart."* I was overwhelmed and sobbed with tears of joy! Our Father seats each of us *next to His heart!* I don't know how He does that, but I know that I am no more special than any of my Brothers and Sisters in Christ. So, in the spiritual realm, *you have been seated next to the Father's heart too!* None of us are less important or less Lovable than the others.

We have a new Father and a new Family. People who *love the ways of the world* won't agree with the message of Jesus. And we who decide to follow Jesus will eventually be ridiculed, slandered and persecuted in some way. Some followers of Jesus are rejected by their own earthly families and Jesus knows what that feels like. For a season, *Jesus' own family* thought he was losing His mind. Jesus Loved His earthly family, but He knew who His *real* Family was.

Then Jesus entered a house, and again a crowd gathered, so that he and his disciples were not even able to eat. When his family heard about this, they went to take charge of him, for they said, "He is out of his mind." Then Jesus' mother and brothers arrived. Standing outside, they sent someone in to call him. A crowd was sitting around him, and they told him, "Your mother and brothers are outside looking for you." "Who are my mother and my brothers?" he asked. Then he looked at those seated in a circle around him and said, "Here are my mother and my brothers! Whoever does God's will is my brother and sister and mother."

Mark 3:20-21, 31-35 NLT

Jesus' earthly family eventually believed He was the Messiah and were led to the Father as well. Our Abba is able to meet every need we have if we will *accept His Love* and *trust His heart.*

For this reason I say to you, do not be worried about your life, as to what you will eat or what you will drink; nor for your body, as to what you will put on. Is life not more than food, and the body more than clothing? Look at the birds of the sky, that they do not sow, nor reap, nor gather crops into barns, and yet your heavenly Father feeds them. Are you not much more important than they? And which of you by worrying can add a single day to his life's span?

Matthew 6:25-27 NASB

When He was 12 years old, Jesus' family took a trip to Jerusalem for the Passover festival and His *coming of age ceremony.* When they left to go back home, they thought Jesus was with other family members or friends. That night they realized Jesus was missing and frantically set out to find Him. *Three days later* they found Jesus in the temple discussing scripture with the priests!

His parents didn't know what to think. "Son," his mother said to him, "why have you done this to us? Your father and I have been frantic, searching for you everywhere. "But why did you need to search?" he asked. "Didn't you know that I must be in my Father's house?" But they didn't understand what he meant. Then he returned to Nazareth with them and was obedient to them. And his mother stored all these things in her heart. Jesus grew in wisdom and in stature and in favor with God and all the people.

Luke 2:48-52 NLT

Jesus wasn't being disobedient or sarcastic. He had just been declared *a young man* so that He could make certain decisions on His own. How would they *not know* He wanted to *be seated in His Abba's House* and learn from Him?

No earthly father is perfect, but Abba is! If you have an imperfect but good dad with good intentions, you are blessed. Some do not. Keep in mind that Adam and Eve didn't have parents to blame but the devil wrecked their lives anyway. We can't always pinpoint the root of our pain, but we know the One who can, and He is the Savior. The Bible tells us that the devil comes to steal, kill and destroy, but Abba sent Jesus to bring us abundant life. You can't change how your story began, but Jesus can change how it ends if you will let Him.

Take all the hurt and grief of this life to Father God and forgive everyone who sinned against you. *Release the pain to God* and your healing will begin. Abba will wrap His arms around you and pull you close to His Heart!

Your Heavenly Father will never abandon you, abuse you, lie to you, belittle, shame or reject you. He knows how awesome you are because *He created you!* Through Jesus, you have been *recreated* into the person God designed you to be all along. You just might not realize it yet.

As you spend time with Abba, He will unwrap rich treasures of His grace and restore your soul one encounter at a time. Abba sent Jesus after you and is so proud to see you escorted to your chair *next to His Heart.*

Father God has *accepted* you, *adopted* you and He *Loves you perfectly!* Now the Holy Spirit is asking you to *be seated in your Abba's House* so you can learn from Him, receive His extravagant Love and freely give it away!

Declaration

I'M SEATED NEXT TO MY ABBA!

14

Incomparable Riches

And God raised us up with Christ and seated us with him in the heavenly realms in Christ Jesus, in order that in the coming ages he might show the incomparable riches of his grace, expressed in his kindness to us in Christ Jesus.

Ephesians 2:6-7 NIV

In *The Beautiful Dream*, as soon as Jesus touched me I was completely free of all evil and filled with perfect Love! *It felt exactly like I was in Heaven!* There was no more sin, sickness, fear, depression, pain — *or anything evil in me or touching me!* What Jesus paid for us to inherit here on earth was way more than we have imagined! These promises are called the *incomparable riches of God's grace* for a reason!

I pray that out of his glorious riches he may strengthen you with power through his Spirit in your inner being, so that Christ may dwell in your hearts through faith. And I pray that you, being rooted and established in love, may have power, together with all the Lord's holy people, to grasp how wide and long and high and deep is the love of Christ, and to know this love that surpasses knowledge — that you may be filled to the measure of all the fullness of God. Now to him who is able to do immeasurably more than all we ask or imagine, according to his power that is at work within us, to him be glory in the church and in Christ Jesus throughout all generations, for ever and ever! Amen.

Ephesians 3:16-21 NIV

God's Word is truth. As Christians, we often miss out on the riches of God's grace because we don't believe they are ours here on earth. Every scene in *The Beautiful Dream* took place while I was living on this earth and in every scene I was free as if I was in Heaven! It was glorious! *Jesus* is the one who comes to us, makes us God's child, and sets us free!

Jesus replied, "Very truly I tell you, everyone who sins is a slave to sin. Now a slave has no permanent place in the family, but a son belongs to it forever. So if the Son sets you free, you will be free indeed.

John 8:34-36 NIV

If you have been *born again*, you are no longer a slave to sin! You are a child of God and *Jesus has set you free!* The riches of God's grace through Jesus are so astounding that it's really hard to believe. But they're real, and they are *already ours* if we can believe Jesus has given them to us!

As we live our lives learning to be *seated in His presence*, we become more and more grounded in our faith—*like a tree*. The seed of the Word of God grows inside us. The roots grow *deep* into God's water table to nourish the tree, and *wide* to anchor the tree in the soil of our hearts.

Oh, the joys of those who do not follow the advice of the wicked, or stand around with sinners, or join in with mockers. But they delight in the law of the LORD, meditating on it day and night. They are like trees planted along the riverbank, bearing fruit each season. Their leaves never wither, and they prosper in all they do. But not the wicked! They are like worthless chaff, scattered by the wind. They will be condemned at the time of judgment. Sinners will have no place among the godly. For the LORD watches over the path of the godly, but the path of the wicked leads to destruction.

Psalm 1:1-6 NLT

When Jesus died on the cross, He paid for us to be *free from all the power of wickedness*. That is why we do not participate in sin.

Being *seated together with God* means we are all like trees with roots that drink from the same river of life, *the Holy Spirit.* The *incomparable riches* of God's grace that we consume at God's Table every day will show up in our lives as *Love for people* and *the absence of evil.*

If you *believe* you are still unholy, unlovable, rejected and destined to become ill, you have planted yourself in a desert. Obviously *we grow like a tree,* so we shouldn't become discouraged if we don't see lots of good fruit from our tree right away. There is no condemnation for those in Christ Jesus! However, *we must position ourselves* beside the river of life, roots deep into God's Water Table. When we are *seated at God's Table* drinking of Him, we will begin to see results. A man after God's own heart, said it like this:

Bless and affectionately praise the LORD, O my soul, and all that is [deep] within me, bless His holy name. Bless and affectionately praise the LORD, O my soul, and do not forget any of His benefits; who forgives all your sins, who heals all your diseases; who redeems your life from the pit, who crowns you [lavishly] with lovingkindness and tender mercy; who satisfies your years with good things, so that your youth is renewed like the [soaring] eagle.

Psalm 103:1-5 AMP

The riches of God's grace include forgiveness of sin, physical healing, emotional healing, mental healing, deliverance, protection, provision and much more. He gives us *all good things* so that we are made new like a healthy child filled with Love! Jesus was nailed to a cross so we could be healed — spirit, soul and body!

He was wounded because of our rebellious deeds, crushed because of our sins; he endured punishment that made us well; because of his wounds we have been healed.

Isaiah 53:5 NET

Jesus took our punishment so we could have perfect peace in our body, soul, and spirit. God wants to bless us, *not punish us.* The Lord doesn't want us to wander off into dangerous territory so sometimes He has to correct and discipline us. He does that because He Loves us so much and wants us safe in His Love.

Father God is smiling at you with pride in His eyes. His spiritual arms are extended, inviting you to run and jump into His embrace! Until we can trust His hands and His smile to be genuine and Loving, it may seem difficult for us to *receive His riches of grace.* But God's Word tells us we can! *The Beautiful Dream* does as well.

God's *incomparable riches* have been purchased for us by Jesus and are available to us through His Spirit. So I asked myself after the dream, "Why did I not *feel* free like I did in the dream?" My journey with the Lord after the dream clarified that a bit. The *process* of drawing closer to Jesus revealed that my soul desperately needed to be restored. He wanted to deliver me and heal my heart in His presence. God wanted my *relationship* with Him to grow! I needed to know how rich His Love for me was so I would grow deeper in His Love and never want to leave His side.

I didn't know what that looked like at first, so I'm sure my attempts to be seated have looked awkward — to say the least. Maybe it's like a little child learning to climb up into their big chair at the family table and pay attention. For our own sake and for the sake of others, we need to mature in the Spirit and learn to pay attention to the Lord.

As I took *spiritual dance lessons* with the Lord and learned to follow His lead, He led me *closer* into His Love and truth. I am learning daily how to be seated and how to stand up for others more gracefully by His power. I can tell you from experience that Jesus is so patient, but He also means what He says. It is vitally important to follow His lead. It's a process of encounters with God that brings healing and breakthrough.

The Beautiful Dream is God's blinking neon sign saying to each of us, "I'm not angry with you and I'm not going to punish you. I see that you Love me. I Love you and I have so much to give you. *Please be seated in my presence.* Learn from Me and my truth will set you free."

What then shall we say to these things? If God is for us, who is against us? He who did not spare His own Son, but delivered Him over for us all, how will He not also with Him freely give us all things?

Romans 8:31-32 NASB

When you say *yes* to Jesus, you become a *righteous and holy child of God.* As children of God, all the riches of grace are ours. In the dream, I realized, "I don't know how to dance!" I only knew that I should *follow his lead.* Well, sometimes He has to lead us *away* from mindsets or behavior that we didn't realize were keeping us from His blessings. Those journeys can take some time. But if you will begin your journey by *knowing the truth about your Foundation in Jesus,* it won't take nearly so long!

In Christ every believer is free of guilt, blame and shame! If you are still feeling ashamed or unloved, the foundation of your faith is not what it needs to be. You will tend to try and *prove your worth* by works, or you will look to *blame others* for your problems. You will see yourself and everyone else from a poverty mindset. But when you know *who we are* in Christ and *what we have in Him,* your thought life and behavior will change. You are rich when you are seated with God in the heavenly realms!

Behold, to obey is better than sacrifice...

1 Samuel 15:22b NKJV

God has *blessed* you and has great plans for your life. As you grow in the Lord you will *follow His Love* into what *He* wants you to do. God asks us to turn every part of our lives over to Him, but He doesn't want us making sacrifices that He has not asked us to make. You cannot receive what God has for you if you are trusting in someone else or your own broken heart.

Learn to listen to God and only do what *the Spirit* is asking you to do. This is how the Church will begin to experience *the incomparable riches of God's grace* flowing from God's Kingdom to earth!

If you have problems, it doesn't mean you aren't saved or not following the Spirit. Stop feeling fearful and ashamed! Our faith is not in *our* faith, *our* belief system, *our* doctrine or *our* ability to be perfect. The riches of Agape Love are already ours because *our faith is in Jesus and we follow Him.* Whether we get around to unwrapping all these rich blessings on this earth or not, they will all be unwrapped for us on the day Jesus takes us from the heavenly realms to Heaven itself! So, by faith, rejoice in Jesus and what He has given us! We are very blessed!

For the LORD God is a sun and shield; the LORD will give grace and glory; no good thing will He withhold from those who walk uprightly. O LORD of hosts, blessed is the man who trusts in You!

Psalm 84:11-12 NKJV

God has given us *incomparable treasures* in the heavenly realms! But you see, we can't take what we treasure on earth with us *and* be seated at God's Table in His Kingdom. God *gave His Greatest Treasure* for us—Jesus! With joy, we empty our hearts of this world so we can receive all He has for us!

Again, the kingdom of heaven is like treasure hidden in a field, which a man found and hid; and for joy over it he goes and sells all that he has and buys that field.

Matthew 13:44 NKJV

Declaration

GOD IS REVEALING
THE INCOMPARABLE RICHES OF HIS GRACE!

15

Be Seated in Authority & Power

You are from God, little children, and have conquered them, because the one who is in you is greater than the one who is in the world.

1 John 4:4 NET

In *The Beautiful Dream* Jesus filled me with His Spirit so that as a beloved child of God, I am victorious!   Jesus has already defeated the devil for me!   I can rest in that truth!

For though we live in the world, we do not wage war as the world does. The weapons we fight with are not the weapons of the world. On the contrary, they have divine power to demolish strongholds. We demolish arguments and every pretension that sets itself up against the knowledge of God, and we take captive every thought to make it obedient to Christ. And we will be ready to punish every act of disobedience, once your obedience is complete.

2 Corinthians 10:3-6 NIV

Our minds will be attacked. We won't win battles as long as we are *disobedient* to the King or allow *thoughts that aren't from Heaven* to reign in our minds. We are victorious when we deny Satan's lies and submit to God's Agape truth!

Then I heard a loud voice in heaven, saying, "Now the salvation, and the power, and the kingdom of our God and the authority of His Christ have come, for the accuser of our brothers and sisters has been thrown down, the one who accuses them before our God day and night. And they overcame him because of the blood of the Lamb and because of the word of their testimony, and they did not love their life even when faced with death.

Revelation 12:10-11 NASB

The blood of Jesus has authority and power! It cancelled all legal accusations against you the moment you said *yes* to Jesus! *Sharing your testimony* about Jesus carries authority and power! Being willing to die to the things of this world and to die physically for the Gospel prepares your body to carry the power and authority of the Spirit!

When Jesus returned to Capernaum, a Roman officer came and pleaded with him, "Lord, my young servant lies in bed, paralyzed and in terrible pain," Jesus said, "I will come and heal him." But the officer said, "Lord, I am not worthy to have you come into my home. Just say the word from where you are, and my servant will be healed. I know this because I am under the authority of my superior officers, and I have authority over my soldiers. I only need to say, 'Go,' and they go, or 'Come,' and they come. And if I say to my slaves, 'Do this,' they do it."

When Jesus heard this, he was amazed. Turning to those who were following him, he said, "I tell you the truth, I haven't seen faith like this in all Israel! And I tell you this, that many Gentiles will come from all over the world—from east and west—and sit down with Abraham, Isaac, and Jacob at the feast in the Kingdom of Heaven. But many Israelites—those for whom the Kingdom was prepared—will be thrown into outer darkness, where there will be weeping and gnashing of teeth," Then Jesus said to the Roman officer, "Go back home. Because you believed, it has happened." And the young servant was healed that same hour.

Matthew 8:5-13 NLT

Faith in God's Word carries authority and power. The Roman officer knew how authority worked. He would give commands and his officers would carry them out. Jesus gave the command in one place, by the Spirit, and the Roman officer's servant was healed in another place! Jesus was seated in the heavenly realms. That is where *our warfare* takes place against the enemy. We can decree and declare God's Word against the works of the enemy anytime. God's motivation, and ours, is always Love!

Bless the LORD, you His angels, you mighty ones who do His commandments, obeying the voice of His word!
Psalm 103:20 AMP

When we *speak the Word* over our situation, not doubting at all, God's angels are able to assist us! *God's angels* carry God's authority and power to help us.

Let all that I am praise the LORD; with my whole heart, I will praise his holy name. Let all that I am praise the LORD; may I never forget the good things he does for me. He forgives all my sins and heals all my diseases. He redeems me from death and crowns me with love and tender mercies. He fills my life with good things. My youth is renewed like the eagle's!
Psalm 103:1-5 NLT

Praise, worship, thanksgiving and rejoicing are powerful in authority and power against the enemy. We *declare* God's Light, Love and Truth with joy and strongholds are broken!

Ask, and it will be given to you; seek, and you will find; knock, and it will be opened to you. For everyone who asks receives, and he who seeks finds, and to him who knocks it will be opened.
Matthew 7:7-8 NKJV

God releases His authority and power when we *ask Him, seek Him* and *knock on His door* in *genuine prayer.* Jesus went on to talk about the Love and generosity of the Father. If we as humans know how to give our children good gifts, we don't need to doubt the goodness of our Father. He is the perfect Father! Faith in Abba's perfect Love is powerful when we pray!

For the one who speaks in a tongue does not speak to people, but to God; for no one understands, but in his spirit he speaks mysteries.

1 Corinthians 14:2 NASB

Praying in the Spirit's unknown heavenly language carries authority and power. The Holy Spirit prays through you!

When the seventy-two disciples returned, they joyfully reported to him, "Lord, even the demons obey us when we use your name!" "Yes," he told them, "I saw Satan fall from heaven like lightning! Look, I have given you authority over all the power of the enemy, and you can walk among snakes and scorpions and crush them. Nothing will injure you.

But don't rejoice because evil spirits obey you; rejoice because your names are registered in heaven." At that same time Jesus was filled with the joy of the Holy Spirit, and he said, "O Father, Lord of heaven and earth, thank you for hiding these things from those who think themselves wise and clever, and for revealing them to the childlike. Yes, Father, it pleased you to do it this way."

Luke 10:17-21 NLT

The name of Jesus in child-like faith carries God's authority and power over the devil and his demonic work. The name, Jesus, means, *"The Lord is salvation."* So every time we pray, declare, or command something evil to leave *in the name of Jesus*, we are declaring that we believe Jesus is the Savior over that situation. We come in *His* name, not in our own power! We come in the power of His Love that drives out evil because Jesus lives in us. When we walk into a situation, Jesus walks in with us!

And then he [Jesus] told them, "Go into all the world and preach the Good News to everyone. Anyone who believes and is baptized will be saved. But anyone who refuses to believe will be condemned. These miraculous signs will accompany those who believe: They will cast out demons in my name, and they will speak in new languages. They will be able to handle snakes with safety, and if they drink anything poisonous, it won't hurt them. They will be able to place their hands on the sick, and they will be healed."

Mark 16:15-18 NLT

Whether you *pray* for the sick, *command* a disease to leave, or just *touch* a person, it is your faith in the Agape Love of God through Jesus that heals them. God receives so much glory!

I will send my terror ahead of you and throw into confusion every nation you encounter. I will make all your enemies turn their backs and run.

Exodus 23:27 NIV

God goes ahead of us to drive out the enemy! This happens when we believe that God Loves us all and we are totally dependent on Him! But those who do not believe in the grace of Jesus do not have Holy Spirit. They will get into some trouble trying to drive demons out in Jesus' name!

A group of Jews was traveling from town to town casting out evil spirits. They tried to use the name of the Lord Jesus in their incantation, saying, "I command you in the name of Jesus, whom Paul preaches, to come out!" Seven sons of Sceva, a leading priest, were doing this. But one time when they tried it, the evil spirit replied, "I know Jesus, and I know Paul, but who are you?" Then the man with the evil spirit leaped on them, overpowered them, and attacked them with such violence that they fled from the house, naked and battered.

The story of what happened spread quickly all through Ephesus, to Jews and Greeks alike. A solemn fear descended on the city, and the name of the Lord Jesus was greatly honored. Many who became believers confessed their sinful practices. A number of them who had been practicing sorcery brought their incantation books and burned them at a public bonfire. The value of the books was several million dollars. So the message about the Lord spread widely and had a powerful effect.

Acts 19:13-20 NLT

The Lord desires to set people free from every work of the devil and *God has chosen His children to do the work.* Cleanse your homes and your hearts of any form of sorcery and witchcraft. *Draw near to God* and rid yourself of all pride, unbelief and compromise, not just so *you* can be free, but *so you can help free others* from the power of the enemy!

And I will give you the keys of the kingdom of heaven, and whatever you bind on earth will be bound in heaven, and whatever you loose on earth will be loosed in heaven.
Matthew 16:19 NKJV

Wow! We are not left to fight the devil on our own power. We are seated with God at His Kingdom Table. In that place of total submission to God, we are given authority over demons so we can carry out God's will here on earth. Is it possible that we are not executing the authority and power that Jesus has entrusted to us against the kingdom of darkness? What would happen if we did?

For the Kingdom of God is not just a lot of talk; it is living by God's power.
1 Corinthians 4:20 NLT

From the beginning, God designed us to *rule with God* on earth. We live in the Kingdom with King Jesus as our Lord and Ruler, so there are no limits to what can be done if we follow His lead. What is impossible for man is *totally possible* with God—for ourselves, our families, our communities and our nations.

See Notes: #4 Declarations and Decrees

Declaration

JESUS HAS GIVEN ME AUTHORITY
TO DESTROY THE WORKS OF THE DEVIL!

16

Dance with the Body of Christ

God's children are referred to as the *Body of Christ*. Just as the head is the control center of the physical body, Jesus is the Head of the Body of Christ. The Holy Spirit dwells inside each one of our physical bodies, but together we are the whole Body of Christ. Together *we are one* with Christ! In this way, Jesus is not only able to *save us*, but to minister *through us*, His Body, to others. In *The Beautiful Dream*, scene two, my husband and I were seated in unity as we shared a common Agape Love and enthusiasm for Jesus. This is a beautiful picture of *the Body of Christ!*

Don't you realize that your body is the temple of the Holy Spirit, who lives in you and was given to you by God? You do not belong to yourself, for God bought you with a high price. So you must honor God with your body.
1 Corinthians 6:19-20 NLT

We were bought at the priceless cost of Jesus's suffering on the cross! Our bodies, souls and spirits *belong to Jesus now* and because of what He has done for us, we joyfully do what He says! We may not always yield perfectly to Him, but *He knows* if we are genuinely trying to follow His lead.

Come to the Lord, the living stone rejected by people as worthless but chosen by God as valuable. Come as living stones, and let yourselves be used in building the spiritual temple, where you will serve as holy priests to offer spiritual and acceptable sacrifices to God through Jesus Christ. ⁶ *For the scripture says,*

> *"I chose a valuable stone, which I am placing as the cornerstone in Zion; and whoever believes in him will never be disappointed."*

1 Peter 2:4-6 GNT

We are like a holy temple being built as living stones upon Jesus, our Cornerstone! The stones need to be placed where the Builder wants them to be. In other words, we need to *be seated in our place* in the Body of Christ. If you are doing what others expect you to do, you may not ever fulfill God's purpose for your life. And if you try to fill every ministry lacking in your church, you may be robbing someone of their joy of serving and maturing in the gifts Holy Spirit has given them. The more we as individuals are *in sync with God's Spirit*, the more we as a Body are healthy and can enjoy the power of the presence of God!

He is the one who holds the whole building together and makes it grow into a sacred temple dedicated to the Lord. In union with him you too are being built together with all the others into a place where God lives through his Spirit.

Ephesians 2:21-22 GNT

Some will attend our churches that haven't given their lives to Jesus yet. There may even be some in our churches who *claim* to be Christians but don't know Jesus. The Body of Christ is every person on earth who *genuinely loves and follows Jesus*. It is *not our job to judge hearts*, but to follow Jesus, the Head, into our purpose in the Body of Christ.

Here is another story Jesus told: "The Kingdom of Heaven is like a farmer who planted good seed in his field. But that night as the workers slept, his enemy came and planted weeds among the wheat, then slipped away. When the crop began to grow and produce grain, the weeds also grew. The farmer's workers went to him and said, 'Sir, the field where you planted that good seed is full of weeds! Where did they come from?' 'An enemy has done this!' the farmer exclaimed. 'Should we pull out the weeds?' they asked. 'No,' he replied, 'you'll uproot the wheat if you do. Let both grow together until the harvest. Then I will tell the harvesters to sort out the weeds, tie them into bundles, and burn them, and to put the wheat in the barn.'"

Matthew 13:24-30 NLT

God has given us guidelines about not tolerating evil behavior and false doctrine in our churches. But beyond that, we are to treat one another with *respect, patience and honor* as we *grow up* in Christ. The Lord has angels who will sort the true followers from the fake ones on Judgment Day. That's not our job to do. Judgment Day has not come yet. So there is still hope for all of us to draw nearer to our Father's heart and be seated! We are *the Body of Christ,* so how we treat one another is how we are treating Jesus, our Lord.

For just as the body is one and yet has many parts, and all the parts of the body, though they are many, are one body, so also is Christ. For by one Spirit we were all baptized into one body, whether Jews or Greeks, whether slaves or free, and we were all made to drink of one Spirit.

1 Corinthians 12:12-13 NASB

Every believer, no matter who they are, where they live, how "sinful" they were before they met Jesus or how strong they have grown spiritually is part of the Body of Christ. We drink of the same Spirit who gives us life! Each of us has been perfectly designed by God to be a *blessing* in the Body of Christ. When we know God and live by the Spirit, He will show each of us what He wants us to do in His Kingdom. The Spirit gives us supernatural *Agape Love* gifts so we can touch lives in a way we never could have done on our own. As we grow in our Love relationship with Jesus, so can the gifts of the Spirit in our lives.

Just as our bodies have many parts and each part has a special function, so it is with Christ's body. We are many parts of one body, and we all belong to each other. In his grace, God has given us different gifts for doing certain things well. So if God has given you the ability to prophesy, speak out with as much faith as God has given you. If your gift is serving others, serve them well. If you are a teacher, teach well. If your gift is to encourage others, be encouraging. If it is giving, give generously. If God has given you leadership ability, take the responsibility seriously. And if you have a gift for showing kindness to others, do it gladly.

Romans 12:4-8 NLT

You are very important in the Body of Christ no matter how young you are in the Lord! God will place some in leadership roles who have *walked in the Spirit* for a while.

Now these are the gifts Christ gave to the church: the apostles, the prophets, the evangelists, and the pastors and teachers. Their responsibility is to equip God's people to do his work and build up the church, the body of Christ. This will continue until we all come to such unity in our faith and knowledge of God's Son that we will be mature in the Lord, measuring up to the full and complete standard of Christ.

Ephesians 4:11-13 NLT

Apostles, prophets, evangelists, pastors and teachers are meant to work together in God's Kingdom on earth. These leaders are to bring people to Jesus and teach new believers to grow up spiritually in the power of the Spirit. Then they can *follow the Spirit* and do God's work as part of the Body.

Not every believer will end up in *full-time ministry* like Peter, John and Paul in the Bible. But no one can remain a spiritual infant for life either. We must *believe* that every Christian can *learn to walk powerfully in the Spirit*. Baby Christians need guidance as they grow from infancy toward maturity. They need to learn about both *humility* and *working in God's power-gifts* at the same time. Otherwise, their spiritual tree will become stunted, sterile, fruitless and may even die. Some will get discouraged and seek out dangerous teachings to satisfy the God-given craving to live from the supernatural realm. We should rejoice with every step of growth a new believer takes and *encourage them* to keep moving forward in Holy Spirit.

As a result, we are no longer to be children, tossed here and there by waves and carried about by every wind of doctrine, by the trickery of people, by craftiness in deceitful scheming; but speaking the truth in love, we are to grow up in all aspects into Him who is the head, that is, Christ, from whom the whole body, being fitted and held together by what every joint supplies, according to the proper working of each individual part, causes the growth of the body for the building up of itself in love.

Ephesians 4:14-16 NASB

Every believer has been called to fill a spot in the Body. It's important that we don't judge the performance of members of the Body like the world does. What matters to God is their Love-relationship with Jesus that inspires them to serve — not the excellence of their natural talents or their appearance. The *smallest* act of kindness done in the Agape power of God's Spirit is *huge* in the Kingdom of God!

... and let's consider how to encourage one another in love and good deeds, not abandoning our own meeting together, as is the habit of some people, but encouraging one another; and all the more as you see the day drawing near.

Hebrews 10:24-25 NASB

God has intended believers to *meet together* as members of the Body. Ask the Lord to lead you to a good church that teaches the truth of the Word of God, seeks to follow the Spirit, reaches outside the church to the lost and blesses people in need. What the building looks like is not important at all. Look deeper by the Spirit for the fruit of the Spirit. Get involved and be faithful to *meet in person* with them.

When God tells you which church to call your own, respect and honor the leaders in the way that *they* believe God has instructed them to lead. Pray for everyone and always extend God's grace to them as God has extended His grace to you.

Jesus pronounced you *clean* the moment you said *yes* to His dance. Your guilt was nailed to the cross and buried in a tomb on earth. The new you was raised to life and seated with God as part of the Body of Christ! If your priority is to be seated daily with *the Head*, you will be able to "find your chair" in the Body of Christ.

Jesus is not ashamed, fearful or prideful so you aren't either. You are *in His Body* and you *have His Spirit.* You are in His Love and able to do anything *He* asks of you. Seek Jesus at His Table and God's wonderful fruit and power-gifts will be given to you by the Holy Spirit for His glory. You are *already* a blessing in *the Body of Christ* and you will continue to be—as you grow up in Jesus!

See Notes: #5 The Church

Declaration

I AM A BLESSING IN THE BODY OF CHRIST!

17

God's Table

The Beautiful Dream is a picture of the Good News of Jesus: Our *salvation*, becoming *established in Christ* on earth, and being *seated* with God in the Spirit. The Table seating eight represents *a new beginning*. Three chairs represent God, *the Trinity*, and the other five chairs represent God's children *redeemed by grace*. Jesus spoke about tables and banquets, and He made a point to sit down with people *at their tables* to share food and conversation. We really need to pay attention to what He is trying to tell us about tables!

The Table in the dream can represent a *Heavenly Board Room* where God is the CEO giving updates, instructions, assignments and hearing from His team. It may represent the *Family Table* where God the Father, Son and Holy Spirit are sharing spiritual food and fellowship with their beautiful children—us! And it could represent the Table in the *Command Center* or *War Room* where God presents to us His victorious strategies against our enemies. It is a multi-purpose Table in *the House of the Lord*.

And just like we often have to remind our small children to have a seat, God is kindly telling us to pay attention and sit down at the Table. There is so much going on that only He knows about. Each of us have a vital role in His plans for His Kingdom. We are all so very honored to be a part of what He is doing on this earth!

But no matter what work He has for us to do, nothing matters if we don't first understand and experience the bounty of God's extravagant Love and grace. Once Jesus touches your heart, you will gladly give up *everything* to be seated with Him!

Meanwhile, Jesus was in Bethany at the home of Simon, a man who had previously had leprosy. While he was eating, a woman came in with a beautiful alabaster jar of expensive perfume made from essence of nard. She broke open the jar and poured the perfume over his head. Some of those at the table were indignant. "Why waste such expensive perfume?" they asked. "It could have been sold for a year's wages and the money given to the poor!" So they scolded her harshly.

But Jesus replied, "Leave her alone. Why criticize her for doing such a good thing to me? You will always have the poor among you, and you can help them whenever you want to. But you will not always have me. She has done what she could and has anointed my body for burial ahead of time. I tell you the truth, wherever the Good News is preached throughout the world, this woman's deed will be remembered and discussed."

Mark 14:3-9 NLT

Jesus saw this woman's heart. She was so full of Love for her Messiah that she poured out what may have been her life savings upon His head. *Jesus saw the hearts of the critics as well.* He knew they didn't really Love the poor. They were so blind with pride that they couldn't *see* what was important in that moment. Their judgmental and critical spirits created a *spiritual stench* at the table—so much so that Jesus had to tell them to *leave her alone!*

When we *pour everything out on Jesus,* all our dreams and plans, our loved ones, our sin, our possessions and our pride, we are showing Him and everyone around us that we owe Him our lives! We are pouring out our Love! His death has brought us to life, and the sweet perfume that fills the room is evidence that we have truly died to our old life. We've buried the dead body of accusation, blame and shame, and have come alive in His Love—*at His Table.*

Then he turned to his host. "When you put on a luncheon or a banquet," he said, "don't invite your friends, brothers, relatives, and rich neighbors. For they will invite you back, and that will be your only reward. Instead, invite the poor, the crippled, the lame, and the blind. Then at the resurrection of the righteous, God will reward you for inviting those who could not repay you."

Luke 14:12-14 NLT

If you invest your time and money into *securing friends* because you *fear* being *ashamed*, maybe you're living from the earthly realm. Agape Love is not conditional. You can't buy it or earn it by your works. It is also *not a law* that says, "Feed the poor or you'll be in trouble!" If you're seated next to the Father's heart, the Spirit will show you how He plans for you to invest in the Kingdom of Agape Love. You will have plenty of Love to share from God's Table!

The Lord is my shepherd, I lack nothing. He makes me lie down in green pastures, he leads me beside quiet waters, he refreshes my soul. He guides me along the right paths for his name's sake. Even though I walk through the darkest valley, I will fear no evil, for you are with me; your rod and your staff, they comfort me. You prepare a table before me in the presence of my enemies. You anoint my head with oil; my cup overflows. Surely your goodness and love will follow me all the days of my life, and I will dwell in the house of the Lord forever.

Psalm 23:1-6 NIV

My Great Shepherd *provides* everything I need. Jesus causes me to stop striving and *rest in His grace*. I drink from His *Living Water* every day, and *my soul finds peace*. Jesus changed the course of my life and is leading me down a *new path filled with His light*. Though I will face fierce battles along this way, I am not afraid because *the Lord is within me*. My faith is in Jesus, and His Word wielded like a sword, will slay the giants in my way.

The Lord has *prepared a Table for me* as the devil and his demons *stand watching hatefully and taunting us*. Jesus takes *His* expensive jar of oil that He paid for with His own life's blood, and *pours it out on my head.* He is anointing me for *my* burial as I die to my old self and come alive in Him to fulfill my special purpose in His Kingdom. The cup of my heart is filled to overflowing with *the wine of the Holy Spirit!* His *goodness and Love* permeates my whole being like a beautiful fragrance. I am amazed because Jesus has escorted me to *His House* and seats me at *His Family Table,* where I will dwell with Him forever — starting right now!

Now Jonathan, Saul's son, had a son who was disabled in both feet. He was five years old when the news of Saul and Jonathan came from Jezreel, and his nurse picked him up and fled. But it happened that in her hurry to flee, he fell and could no longer walk. And his name was Mephibosheth.

2 Samuel 4:4 NASB

King Saul tried to kill young David many times, but David remained faithful and served him anyway. He had opportunities to kill Saul in self-defense, but instead, he honored Saul's anointed position and resisted temptation. Saul's son, Jonathan, however, was David's best friend. They were such close friends that they made a covenant to support one another no matter what happened. Jonathan grieved over his father's hatred for David.

After King Saul and Jonathan were killed by the Philistines, David and his men recovered Israel from the enemy. King David was concerned about *Saul's family* because many of them had been slaughtered by the Philistines during the battle. One of Saul's household servants, Ziba, told King David about Mephibosheth, and David sent for him.

His name was Mephibosheth; he was Jonathan's son and Saul's grandson. When he came to David, he bowed low to the ground in deep respect. David said, "Greetings, Mephibosheth." Mephibosheth replied, "I am your servant."

"Don't be afraid!" David said. "I intend to show kindness to

you because of my promise to your father, Jonathan. I will give you all the property that once belonged to your grandfather Saul, and you will eat here with me at the king's table!"

Mephibosheth bowed respectfully and exclaimed, "Who is your servant, that you should show such kindness to a dead dog like me?"

Then the king summoned Saul's servant Ziba and said, "I have given your master's grandson everything that belonged to Saul and his family. You and your sons and servants are to farm the land for him to produce food for your master's household. But Mephibosheth, your master's grandson, will eat here at my table." (Ziba had fifteen sons and twenty servants.) Ziba replied, "Yes, my lord the king; I am your servant, and I will do all that you have commanded."

And from that time on, Mephibosheth ate regularly at David's table, like one of the king's own sons. Mephibosheth had a young son named Mica. From then on, all the members of Ziba's household were Mephibosheth's servants. And Mephibosheth, who was crippled in both feet, lived in Jerusalem and ate regularly at the king's table.

2 Samuel 9:6-13 NLT

God called David a man after His own heart. Is there any wonder why? David had a *personal relationship with God* and modeled His grace beautifully. Though David was probably around 20 years old when Samuel anointed him to be the next king of Israel, David didn't take his crown until *God* gave the command. He was very brave and powerful in battle, yet he refrained from retaliating against King Saul's attempts to murder him.

After becoming king, David looked for a way to bless those who had cursed him. To his surprise, Jonathan's son was still alive. David was so happy to have Mephibosheth seated *daily* at his family table and to take care of all his needs. King David lavishly and excessively kept his covenant with Jonathan. There were no selfish motives in his heart. He just Loved well. David was like Jesus in so many ways!

Our King has taken us in to *His House* and *seated us at His Table*. Who are we that the Lord would invite us, the broken ones, to sit at His Table? Imperfect as we are, the Lord Loves us! He restores our dignity and makes us Family! We are not shamed as dogs or treated as hired servants. We are *heirs* and enjoy a *rich inheritance* in Christ Jesus! He instructs us to see one another *in this light* where we are seated with Him *at His Table* in the heavenly realms.

Let us bow before our King, praise Him for His extravagant expressions of Love and enjoy the grace and mercy of His Majesty's Table! Jesus has anointed our heads with His oil and crowned us with Loving-kindness, declaring us to be royal sons and daughters. Let us keep our covenant with the Son of God, our King, and pour out the fragrant oil of our lives upon Jesus by sharing His tender mercies with others! Where is Mephibosheth!? Find him and invite him to the King's Table!

Declaration

JESUS HAS PREPARED A TABLE FOR ME!

18

The Son's Table

Jesus shared His Table with His twelve disciples just hours before He was arrested. Jesus explained that He would give His body to be broken and His blood to be poured out for us. This *new covenant* would set us free from death and bring us into life in the Spirit!

When the time came, Jesus and the apostles sat down together at the table. Jesus said, "I have been very eager to eat this Passover meal with you before my suffering begins. For I tell you now that I won't eat this meal again until its meaning is fulfilled in the Kingdom of God." Then he took a cup of wine and gave thanks to God for it. Then he said, "Take this and share it among yourselves. For I will not drink wine again until the Kingdom of God has come."

He took some bread and gave thanks to God for it. Then he broke it in pieces and gave it to the disciples, saying, "This is my body, which is given for you. Do this in remembrance of me." After supper he took another cup of wine and said, "This cup is the new covenant between God and his people—an agreement confirmed with my blood, which is poured out as a sacrifice for you."

Luke 22:14-20 NLT

Jesus knew He would begin drinking from a different cup prepared by His Father — *the cup of suffering for our sins!*

He [Jesus] went a little farther and fell on His face, and prayed, saying, "O My Father, if it is possible, let this cup pass from Me; nevertheless, not as I will, but as You will."

Matthew 26:39 NKJV

That same night religious leaders hired one of Jesus' disciples named Judas to help them find Jesus. They took the holy Son of God and tortured Him like He was an evil criminal. The next day they crucified Jesus and He died on the cross that afternoon.

His body was bruised by His accusers, torn with slicing whips, pierced by a crown of thorns, splintered by a rough wooden cross, nailed through and speared, so that we could eat the Bread of Life broken for us—Jesus! But three days later, the Holy Spirit raised Jesus from the dead! A new covenant was born—not a covenant of the law, *but of the Spirit!* Our lives are completely changed!

Don't be drunk with wine, because that will ruin your life. Instead, be filled with the Holy Spirit, singing psalms and hymns and spiritual songs among yourselves, and making music to the Lord in your hearts. And give thanks for everything to God the Father in the name of our Lord Jesus Christ.

Ephesians 5:18-20 NLT

The Holy Spirit comes to live inside us when we enter into *covenant relationship with Jesus.* We don't need earthly wine or drugs to make us forget our sorrows. When we choose to drink of the Spirit, our hearts are filled with God's glory—His Love, joy, peace and all the goodness of God!

"I am the bread of life," Jesus told them. "Those who come to me will never be hungry; those who believe in me will never be thirsty."

John 6:35 GNT

The Ten Commandments and God's other laws were given under the *old covenant.* God's laws are holy and good, but no one can be cleansed by them. The purpose of God's law is to give us a *sin conscience* and to show us that we need a Savior. Trying to live by the holy law produces more sin and guilt because *we can't become holy by our own effort.*

Jesus didn't come to get rid of God's laws, but to *fulfill* them. The *new covenant* cleanses us and gives us power to resist sin by the Spirit! It is the responsibility of parents to teach their children right from wrong (the law), so they will develop a *conscience* and realize they need a Savior. But at the same time, parents *must live by the Spirit* so that Agape Love and grace are the atmosphere of their homes.

A Canaanite woman who lived in that region came to him. "Son of David!" she cried out. "Have mercy on me, sir! My daughter has a demon and is in a terrible condition." But Jesus did not say a word to her. His disciples came to him and begged him, "Send her away! She is following us and making all this noise!" Then Jesus replied, "I have been sent only to the lost sheep of the people of Israel."

At this the woman came and fell at his feet. "Help me, sir!" she said. Jesus answered, "It isn't right to take the children's food and throw it to the dogs." "That's true, sir," she answered, "but even the dogs eat the leftovers that fall from their masters' table." So Jesus answered her, "You are a woman of great faith! What you want will be done for you." And at that very moment her daughter was healed.

Matthew 15:22-28 GNT

This woman, not a Jew, knew if she only ate a crumb of the Bread of Life her daughter would be delivered and healed! Jesus was *testing* her to see if she *believed* God Loved her. She passed the test! Jesus invited her to *His Table*, not to crawl on the floor like a dog, or to be treated like a slave. Jesus invited her and her daughter to be forgiven, healed and delivered in His presence! Others may have seen a dog, but *Jesus saw His Bride* and welcomed her to the Table!

Paul noticed that some believers in the church in Corinth were showing up to the table early with their rich friends, eating all the bread and getting drunk on the wine. They were leaving none for their Brothers and Sisters who were financially poor. Pride has *no chair* at the Son's Table.

So anyone who eats this bread or drinks this cup of the Lord unworthily is guilty of sinning against the body and blood of the Lord. That is why you should examine yourself before eating the bread and drinking the cup. For if you eat the bread or drink the cup without honoring the body of Christ, you are eating and drinking God's judgment upon yourself. That is why many of you are weak and sick and some have even died. But if we would examine ourselves, we would not be judged by God in this way. Yet when we are judged by the Lord, we are being disciplined so that we will not be condemned along with the world.

1 Corinthians 11:27-32 NLT

In *The Beautiful Dream,* my Brothers and Sisters stood up for me as God did. Seated at the Son's Table, we see one another as the Lord does. We don't put shame on others because we don't have any shame in us! Jesus took it away when we said *yes* to Him! We only have Agape Love to give away.

Each one of our Brothers and Sisters in Christ are a temple of the Holy Spirit. They have been *cleansed* and the *Holy Spirit* lives in them. To look down upon them is slandering the Spirit and His work in their lives. According to Jesus, this is *very dangerous* spiritually. How we treat one another is how we are treating Holy Spirit whose power brought about their rebirth.

I am the vine; you are the branches. If you remain in me and I in you, you will bear much fruit; apart from me you can do nothing. If you do not remain in me, you are like a branch that is thrown away and withers; such branches are picked up, thrown into the fire and burned.

If you remain in me and my words remain in you, ask whatever you wish, and it will be done for you. This is to my Father's glory, that you bear much fruit, showing yourselves to be my disciples.

As the Father has loved me, so have I loved you. Now remain in my love. If you keep my commands, you will remain in my love, just as I have kept my Father's commands and remain in his love. I have told you this so that my joy may be in you and that your joy may be complete. My command is this: Love each other as I have loved you.

John 15:5-12 NIV

We *remain* in Jesus, the Vine, by drinking continually of His Spirit and obeying His Word. The result is eternal life, Agape Love and lots of good fruit! Stay connected to Jesus!

And the Holy Spirit also testifies that this is so. For he says, "This is the new covenant I will make with my people on that day, says the LORD: I will put my laws in their hearts, and I will write them on their minds." Then he says, "I will never again remember their sins and lawless deeds." And when sins have been forgiven, there is no need to offer any more sacrifices. And so, dear brothers and sisters, we can boldly enter heaven's Most Holy Place because of the blood of Jesus.

Hebrews 10:15-19 NLT

This *new covenant* is like wedding vows spoken between Jesus and His adoring Bride. He promises to never remember our sin and we promise to stay in Love with Him and follow His lead! Our King is preparing a beautiful wedding banquet and sending us out to invite anyone who will be *clothed in His righteousness!*

Jesus spoke to them again in parables, saying: "The kingdom of heaven is like a king who prepared a wedding banquet for his son. He sent his servants to those who had been invited to the banquet to tell them to come, but they refused to come.

Then he sent some more servants and said, 'Tell those who have been invited that I have prepared my dinner: My oxen and fattened cattle have been butchered, and everything is ready. Come to the wedding banquet.' But they paid no attention and went off—one to his field, another to his business. The rest seized his servants, mistreated them and killed them.

The king was enraged. He sent his army and destroyed those murderers and burned their city. Then he said to his servants, 'The wedding banquet is ready, but those I invited did not deserve to come. So go to the street corners and invite to the banquet anyone you find.' So the servants went out into the streets and gathered all the people they could find, the bad as well as the good, and the wedding hall was filled with guests.

But when the king came in to see the guests, he noticed a man there who was not wearing wedding clothes. He asked, 'How did you get in here without wedding clothes, friend?' The man was speechless. Then the king told the attendants, 'Tie him hand and foot, and throw him outside, into the darkness, where there will be weeping and gnashing of teeth. For many are invited, but few are chosen.'"

Matthew 22:1-14 NIV

We have moved from the *old covenant law* to the *new covenant of grace,* where we live by the Spirit from the heavenly realms. If we're dressing ourselves in our own self-righteous works we will be unprepared on the day of the wedding banquet. We will be fearful and ashamed. But if we're in Love with the Son and seated next to our Father, we will be dressed in acts of Agape Love. So let's be clothed in the righteousness of Jesus Christ and invite others to come to the Son's wonderful *Table of grace!*

See Notes: #6 Old Covenant – New Covenant

Declaration

I'M SEATED ACROSS FROM THE SON OF GOD!

19

The Father's Table

And I will be your Father, and you will be my sons and daughters, says the LORD Almighty.

2 Corinthians 6:18 NLT

A deep revelation of *the astounding Love of our Father God* will open our hearts to the glory of His grace!

Jesus told them this story: "A man had two sons. The younger son told his father, 'I want my share of your estate now before you die.' So his father agreed to divide his wealth between his sons. A few days later this younger son packed all his belongings and moved to a distant land, and there he wasted all his money in wild living. About the time his money ran out, a great famine swept over the land, and he began to starve. He persuaded a local farmer to hire him, and the man sent him into his fields to feed the pigs. The young man became so hungry that even the pods he was feeding the pigs looked good to him. But no one gave him anything.

When he finally came to his senses, he said to himself, 'At home even the hired servants have food enough to spare, and here I am dying of hunger! I will go home to my father and say, "Father, I have sinned against both heaven and you, and I am no longer worthy of being called your son. Please take me on as a hired servant."'

So he returned home to his father. And while he was still a long way off, his father saw him coming. Filled with love and compassion, he ran to his son, embraced him, and kissed him. His son said to him, 'Father, I have sinned against both heaven and you, and I am no longer worthy of being called your son,'

But his father said to the servants, 'Quick! Bring the finest robe in the house and put it on him. Get a ring for his finger and sandals for his feet. And kill the calf we have been fattening. We must celebrate with a feast, for this son of mine was dead and has now returned to life. He was lost, but now he is found.' So the party began.

Meanwhile, the older son was in the fields working. When he returned home, he heard music and dancing in the house, and he asked one of the servants what was going on. 'Your brother is back,' he was told, 'and your father has killed the fattened calf. We are celebrating because of his safe return.' The older brother was angry and wouldn't go in. His father came out and begged him, but he replied, 'All these years I've slaved for you and never once refused to do a single thing you told me to. And in all that time you never gave me even one young goat for a feast with my friends. Yet when this son of yours comes back after squandering your money on prostitutes, you celebrate by killing the fattened calf!'

His father said to him, 'Look, dear son, you have always stayed by me, and everything I have is yours. We had to celebrate this happy day. For your brother was dead and has come back to life! He was lost, but now he is found!'"

Luke 15:11b-32 NLT

There is nothing in this story about the son having to *clean himself up* before his father could hug him. The boy had *repented of his sins* and came back home. The father ran to meet him, embraced his starving body and kissed his precious dirty face! Then He began to order the finest for His beloved son!

Our Abba Father welcomes us in the same way! He is always *longing* for His lost kids to come home. The Father doesn't make us *prove ourselves through good works* before we can enter

His presence. Abba hugged and kissed us with the death of His own Son, Jesus, even while we wore the stench of sin and death! Then He clothed us in robes of His righteousness, placed a ring on our finger and sandals on our feet. He Loves us because we are His children — *not because of what we've done.*

Satan often lures by earthly culture, philosophies, pleasure and pride, but *there is no real food on the world's table.* Satan will *steal* from you and then point a finger of accusation at you. The deceiver does this — *not Abba!*

When we stray from the Father and find ourselves in a mess, deliberately or unintentionally, we often take on the same attitude as the prodigal son. "I'm not worthy. I'm bad. If I *work really hard*, maybe the Father will send some *leftovers* out to the barn for me to eat. I'll just let God *punish and shame me now* and maybe He'll let me *sneak into Heaven* when I die. I'll keep a low profile and nobody will notice I'm here." We may not say those words, but sometimes that is our mindset, and it breaks the Father's heart!

When we think this way, we diminish the cross of Jesus because *we think we have to suffer for our sin* in order to receive our Fathers' grace. The Blood of Jesus cleanses us from *all* sin — not some sin — *all of it!* We also diminish the Father's extravagant Love for us.

When we *repent*, change our direction and come home, our Father sees His precious and dearly Loved sons and daughters! He just wants us seated, safe at His Table in His House again! Abba knows the great potential that is inside you, but that is not His first concern. Agape Love is His first concern. He wants you to know the height, depth and width of His Love so you will never *work for* His Love. You will be *filled with Him* and work from the power and strength of His Love!

When you turn around and start your journey home, *Abba* is watching and runs to meet you on the path! He calls for all of Heaven to celebrate! He prepares a feast for you at the Family

Table—so undeserved yet *extravagant!* He is so happy when your chair at His Table is not empty!

In many prosperous cultures today, a child grows up being urged toward independence. He leaves home with family celebrations and returns only to visit. But *in the Kingdom,* we are *completely dependent* on our Abba forever! When we cherish the Father's Table, every good gift flows to us from His Loving presence. The *inheritance* for His children never runs out as they get to know Him at His Table! Yes, our Father has work for us to do. But it doesn't seem like work when we are *rejoicing with one another in His Love!*

The youngest son came back home with a religious mindset, hoping he could *work hard as hired servant* and just survive. But instead, he received his identity back—as the *beloved son* of his father! He saw his father from *a different perspective*—a perspective of immense love!

The older son also had a religious mindset. He was not doing outward sin in the world, but *his heart was full of evil.* He lost touch with the father's love while still living at home. Nobody noticed until "little brother" came back home. *When put to the test,* the true state of his heart was *exposed!* He was full of pride and void of mercy and grace.

Like the jealous son, many believe that their value and identity as a Christian is *achieved by works.* They aren't happy when someone repents and receives *undeserved favor.* Instead, they keep bringing up their past. A *religious spirit* has taken hold of their heart. They have forgotten who gave them *new birth* and why they are *so blessed.* Each one of us has received *undeserved favor* and our Father deserves *all the glory!* Rejoice at the Father's Table of grace!

Be merciful, just as your Father is merciful.

Luke 6:36 NET

Our Father is so merciful! Do you believe it? Well, let's go back to that wonderful scripture we know so well:

For God so loved the world that he gave his one and only Son, that whoever believes in him shall not perish but have eternal life. For God did not send his Son into the world to condemn the world, but to save the world through him.

John 3:16-17 NIV

The Father Loved *everybody* in the world and sent His Son, Jesus, to save us. He doesn't have condemnation on His mind! The Father has pure Love and acceptance for us and *really wants us to believe it, receive it, rejoice in it and live in it!*

Understanding and believing in the Love of the Father is difficult for so many. The Father is Spirit, and it may seem hard for us to love someone we can't see. No earthly father is perfect, so we're left on the ground level, trying to reach up to a vague Love we have never experienced. That's why Jesus has taken you to the heavenly realms and seated you next to your *Abba.*

Father God wants you to sit next to His heart, *not* so He can keep an eye on you and shame you when you do something wrong. He wants to express His Love to you, *honor you*, and help you. *Abba* wants you close, so He can *protect you.* He wants you near so you can feel comfortable asking Him for whatever you need. Your Father wants you to feel special because *you are special to Him.*

Perhaps your heart is bruised and you need some extra Loving care. That's why you're seated next to your *Papa.* You're important to Him and He knows you're not convinced of that yet. After all, you were adopted and you're still learning about your amazing Father. You can sit next to Him — where *important* people sit. He is going to include you in everything that happens at the Table. You are going to learn the way *He* does things, the way *He* speaks, and especially the way *He* Loves. You know Jesus, and now it's time to know your *Abba!*

...for the Father Himself loves you, because you have loved Me

117

and have believed that I came forth from the Father.

John 16:27 NASB

In *The Beautiful Dream*, Jesus didn't tell me to get in the light or to get happy. He just asked me in the Spirit if I would dance with Him. I said *yes* to following His lead and *He* filled me with unimaginable Love and joy! The transformation was so powerful that I couldn't keep quiet about Him on the earth. Jesus then led me to God's light in the heavenly realms to be seated with my Father. The Love I felt throughout the dream was so immense and intense that I can't put it into words. I would have been thrilled to sit anywhere at that Table, but Jesus placed me next to my Abba—the One who sent Jesus to rescue me! Our Father is so thrilled when we come Home! He wants us always to be seated next to His heart!

Church, *get your hearts ready* because the prodigals are repenting and coming home to Abba! The religious ones will look down on them with arrogant eyes, but to those who Love the Father, they will look beautiful! The prodigals are going to *feel ashamed* but it's our joy to welcome them and celebrate the grace of Jesus over them! So run and get the Father's best robe to cover their fear and shame. Get the sandals of God's peace for their feet and their covenant ring of inheritance.

Welcome your prodigals to the Table unconditionally and say to them, "You are not a hired servant! You are the Father's child! The Lamb has been slain and the food is prepared! Eat the *Bread* and drink of the *wine of the Spirit!* You're safe in the Father's House now, so embrace Him and be seated with us, your Brothers and Sisters. We Love you! *Abba* Loves you and that will never, ever change!"

Declaration

I'M SEATED NEXT TO MY FATHER'S HEART!

20

The Holy Spirit's Table

In *The Beautiful Dream*, the Lady in pink was in charge. She, *well, just the dress*, was the only one I actually *saw* in the room, though I was *aware* of the others. The Holy Spirit is *like* the most perfect mother you could imagine—protective, loving, joyful, peaceful, hilarious, patient, kind, good, faithful, gentle and self-controlled. The Spirit is *wisdom* and teaches God's children *who pay attention*. The Spirit is *all-powerful*, but He *grieves* over those who stray from the Father's Love. Because the Father, the Son and the Spirit are One, we refer to the Holy Spirit in the masculine form, and sometimes as *"Holy Spirit."*

However, when He, the Spirit of truth, has come, He will guide you into all truth; for He will not speak on His own authority, but whatever He hears He will speak; and He will tell you things to come. He will glorify Me, for He will take of what is Mine and declare it to you. All things that the Father has are Mine. Therefore I said that He will take of Mine and declare it to you.

John 16:13-15 NKJV

The Father and Son often speak through Holy Spirit, and the Spirit empowers all of God's children to do His will. John the Baptist said:

I baptize with water those who repent of their sins and turn to God. But someone is coming soon who is greater than I am—so much greater that I'm not worthy even to be his slave and carry

119

his sandals. He will baptize you with the Holy Spirit and with fire.

Matthew 3:11 NLT

John the Baptist was the prophet God spoke through who prepared people to receive the ministry of Jesus. He preached the message of *repentance* and *water baptism.* John also prophesied that Jesus would baptize people in the Holy Spirit and God's fire! And He did!

Gathering them together, He commanded them not to leave Jerusalem, but to wait for what the Father had promised, "Which," He said, "you heard of from Me; for John baptized with water, but you will be baptized with the Holy Spirit not many days from now."

So, when they had come together, they began asking Him, saying, "Lord, is it at this time that You are restoring the kingdom to Israel?"

But He said to them, "It is not for you to know periods of time or appointed times which the Father has set by His own authority; but you will receive power when the Holy Spirit has come upon you; and you shall be My witnesses both in Jerusalem and in all Judea, and Samaria, and as far as the remotest part of the earth." And after He had said these things, He was lifted up while they were watching, and a cloud took Him up, out of their sight.

Acts 1:4-9 NASB

The Spirit's fire burns away impurity in those who repent and yield to His presence. As Christians, we want the fire of the Holy Spirit to remain active so that we can burn with His presence and be empowered to tell others about Jesus!

Blessed is the one who has found wisdom, and the one who obtains understanding. For her benefit is more profitable than silver, and her gain is better than gold. She is more precious than rubies, and none of the things you desire can compare with her. Long life is in her right hand; in her left hand are riches and honor. Her ways are very pleasant, and all her paths are peaceful. She is like a tree of life to those who grasp onto her, and everyone who takes hold of her will be blessed.

By wisdom the LORD laid the foundation of the earth; he established the heavens by understanding. By his knowledge the primordial sea was broken open, so that the clouds drip down dew. My child, do not let them escape from your sight; safeguard sound wisdom and discretion. So they will become life for your soul, and grace around your neck. Then you will walk on your way with security, and you will not stumble. When you lie down you will not be filled with fear; when you lie down your sleep will be pleasant.

Do not be afraid of sudden disaster, or when destruction overtakes the wicked; for the LORD will be the source of your confidence, and he will guard your foot from being caught in a trap.

Proverbs 3:13-26 NET

The Spirit inside us gives us wisdom, understanding, long life, riches, honor, direction, peace, life, blessing, sound judgment, discretion, safety, stability, Love, sweet sleep, the presence of the Lord, freedom *and the list continues!*

But their minds were hardened; for until this very day at the reading of the old covenant the same veil remains unlifted, because it is removed in Christ. But to this day whenever Moses is read, a veil lies over their hearts; but whenever someone turns to the Lord, the veil is taken away. Now the Lord is the Spirit, and where the Spirit of the Lord is, there is freedom. But we all, with unveiled faces, looking as in a mirror at the glory of the Lord, are being transformed into the same image from glory to glory, just as from the Lord, the Spirit.

2 Corinthians 3:14-18 NASB

After Moses spoke with God, his face was so bright with God's glory that he wore a veil so people could look at him! But now, because the Spirit lives inside us *we can all enter into God's glory!* The Table of the Holy Spirit is where our *transformation* takes place. As we meet face to face with Jesus in the heavenly realms, being taught and powerfully touched by Holy Spirit, *we are changed with ever-increasing glory.* The veil of the old covenant has been removed! *Be seated with Holy Spirit* and allow God's glory to rise in you!

You may be praying and begin groaning or crying with a deep sense of connection with God. This is Holy Spirit praying for you and through you to God.

In the same way, the Spirit helps us in our weakness. We do not know what we ought to pray for, but the Spirit himself intercedes for us through wordless groans. And he who searches our hearts knows the mind of the Spirit, because the Spirit intercedes for God's people in accordance with the will of God.
Romans 8:26-27 NIV

The Spirit wants to empower us with gifts, but not without His fruit! Genuine good fruit is proof that we *crucified our sinful nature* and *embraced God's nature,* which is His presence.

But the Holy Spirit produces this kind of fruit in our lives: love, joy, peace, patience, kindness, goodness, faithfulness, gentleness, and self-control. There is no law against these things. Those who belong to Christ Jesus have nailed the passions and desires of their sinful nature to his cross and crucified them there. Since we are living by the Spirit, let us follow the Spirit's leading in every part of our lives. Let us not become conceited, or provoke one another, or be jealous of one another.
Galatians 5:22-26 NLT

Many wonderful people have heard part of the Gospel but are still *missing* the very important truth about the Spirit.

While Apollos was in Corinth, Paul traveled through the interior regions until he reached Ephesus, on the coast, where he found several believers. "Did you receive the Holy Spirit when you believed?" he asked them. "No," they replied, "we haven't even heard that there is a Holy Spirit." "Then what baptism did you experience?" he asked. And they replied, "The baptism of John." Paul said, "John's baptism called for repentance from sin. But John himself told the people to believe in the one who would come later, meaning Jesus."

As soon as they heard this, they were baptized in the name of the Lord Jesus. Then when Paul laid his hands on them, the Holy Spirit came on them, and they spoke in other tongues and prophesied. There were about twelve men in all.

Acts 19:1-7 NLT

You can say *yes* to Jesus *and* receive Holy Spirit's power, just like they did in Ephesus!

"So I say to you, ask, and it will be given to you; seek, and you will find; knock, and it will be opened to you. For everyone who asks receives, and the one who seeks finds, and to the one who knocks, it will be opened.

Now which one of you fathers will his son ask for a fish, and instead of a fish, he will give him a snake? Or he will even ask for an egg, and his father will give him a scorpion? So if you, despite being evil, know how to give good gifts to your children, how much more will your heavenly Father give the Holy Spirit to those who ask Him?"

Luke 11:9-13 NASB

Respectfully, in light of the dream, let us imagine Holy Spirit as the best mother in the world. The moment a mother knows a little one is coming she prepares a crib where the baby can sleep. *Holy Spirit wants God's newborns to learn to rest in God's grace.* A mother rocks her babies close, assuring them that they are safe and loved. *Holy Spirit is always close, wanting us to receive God's Agape Love.* A mother nourishes and nurtures, keeping her bundle of joy thriving in health. *Holy Spirit attentively feeds us God's Word and takes care of our needs.*

A mother loves her boys and girls at every stage of their growth. *Holy Spirit Loves all of God's children uniquely and unselfishly, whether they are male, female, young or old in Christ.* A mother doesn't make her baby earn her love and attention. *Holy Spirit reminds us that our works didn't bring us into God's Love. God's Love came to us through Jesus, and we received Him! He brought us to the heavenly realms where we could never go on our own. He has blessed us to overflowing with gifts. Without Him we would be spiritually starving, impoverished, and facing eternal death.*

A mother helps each of her children learn to walk, run and play — to read, write and create — to communicate, think productively and belly laugh — to Love others boundlessly, encourage truthfully and give generously. *Holy Spirit helps us with every area of our growth, in the spiritual realm as well as the natural realm — spirit, soul and body.*

A mother wants her children to be able to receive and give Love so they can thrive in life. *Holy Spirit knows that for God's children to really live, they must experience a baptism of the Father's Love and be able to give His Love away to others.*

The earthly realm and the heavenly realm are so different. According to scripture, in the earthly realm, when a child grows up and gets married, they are supposed to *leave their parent's home* and cling to their spouse. But in the heavenly realms, the Spirit is the One who connects us to our Father and Jesus, our Groom! Our eternity begins now at God's Table in the heavenly realms. Learn to Love the Holy Spirit and pay attention to the One who is preparing us to *dwell in the House of the Lord forever —* in Heaven!

Declaration

THE HOLY SPIRIT GUIDES ME INTO ALL TRUTH!

21

The Flesh vs. the Spirit

Jesus returned to the Mount of Olives, but early the next morning he was back again at the Temple. A crowd soon gathered, and he sat down and taught them. As he was speaking, the teachers of religious law and the Pharisees brought a woman who had been caught in the act of adultery. They put her in front of the crowd. "Teacher," they said to Jesus, "this woman was caught in the act of adultery. The law of Moses says to stone her. What do you say?" They were trying to trap him into saying something they could use against him, but Jesus stooped down and wrote in the dust with his finger.

They kept demanding an answer, so he stood up again and said, "All right, but let the one who has never sinned throw the first stone!" Then he stooped down again and wrote in the dust. When the accusers heard this, they slipped away one by one, beginning with the oldest, until only Jesus was left in the middle of the crowd with the woman.

Then Jesus stood up again and said to the woman, "Where are your accusers? Didn't even one of them condemn you?" "No, Lord," she said. And Jesus said, "Neither do I. Go and sin no more."

John 8:1-11 NLT

The law *condemned* this woman, but the words Jesus spoke, and perhaps wrote in the sand, drove her accusers away. The religious leaders blindly confronted the sinless Lamb of God who would silence "the accuser" forever with His Blood! They carelessly debated the Word of God himself in the temple courts, and lost! She was forgiven and set free by the Love and grace of Jesus! Then Jesus said, "Go now and leave your life of sin." With her sins removed by Jesus, she was a brand new person with a brand new life!

Humans can reproduce only human life, but the Holy Spirit gives birth to spiritual life.

John 3:6 NLT

There is a realm of the "flesh" and a realm of the Spirit. *The Beautiful Dream* shows us that we cannot live life from an earthly perspective. We must live by the Spirit, seated with God in the heavenly realms!

"Yes, I am the bread of life! Your ancestors ate manna in the wilderness, but they all died. Anyone who eats the bread from heaven, however, will never die. I am the living bread that came down from heaven. Anyone who eats this bread will live forever; and this bread, which I will offer so the world may live, is my flesh."

Then the people began arguing with each other about what he meant. "How can this man give us his flesh to eat?" they asked.

So Jesus said again, "I tell you the truth, unless you eat the flesh of the Son of Man and drink his blood, you cannot have eternal life within you. But anyone who eats my flesh and drinks my blood has eternal life, and I will raise that person at the last day. For my flesh is true food, and my blood is true drink. Anyone who eats my flesh and drinks my blood remains in me, and I in him. I live because of the living Father who sent me; in the same way, anyone who feeds on me will live because of me. I am the true bread that came down from heaven. Anyone who eats this bread will not die as your ancestors did (even though they ate the manna) but will live forever.

John 6:48-58 NLT

Only the sinless flesh of Jesus Christ could take the punishment for the sins of the world. *Jesus' torn flesh* freed us from *death* and gives us *life* by His Spirit. Jesus Himself is the Bread of Life! His body was bruised and torn like bread and His blood poured out so that we could be sustained for eternity by the Spirit! Just like a body must take in food in order to live on earth, our spirit must take in *Jesus* in order to live now and forever. We cannot live spiritually unless we *feed on Jesus* through fellowship with His Spirit. Jesus instructed us to come together and *remember* His death by reverently eating a small serving of unleavened bread and drinking of "the fruit of the vine."

It is the Spirit who gives life; the flesh provides no benefit; the words that I have spoken to you are spirit, and are life.
John 6:63 NASB

Before we met Jesus, we lived in the realm of *the flesh*, which is *human effort and sinful desires* that produces death. But when we were *born again*, Jesus gave us His Spirit and we *died to our flesh*. We stopped trying to attain perfection by our own works and like Jesus told the woman to do, we stopped sinning.

Now we receive *life* from the Word of God and the Holy Spirit. When we devour the Word, sometimes called the Bread of Life, the Spirit of Jesus is on the Word giving us life! It's like we are *eating His righteous flesh* — the Bread that gives us life! And when we yield to the Spirit, sometimes called *the Wine*, it's like we are drinking His Blood, not literally but spiritually, and Jesus' Blood gives us life!

Our *desire to sin* is called *the flesh* because it is closely related to the cravings of our body, mind, will and emotions. Every sin of ours was *crucified* when Jesus died on the cross. Through the power of Holy Spirit we can *put our sinful flesh-nature to death* and live in the realm of the Spirit who gives us life!

For when we were in the realm of the flesh, the sinful passions aroused by the law were at work in us, so that we bore fruit for death.
Romans 7:5 NIV

The Jewish religious leaders of Jesus' day didn't *practice the grace of God*. They lived by the law and *practiced accusation* instead of offering mercy. Their greatest king of the ages, David, had committed adultery and repented, asking God to forgive him and give him a clean heart. The Lord forgave him, restored him, and called him *a man after God's own heart*. But these *teachers of the law* didn't learn from King David. They didn't see a soul that could receive God's forgiveness. They were about to stone her to death and she would have spent eternity in hell! Their flesh was *very much alive* producing only death and driving them into deeper darkness. The grace of the Spirit will lead us to display the life-giving Love of the One inside us.

So now there is no condemnation for those who belong to Christ Jesus. And because you belong to him, the power of the life-giving Spirit has freed you from the power of sin that leads to death.

The law of Moses was unable to save us because of the weakness of our sinful nature. So God did what the law could not do. He sent his own Son in a body like the bodies we sinners have. And in that body God declared an end to sin's control over us by giving his Son as a sacrifice for our sins. He did this so that the just requirement of the law would be fully satisfied for us, who no longer follow our sinful nature but instead follow the Spirit.

Those who are dominated by the sinful nature think about sinful things, but those who are controlled by the Holy Spirit think about things that please the Spirit. So letting your sinful nature control your mind leads to death. But letting the Spirit control your mind leads to life and peace. For the sinful nature is always hostile to God. It never did obey God's laws, and it never will. That's why those who are still under the control of their sinful nature can never please God. But you are not controlled by your sinful nature. You are controlled by the Spirit if you have the Spirit of God living in you. (And remember that those who do not have the Spirit of Christ living in them do not belong to him at all.)

And Christ lives within you, so even though your body will die because of sin, the Spirit gives you life because you have been made right with God. The Spirit of God, who raised Jesus from the dead, lives in you. And just as God raised Christ Jesus from the dead, he will give life to your mortal bodies by this same Spirit living within you.

Therefore, dear brothers and sisters, you have no obligation to do what your sinful nature urges you to do. For if you live by its dictates, you will die. But if through the power of the Spirit you put to death the deeds of your sinful nature, you will live.

Romans 8:1-13 NLT

Holy Spirit frees us from sin's power! Jesus says it is impossible to follow the Spirit from the heavenly realms and also follow *ourselves* in the earthly realm. *Not* following the Spirit *is* following our own *flesh*, even if we think our choices are good. The *flesh*, also called *the sinful nature, sinful desires, human effort, earthly reasoning, the natural man, etc.* is against the Spirit. It's sneaky. It likes to make you think it's not so bad so it can grow and rule over you. You must rule over it! We can *die to ourselves* by *listening to the Spirit and the Word,* and telling our *"flesh"* to die. Don't let the earthly realm rule you!

I have been crucified with Christ and I no longer live, but Christ lives in me. The life I now live in the body, I live by faith in the Son of God, who loved me and gave himself for me.

Galatians 2:20 NIV

Paul wrote letters to the churches he had started, encouraging them in the Lord. There was usually a correction included in the letter that dealt specifically with the church he was writing to. He had to rebuke both men and women. In Corinth and Ephesus there were many women in the churches that were still *living by the flesh*. It is possible that the demonic strongholds of pagan goddess worship in those regions were still at work in them. They were behaving disrespectfully during the church meetings. Paul had to tell those women to *be quiet* because they were disrupting what Holy Spirit was trying to do.

When believers live by *the law of the flesh* and from *the earthly realm,* sometimes they have to be *rebuked by the law* until they can learn to walk by the Spirit. But when we live from God's Table, we see one another from God's perspective. We do have roles to play as men and women of God on earth. God wants us to rejoice in the biological gender He created us with. But by focusing only on the earthly, we can mess up God's divine plan to empower both men and women for His glory!

Deborah who was one of God's judges and prophetesses prophesied to Barak to fight against Sisera's army. Barak said he would only go if she came with him. Deborah *respectfully* advised him that if she went, the honor would go to a woman. *He was fine with that!*

During the battle, a woman named Jael drove a tent peg into Sisera's head and on that day Israel defeated their mighty enemy! Just as Deborah had prophesied, the honor was given to a woman—Jael! And I would suggest that the honor also rested upon Deborah. I think Barak deserves credit too!

It was the Lord who caused them to be victorious! But they had to obey the Lord's instructions. They were listening to the Holy Spirit. Barak was not a wimp, and neither was Deborah. Jael certainly wasn't! They conquered fleshly fear and pride, and worked together to win a victory for God's Kingdom!

See Notes: #7 Renewing Your Mind

Declaration

I LIVE BY THE SPIRIT — NOT BY THE FLESH!

22

TABLE TALK: *Living Water Dream*

I was inside a shopping mall standing in front of a small public sink. The problem was that instead of a water faucet, the clean-looking water was coming up out of the drain through something that looked like dark chewing tobacco. Beside me to my right, was a line of people waiting to wash their hands. As I looked into the sink, I may have made a face because I didn't want to put my hands in that water. I tried getting just my fingers wet but I couldn't without touching the dirty tobacco.

As I tried to wash them, I closed my eyes and said Luke 10:19 aloud, "... *and nothing shall harm you.*" When I opened my eyes, there in front of me was a different sink with a faucet. Clean water was flowing over my hands! I could even see scratches where the sink had been scrubbed clean many times. The water flushed right down the drain! Surprised, I looked over to the people in line and said, "Did you see that? I said, '*and nothing shall harm you*' and the sink changed!" Then I woke up.

I believe the people in line were believers in Christ. The darkness around us can make us feel *vulnerable* or *dirty* even if we choose not to participate in it. But as world culture bombards our senses, we can grow accustomed to living from the earthly realm. When our Christian friends participate in behavior that Holy Spirit has told us to separate ourselves from, it's tempting to *compromise* our own faith-convictions to save the friendship. If we live like that, we have become double-minded. We're washing from a dirty sink.

Come close to God [with a contrite heart] and He will come close to you. Wash your hands, you sinners; and purify your [unfaithful] hearts, you double-minded [people].

James 4:9 AMP

Living Water does not flow from the earthly realm. It's cleansing flow comes from *God's throne* and from *Jesus*. When we are *seated with God* His pure Living Water washes us clean, everywhere we need to go here on earth. *Nothing can harm us!*

Then the angel showed me the river of the water of life—water as clear as crystal—pouring out from the throne of God and of the Lamb,

Revelation 22:1 NET

Jesus got a towel and a washbasin, and like a servant, knelt down to wash His disciple's feet. Peter objected, but Jesus said *he couldn't be His disciple if he didn't let Him do this.*

Jesus said, "Those who have taken a bath are completely clean and do not have to wash themselves, except for their feet. All of you are clean—all except one [Judas Iscariot]."

John 13:10 GNT

After washing their feet, Jesus told them they would now need to *wash one another's feet*—also implying that they couldn't be His disciple if they didn't wash each other's feet. Do not let *the world* build up on your Brother's feet. Spiritually position yourself *low in humility* and let Jesus wash their feet through you by extending God's grace. The Holy Spirit will show you how to do that if you will pay attention to Him.

Be single-minded! Hold out your hands at the Table. Fresh clean Living Water is always flowing through the Spirit because *you have chosen to be seated with God!* You are forgiven, healed, delivered, protected and provided for! And every time you wash your Brother's and Sister's feet with Living Water your own hands are being cleansed as well! *Nothing will harm you!*

23

Dancing with the Prince of Peace

The people walking in darkness have seen a great light; on those living in the land of deep darkness a light has dawned... For to us a child is born, to us a son is given, and the government will be on his shoulders. And he will be called Wonderful Counselor, Mighty God, Everlasting Father, Prince of Peace.

Isaiah 9:2, 6 NIV

Darkness has seeped into the nations in such a way that it has taken us by surprise. A sudden display of evil in the world has brought a new wave of fear and anxiety to many people. The things they trusted in to calm their stress and heal their anxiety no longer work. If the children of God are filled with anxiety and fear, how will we be able to help the lost find peace?

How beautiful on the mountains are the feet of those who bring good news, who proclaim peace, who bring good tidings, who proclaim salvation, who say to Zion, "Your God reigns!"

Isaiah 52:7 NIV

The Biblical Hebrew word for peace, *shalom*, means complete and whole. When Jesus touched me in *The Beautiful Dream*, He made me whole! Everything was made right, as if I had never been touched by the kingdom of darkness! Our Prince of Peace came, was crucified and rose again so that we could be *at peace with God*. No person, drug, possession, pleasure or achievement can give you *shalom* peace—only Jesus. If there is hope for real peace in the world, it will be by sharing the Gospel of Jesus. Let's keep our feet on *the Mountain of the Lord!*

And suddenly there was with the angel a multitude of the heavenly host praising God and saying: Glory to God in the highest, and on earth peace, goodwill toward men!

Luke 2:13-14 NKJV

The angels proclaimed this *shalom* peace to shepherds in the field, on the night Jesus was born!

In peace I will both lie down and sleep, for You alone, LORD, have me dwell in safety.

Psalm 4:8 NASB

If we believe in Jesus, He not only gives us peace with God for judgment day, but also now! He gives us peace of mind, even as we lay our heads down at night. It is the Lord within us who calms the soul and allows us to rest. He never sleeps. The Lord watches over us day and night because *we put our trust in Him.* Peace is a benefit of staying close to God.

A heart at peace gives life to the body, but envy rots the bones.

Proverbs 14:30 NIV

Not knowing *who you are in God* will cause you to feel inferior to others. You will lose your peace and become *jealous* or *envious* of the blessings that others are experiencing. The devil has lied to you. You are *complete* in Christ! Jealousy and envy can literally make you sick so that the *shalom* peace of God isn't able to rise to bless you! You must not *compare yourself to others* or you will not enjoy the peace of mind He has given you.

The Father has welcomed you as *His very own* royal son or daughter and Loves you completely and perfectly, not preferring anyone else more or less than you. The Holy Spirit is always with you bringing you gifts from God and nourishing you supernaturally — body, soul and spirit — as you ask in faith.

When you allow God to wrap His goodness and Love around you and inside you, you can understand that there is no need to be jealous or envious of anyone. In Christ, you are exactly who you are supposed to be — *already!*

But the fruit of the Spirit is love, joy, peace, forbearance [patience], kindness, goodness, faithfulness, gentleness and self-control.

Galatians 5:22-23a NIV

The Holy Spirit inside us gives us supernatural Love, Joy, *Peace* and many other riches of God's grace!

But the Helper, the Holy Spirit whom the Father will send in My name, He will teach you all things, and remind you of all that I said to you. Peace I leave you, My peace I give you; not as the world gives, do I give to you. Do not let your hearts be troubled, nor fearful.

John 14:26-27 NASB

These are some of the words Jesus spoke to His disciples to prepare them for His death and resurrection. What was He going to leave with them? His peace! Peace is ours! No matter what your circumstances are, you have peace because you have the Prince of Peace living inside you — Jesus! Reject the devil's lies and hold on to the truth. Holy Spirit reveals the Word who is Jesus, and we can unwrap the gift of *shalom* peace.

Search me, God, and know my heart; put me to the test and know my anxious thoughts; and see if there is any hurtful way in me, and lead me in the everlasting way.

Psalm 139:23-24 NASB

The Spirit is the Wonderful Counselor! He knows what is making us anxious. Praying in the Spirit with a heart that is trusting God brings peace to your spirit, soul and body.

You will keep in perfect peace all who trust in you, all whose thoughts are fixed on you!

Isaiah 26:3 NLT

If you worry that God is determined to catch you doing wrong so He can *punish* you, you're mistaken. If you worry that the people you are responsible for will suffer because of you and you will get the *blame*, you're being misguided. If you worry that God is not going to answer your prayers, you're falling right into the devil's trap of *unbelief*. The Father sent Jesus to *save* you — not to condemn you. Our faith must rest in the Prince of Peace who came to rescue us, not in our own abilities. Our peace comes when we follow His Spirit who will always tell us what to do next. And if everything seems to be falling apart but we're trusting God, we will have peace of mind — in Christ.

For some of you, punishment and accusation happened at your family table or anytime your family was together — *sometimes for no reason at all*. But at God's Table in the heavenly realms you are just Loved! So, be seated in God's peace.

As far as the east is from the west, so far does he remove our sins from us.
Psalm 103:12 GNT

You can sit down at the Table in perfect shalom peace.

Since God chose you to be the holy people he loves, you must clothe yourselves with tenderhearted mercy, kindness, humility, gentleness, and patience. Make allowance for each other's faults, and forgive anyone who offends you. Remember, the Lord forgave you, so you must forgive others. Above all, clothe yourselves with love, which binds us all together in perfect harmony. And let the peace that comes from Christ rule in your hearts. For as members of one body you are called to live in peace. And always be thankful.
Colossians 3:12-15 NLT

God's Family lives in the atmosphere of *shalom peace* by being seated with God in the heavenly realms. To receive personal peace in our hearts and live from the Table, we have to be at peace with our Brothers and Sisters in Christ.

Blessed are the peacemakers, for they will be called children of God.

Matthew 5:9 NIV

All of our hatred, unforgiveness, bitterness, jealousy and pride was placed on our *Prince of Peace* when He was nailed to the cross. Those things need to be buried in the earth so we can be seated with God in the heavenly realms. He forgave us when we said *yes* to Him and *we are no longer troublemakers!* When we chose to follow Jesus, He deposited His peace inside us and we became peacemakers. We carry the Prince of Peace wherever we go!

Does that mean that if people don't respond to us peacefully we have not carried the peace of God to them?

If someone has done you wrong, do not repay him with a wrong. Try to do what everyone considers to be good. Do everything possible on your part to live in peace with everybody. Never take revenge, my friends, but instead let God's anger do it. For the scripture says, "I will take revenge, I will pay back, says the Lord."

Romans 12:17-19 GNT

It is our goal to live in peace with everybody. There will always be bullies but that's not who *we* are. We have been transformed. We are *courageous* and *bold* like Jesus. We *protect* and *stand up for truth, righteousness and justice* as the Spirit leads. But we don't allow our flesh to rule, provoking others to anger or taking revenge. One of the fruits of the Spirit is self-control. We can accomplish great feats for God by following the Spirit. But reacting impulsively by the *flesh* will backfire on us.

You may have to fire someone at your job or correct your children, but you don't have to do it in anger. The Prince of Peace will shine through you, but *not everyone will respond well to His presence.* Jesus warned us about this. Carrying the Prince of Peace inside you can cause terrible reactions. Stay in peace.

Do you think that I came to provide peace on earth? No, I tell you, but rather division; for from now on five members in one household will be divided, three against two and two against three.

Luke 12:51-52 NASB

Jesus came to earth *offering* peace with God, but not everyone will accept His offer. Some will become angry simply because we Love Him. But *do not dance with anger.* It will destroy you. *Dance with the Lord of Peace.* You can have peace of mind in the midst of difficult circumstances by staying close to Jesus.

I have told you these things, so that in me you may have peace. In this world you will have trouble. But take heart! I have overcome the world.

John 16:33 NIV

Peace of mind is possibly the most treasured gift of all in a world filled with trouble. There is no need to be afraid or to worry! Jesus came to bring peace — peace of mind and peace within the Body of Christ. Peace is a *fruit* of the Holy Spirit. His peace can *grow* in our hearts when we become *convinced* that God Loves us unconditionally and extravagantly.

You will be a peacemaker when chaos and fear grip those around you. That's because you know God and you spend time with Him in the Spirit. You carry the atmosphere of Heaven in and around you because you are seated with the Prince of Peace, the Wonderful Counselor and the Everlasting Father. Jesus is walking around on this earth with you and His perfect peace will touch others through you! Shalom!

Declaration

**I HAVE PEACE OF MIND
BECAUSE THE PRINCE OF PEACE LIVES IN ME!**

24

Dancing from the Heart

In the first and third scenes of *The Beautiful Dream*, we communicated without opening our mouths. There were words, but *they were spoken from the heart in the spirit realm*. God can hear what our hearts are saying. If we listen carefully, we can also hear what He is saying to us. Our hearts are speaking in the spiritual realm even when we don't realize it. The enemy speaks in the spirit realm as well. We need to learn to *know who is speaking* so we can yield to the right voice! What is being said *from our hearts* is the substance of our faith, whether good or bad.

The way of the righteous is like the first gleam of dawn, which shines ever brighter until the full light of day. But the way of the wicked is like total darkness. They have no idea what they are stumbling over. My child, pay attention to what I say. Listen carefully to my words. Don't lose sight of them. Let them penetrate deep into your heart, for they bring life to those who find them, and healing to their whole body, Guard your heart above all else, for it determines the course of your life.

Proverbs 4:18-23 NLT

If God is speaking in the spirit realm and Satan's demons are also speaking, *it is our responsibility to guard the door of our heart* and only allow truth to enter. Demons will try to make you think that a lie they spoke was your own inner thought. For instance, you know that God Loves you. But then one day you might have the thought, "I wonder if God Loves me." Fear strikes at your heart. May I suggest that the "thought" was probably not yours—but a demon *impersonating* your inner voice in the spirit realm. *You know that God Loves you!* At that moment, you must *reject* the lie so that it doesn't become what you *believe* in your heart.

God *created* the universe with His *Words* and God gives us authority to *speak His Word, creating change for His glory.* If Satan can get you to believe his lies are coming from your own heart, he will be able to make you live in fear. Learn to respond with, "That's not me. That's a lie." Then *speak God's Word*, which is truth, over your mind and heart!

So, how do you know if what you heard in the spirit realm was *from your own heart?* You will know by the words that regularly come out of your mouth. If you are always saying things like, "God is for me and not against me," and "I am victorious because I am in Christ," then that's what is in your heart. But if you often *say* things like, "I'm so stupid! I'm just a failure!" you have allowed that lie to occupy a room in your heart.

Ask God to forgive you for believing the lie and *He will forgive you.* Forgive anyone who said those words to you or implied them by their actions. Denounce, renounce and reject that belief aloud before God. Command that lie to leave you in Jesus' name. Then start *renewing your mind* by dwelling on scripture that builds up your faith. Do this briefly and prayerfully during the day or night from your heart *as the Spirit leads you.* Don't let it become a method or a ritual! It is Jesus, the Word, speaking through you. Your words and actions will change over time and your joy will return! When that happens, God's light is shining brighter and brighter like the sun arising in the morning. You (and Jesus) are driving the devil away from the territory God has given you.

Later, if you are tempted to believe that lie again, *reject it in Jesus name!* Speak the Word to the lie. It doesn't have a right to attach itself to you. Your heart belongs to Jesus now, and over time, His Word will grow and produce very good fruit!

We are either *speaking* God's truth producing life, or speaking the devil's lies producing death and unbelief. These mind words scattered around like seeds *in our hearts*, whether from God *or* evil, will produce a bumper crop over time. They will be seen in our actions, heard in our words, felt in our emotions and manifested in our bodies as blessings *or* curses.

God's Word will keep the enemy's voice from becoming your own belief system. The voice of the liar, Satan, will diminish and God's Love and truth will confirm *who you truly are* — a beloved child of God!

The heart is more deceitful than all else and is desperately sick; who can understand it? I, the Lord, *search the heart, I test the mind, to give to each person according to his ways, according to the results of his deeds.*

Jeremiah 17:9-10 NASB

Contrary to modern thought, *following your own heart* will lead you down the wrong path. Follow the Holy Spirit!

Enter through the narrow gate; for the gate is wide and the way is broad that leads to destruction, and there are many who enter through it. For the gate is narrow and the way is constricted that leads to life, and there are few who find it.

Matthew 7:13-14 NASB

Christians can carelessly seek the world's wisdom instead of following the Spirit and the Word. What you *choose to put in your mind* will in time make its way into your heart.

... because their minds are dull, and they have stopped up their ears and have closed their eyes. Otherwise, their eyes would see, their ears would hear, their minds would understand, and they would turn to me, says God, and I would heal them.'

Matthew 13:15 GNT

What realm are you paying attention to — the earthly realm or the realm of the Spirit? Your heart can become calloused by exchanging *your Love relationship with God* for something else. Pride says, "I don't have to consult with God about everything!" Our hearts are intertwined with Jesus now! He cares about *every concern* of our lives — and we care about His.

Yes, the Sovereign LORD is coming in power. He will rule with a powerful arm. See, he brings his reward with him as he comes. He will feed his flock like a shepherd. He will carry the lambs in his arms, holding them close to his heart. He will gently lead the mother sheep with their young.

Isaiah 40:10-11 NLT

Without our Shepherd guiding us, we, like sheep, will wander off into dangerous territory. Our Great Shepherd has given us freedom by His Spirit so we can follow Him into the abundant life He offers. Sometimes the Lord has to correct us *to keep us in His Love and close to His heart,* but He is not abusive! He carries the weak, and gently leads those who nurture others. Together at His Table, the Father, the Son and Spirit lead us to green pastures!

Our hearts are like soil in a farmer's field. Good soil receives the seed of the Word and *produces a good crop.* Jesus told a parable about a farmer who scattered seed over his field. Later He explained it to His disciples like this:

This is the meaning of the parable: The seed is God's word. The seeds that fell on the footpath represent those who hear the message, only to have the devil come and take it away from their hearts and prevent them from believing and being saved.

The seeds on the rocky soil represent those who hear the message and receive it with joy. But since they don't have deep roots, they believe for a while, then they fall away when they face temptation.

The seeds that fell among the thorns represent those who hear the message, but all too quickly the message is crowded out by the cares and riches and pleasures of this life. And so they never grow into maturity.

And the seeds that fell on the good soil represent honest, good-hearted people who hear God's word, cling to it, and patiently produce a huge harvest.

Luke 8:11-15 NLT

Just hearing God's Word doesn't mean you'll grow roots and flourish in Jesus. As believers, we have to listen by the Spirit in the heavenly realms where we have been seated. Others can encourage, but no one can make you pay attention to the Holy Spirit. You are responsible to guard your own heart.

And I will give you a new heart, and I will put a new spirit in you. I will take out your stony, stubborn heart and give you a tender, responsive heart. And I will put my Spirit in you so that you will follow my decrees and be careful to obey my regulations.

Ezekiel 36:26-27 NLT

The Word, Jesus, reveals the condition of the soil of your heart and also breaks up the soil making it more receptive. Read scripture and listen to God speak. Apply it to your heart by *rejecting* wrong thoughts and *repenting* of wrong actions. Say the Word of God *from your heart* and Jesus will pulverize the stones of doubt and fear that keep you from victory. Renewing our minds in the Word is not some kind of natural therapy to bring us relief. It is part of our relationship with Jesus! Jesus is the Word and He sets us free through His Word!

Do not be anxious about anything, but in every situation, by prayer and petition, with thanksgiving, present your requests to God. And the peace of God, which transcends all understanding, will guard your hearts and your minds in Christ Jesus. Finally, brothers and sisters, whatever is true, whatever is noble, whatever is right, whatever is pure, whatever is lovely, whatever is admirable — if anything is excellent or praiseworthy — think about such things.

Philippians 4:6-8 NIV

It's not just a "Please, God" kind of begging but a "Thank You, God" kind of asking because we know *the heart of the Father* is full of kindness, favor and blessing. When you're tempted to worry or be afraid, say the scripture Philippians 4:6-7 from the deepest part of your heart. Then do exactly what it says. *Present* your request to God in prayer. *Give* the request to Him and then *thank* Him that He will take care of it. Believe He has heard you and is pleased with your request. The Lord will fill your heart with peace.

Life on earth won't be perfect. But when we trust God and dwell on *His truth*, our *hearts* get closer to His and are filled with His peace. Guard the seed of the Word in your heart because that seed is Jesus! Cultivate your soil in the heavenly realms where Living Water flows and the light is bright!

Listen for the Lord to speak to you, *heart to heart*. Ask the Spirit to silence the voices of today's stress, your past mistakes, and your worries about the future. Remember that *you are already cleansed* by the Blood of Jesus! You don't have to worry when the enemy whispers His lies and accusations. You belong to Jesus and you are safe! God really, really does Love you!

The process of maturity is your *heart-to-heart relationship* with God. You can communicate with God in the Spirit anywhere at any time, aloud or in complete silence. He is so powerful, but most of the time He will speak to you quietly and tenderly. Get to know God and allow Him to pursue your heart and express His Love to you deeply in the Spirit. You will never desire the world's love again. This is how we dance with Jesus from the heart!

Declaration

I HAVE A LOVE RELATIONSHIP WITH GOD!

25

He Asked to See Me Again

Jesus asked if He could *see* me again! Jesus promised that in the last days He would return to earth to rescue those who follow Him. But I think this phrase in the dream is speaking about Jesus wanting *an appointment* with me. The question is, "Do I want to see Him?" *In The Beautiful Dream*, I couldn't wait to see Him again! I was so in Love! Jesus came and took me to the heavenly realms to be seated with God where I can meet with Him *all the time!*

Zacchaeus

Zacchaeus was short and wanted so much to *see* Jesus that he *ran ahead* of the crowd and climbed a tree. It was no coincidence that Jesus came near where he lived.

Jesus entered Jericho and made his way through the town. There was a man there named Zacchaeus. He was the chief tax collector in the region, and he had become very rich. He tried to get a look at Jesus, but he was too short to see over the crowd. So he ran ahead and climbed a sycamore-fig tree beside the road, for Jesus was going to pass that way. When Jesus came by, he looked up at Zacchaeus and called him by name. "Zacchaeus!" he said. "Quick, come down! I must be a guest in your home today."

Zacchaeus quickly climbed down and took Jesus to his house in great excitement and joy. But the people were displeased. "He has gone to be the guest of a notorious sinner," they grumbled. Meanwhile, Zacchaeus stood before the Lord and said, "I will give half my wealth to the poor, Lord, and if I have cheated people on their taxes, I will give them back four times as much!" Jesus responded, "Salvation has come to this home today, for this man has shown himself to be a true son of Abraham. For the Son of Man came to seek and save those who are lost."

Luke 19:1-10 NLT

Zacchaeus encountered Jesus and *nothing else mattered!* Suddenly, Zacchaeus Loved and honored people the way Jesus had Loved and honored him. The Holy Spirit has that wonderful affect on our hearts when we meet the Lord! But we have to *want* to see Him and joyfully invite Him to mess up our old way of thinking and living! We were *too short* to see God, so *He took us up* to the heavenly realms to be seated with Him at His Table! No more *hoping* to see Him. Because of the Holy Spirit we are *always* with the Lord!

The Nameless Woman
Sometimes God's children wait until they are in *desperate need* to get to know Him intimately. But the Lord is compassionate toward those who seek Him—*whenever* they decide to do so. Jesus is always ready and willing to bring us wholeness if we'll look for Him wholeheartedly.

As Jesus went with him, he was surrounded by the crowds. A woman in the crowd had suffered for twelve years with constant bleeding, and she could find no cure. Coming up behind Jesus, she touched the fringe of his robe. Immediately, the bleeding stopped. "Who touched me?" Jesus asked.

Everyone denied it, and Peter said, "Master, this whole crowd is pressing up against you." But Jesus said, "Someone deliberately touched me, for I felt healing power go out from me..."

When the woman realized that she could not stay hidden, she began to tremble and fell to her knees in front of him. The whole crowd heard her explain why she had touched him and that she had been immediately healed. "Daughter," he said to her, "your faith has made you well. Go in peace."

Luke 8:42b-48 NLT

This precious woman had suffered for so many years, but not only because of her health. Women in that society were looked upon as *much less valuable than men,* and there were *many* cultural limitations placed upon them. Jewish law prohibited a woman to go out in public during her monthly cycle. She was breaking all the rules, desperately counting on Jesus to set her free from *her illness* — and He did!

Jesus wasn't happy with her slipping away *half-healed.* He wanted to *encounter her personally,* so He called her out! She feared that she had done something wrong! But instead of *shaming* her, Jesus *honored* her. He declared, for all to hear, that *her faith* was the reason she was healed. Then He blessed the woman with *shalom* peace, meaning that she was now made whole — spirit, soul and body! Jesus *removed the disgrace and trauma* she had experienced since birth and filled her with the Father's Love! She got to look into the eyes of her Messiah and Savior face to face. Jesus set up the appointment — and she got to *see Him!*

Do you want to *see* Him today, or is your life too busy? Perhaps you have approached the Lord and you thought that nothing happened, so you started looking for relief in other places. I've got good news for you. When you call on the Lord in humility and faith, *something good always happens,* even if you don't *feel* anything. So like the desperate woman, press through your crowded schedule, kneel on the ground and touch the hem of His robe. If you will *be seated,* perhaps you will *lock eyes* with Jesus too!

Hagar
Broken, abused and rejected, *Hagar,* Abraham and Sarah's slave, fled into the desert. She had been used and discarded. Hagar felt alone, worthless, unloved and invisible, but the Lord *saw* Hagar, came to her and comforted her! He prophesied into her

future, and the future of her unborn son, Ishmael, and showed her what to do next. Hagar was undoubtedly overwhelmed by God's Love! *She saw Jesus* who was keeping watch over her!

She [Hagar] gave this name to the LORD who spoke to her: "You are the God who sees me," for she said, "I have now seen the One who sees me."

Genesis 16:13 NIV

The Lord still *sees* and *Loves* the Arab people who descended from Abraham and Hagar's son, Ishmael! Even today, many of these precious people are *seeing* Jesus face to face and in dreams and visions, and are receiving Him as their Savior. Hagar's children are meeting Jesus! For thousands of years, Ishmael and Isaac's children have warred against each other. But now, many are seated together at the Table in the heavenly realms as Brothers and Sisters in God's Love! *Hagar,* you are *not* alone, worthless, unloved and invisible! You are *so very important* to God! He loves you! Because of Jesus you are no longer a slave! *God sees you,* wants to meet with you, encourage you, fill you with His Spirit and call you into your destiny!

Esther
Maybe you want to *see* Jesus again, but you are afraid of what He might ask you to do. We've all been in that awkward place. It's a little bit like a child who doesn't want to grow up. God has amazing plans for us, but if we hide behind our fears, we'll never experience the joys of fulfilling our purpose and destiny here on earth!

Esther was a young Jewish orphan, who because of her beauty and grace, was chosen to marry King Xerxes — the pagan king of the Persian Empire. This was not a perfect love story at all. However, God helped Esther to be extremely brave so that the Jewish people were saved from destruction. The people of Israel were in bondage because of their disobedience to God. They were about to face persecution and annihilation when the Lord spoke to Esther through Mordecai, her cousin.

Through a messenger, Mordecai urged Esther to go into the presence of King Xerxes. Esther was to tell the king about evil schemes planned against the Jewish people. These schemes were secretly put together by the king's right hand man, and she was to beg King Xerxes for mercy. But instead, Esther sent word to Mordecai that *she would surely die* if she approached the king uninvited!

So Hathach gave Esther's message to Mordecai. Mordecai sent this reply to Esther: "Don't think for a moment that because you're in the palace you will escape when all other Jews are killed. If you keep quiet at a time like this, deliverance and relief for the Jews will arise from some other place, but you and your relatives will die. Who knows if perhaps you were made queen for just such a time as this?"

Then Esther sent this reply to Mordecai: "Go and gather together all the Jews of Susa and fast for me. Do not eat or drink for three days, night or day. My maids and I will do the same. And then, though it is against the law, I will go in to see the king. If I must die, I must die."

Esther 4:12-16 NLT

Esther went before *the King of Heaven* in prayer and fasting, along with all the Jewish people. And because *she believed that God saw her*, she and all the Jewish people were saved! The Holy Spirit's power came upon her, and she carried out the will of God so beautifully!

Jesus is asking to *see* you again. You have this great honor to meet with God daily and execute what He has for you to do. Some of God's children will share the Gospel with the nations. Many will serve in governmental positions, education, business and hired jobs. Others will care for those who cannot care for themselves. God's children are uniquely placed and scattered all over the earth in millions of occupational platforms *for His purposes to be accomplished.*

Fulfilling God's destiny for our lives does not come

automatically. *It takes courage!* Like Esther, we must desire *His will* above our own comfort and safety. And at God's Table, He empowers us to do what we could never do on our own. But we have to *want* to see Jesus again, no matter what He might ask us to do. Then we can draw close to Him and He will meet with us! God will equip and empower us for His glory!

Jesus wants to meet with you. You may feel like you don't have what it takes to encounter God in an intimate relationship, but you do. You are able to meet with Jesus and follow Him! But following Jesus is not following a set of rules. It's following the Person of Jesus Christ through the Spirit. If you are sincere and you *want* to encounter the Lord, you will, and even more and more as time goes by. You can begin by reading His Word and listening to what God is saying to your heart. Talk with God as you read and worship Him in song, connecting to His heart. The ways God meets with you will increase if you keep asking, seeking and knocking on the door of His heart!

I will see you again and you will rejoice, and no one will take away your joy. In that day you will no longer ask me anything. Very truly I tell you, my Father will give you whatever you ask in my name.

John 16:22b-23 NIV

Do not underestimate the importance of your *appointments* with the King of Kings in the heavenly realms! Yours is the perfect Love story! Run ahead and climb a tree. Press through the crowd and touch His robe. Always desire to *see* and *meet with* the One who Loves you and is watching over you! Be ready to lay your earthly crowns on the Table for the sake of your King. One encounter with Jesus and nothing matters more than *seeing Him again at His Table* and making *His* dreams come true!

Declaration

I HAVE AN APPOINTMENT WITH MY KING!

26

Be Seated in the Word

In the beginning was the Word [Jesus], and the Word was with God, and the Word was God. He was with God in the beginning. Through him all things were made; without him nothing was made that has been made. In him was life, and that life was the light of all mankind. The light shines in the darkness, and the darkness has not overcome it.

John 1:1-5 NIV

Jesus Christ *is the Word.* His Spirit causes the written Word to give us life and light as we read it and hear it.

Then he opened their minds so they could understand the scriptures...

Luke 24:45 NET

Jesus opens our minds to what *He* is saying in His Word! When we read it yielded completely to His Spirit, God gives us revelation. He shares His heart with us!

You were cleansed from your sins when you obeyed the truth, so now you must show sincere love to each other as brothers and sisters. Love each other deeply with all your heart. For you have been born again, but not to a life that will quickly end.

Your new life will last forever because it comes from the eternal, living word of God. As the Scriptures say, "People are like grass; their beauty is like a flower in the field. The grass withers and the flower fades. But the word of the Lord remains forever." And that word is the Good News that was preached to you.

1 Peter 1:22-25 NLT

When we heard the Word, believed it and received Jesus it was like a seed *implanted into our hearts.* That seed is *alive and eternal* because it is the Spirit and the Word inside us. The Word, Jesus, gives us eternal life! It is our responsibility to nurture the Word.

Do you not yet understand that whatever enters the mouth goes into the stomach and is eliminated? But those things which proceed out of the mouth come from the heart, and they defile a man. For out of the heart proceed evil thoughts, murders, adulteries, fornications [sexual sins], thefts, false witness, blasphemies. These are the things which defile a man, but to eat with unwashed hands does not defile a man."

Matthew 15:17-20 NKJV

What we *say* is what is in our hearts. And what is in our hearts will come out of our mouth, creating a fortress within us and planting seeds in the lives of those around us – either for the kingdom of darkness or the Kingdom of God. Everything God has spoken in His Word is good. It came from His heart and produces eternal life! When we *know* the Word, Jesus, declaring His Word becomes a powerful weapon for God's Kingdom! Through the Spirit, we can *speak God's Word* over ourselves, our family, friends, church, community and the nations!

For the word of God is living and active, and sharper than any two-edged sword, even penetrating as far as the division of soul and spirit, of both joints and marrow, and able to judge the thoughts and intentions of the heart. And there is no creature hidden from His sight, but all things are open and laid bare to the eyes of Him to whom we must answer.

Hebrews 4:12-13 NASB

Satan will try to distract you from reading God's Word in the Spirit because he knows *it is alive with power!* Reading God's Word is sitting down with Jesus and letting His double-edged

152

sword *fight for you* and *do surgery on you.*

So then faith comes by hearing, and hearing by the word of God.
Romans 10:17 NKJV

Hearing the Word of God causes your faith seed to grow!

[Jesus prayed for us] Sanctify them [make them holy] in the
truth; your word is truth.
John 17:17 NASB

The Bible says that Jesus is the Word and He is also the Truth.
There is no faith if we don't believe that the Word is Truth.

I have treasured Your word in my heart, so that I may not sin
against You.
Psalm 119:11 NASB

Those who *know Jesus* want to know His Word because they
want to Love and obey their King more than anything!

To the Jews who had believed him, Jesus said, "If you hold to
my teaching, you are really my disciples. Then you will know
the truth, and the truth will set you free."
John 8:31-32 NIV

Every believer is a disciple of Jesus if they *learn* from Him and
hold tight to what He says. His Word sets us free!

Your word is a lamp to my feet and a light to my path.
Psalm 119:105 AMP

The *written* Word of God is a *portal* to the Spirit realm. It is your
roadmap to freedom! The more you *believe the Word,* the more
His truth comes alive in you and can set you free.

Now no one lights a lamp and covers it over with a container,
or puts it under a bed; but he puts it on a lampstand so that
those who come in may see the light. For nothing is concealed

*that will not become evident, nor anything hidden that will not
be known and come to light. So take care how you listen; for
whoever has, to him more will be given; and whoever does not
have, even what he thinks he has will be taken away from him.*

Luke 8:16-18 NASB

God's Word gives you *spiritual* and *practical* guidance. *Pay close
attention* and you will be filled with light!

*Do not merely listen to the word, and so deceive yourselves. Do
what it says.*

James 1:22 NIV

In the third scene of the dream, I was *not paying attention to the
Spirit speaking.* Just knowing scripture in your head will not
keep you from deception. But if you're *really listening for Him,*
you'll obey what the Spirit says.

*No one lights a lamp and then hides it or puts it under a basket.
Instead, a lamp is placed on a stand, where its light can be seen
by all who enter the house. Your eye is like a lamp that provides
light for your body. When your eye is healthy, your whole body
is filled with light. But when it is unhealthy, your body is filled
with darkness. Make sure that the light you think you have is
not actually darkness. If you are filled with light, with no dark
corners, then your whole life will be radiant, as though a
floodlight were filling you with light.*

Luke 11:33-36 NLT

The Word is Jesus and He is the Light of the World, so His
Word is light. It's better to go to God in the secret place and
allow Him to purge us there. Otherwise, God will allow us to
say or *do* inappropriate things, causing us to feel embarrassed so
we can realize that there is still a *dark corner* in our hearts. If we
feel embarrassed or afraid by what others say or do to us, that
indicates a dark corner in our hearts as well. We need the light
of Jesus to bring us into His truth that sets us free. Any
darkness in our hearts will keep us from being able to be seated
close to the Father's heart where the light of His glory is.

The fire of God's glory is rising. If we are not already seated in His light, the glory will consume us—*not in a good way.* We need the fire of the Word of God to *purify us* now, so we can embrace the fire of His glory when Holy Spirit comes in power!

If you notice a believer not guarding their tongue, do not be quick to judge. God is probably taking them through the fire to purify them. Pray for them in the secret place and for yourself that *your eyes will see them correctly.* Otherwise, you may find yourself in the same fiery trial as they are in.

God has provided His Word as a *weapon* for His children to use against all the works of the devil!

Again, the devil took him [Jesus] to a very high mountain and showed him all the kingdoms of the world and their splendor. "All this I will give you," he said, "if you will bow down and worship me." Jesus said to him, "Away from me, Satan! For it is written: 'Worship the Lord your God, and serve him only."" Then the devil left him, and angels came and attended him.
Matthew 4:8-11 NIV

If *Jesus* who never sinned spoke His own Words against the devil, how much more should we declare God's Word against anything that is not from God!? The Word is an *offensive* and *defensive* weapon we should use at all times.

Jesus spoke only the words He heard His Father say. The more we follow His lead in this way the better off we'll be. When we *speak* God's promises we are planting seeds of life! If you *rehearse* bitterness, you will *produce* bitterness. If you keep *thinking* and *saying* you are miserable, unlovable, sinful, weak and worthless, you will likely reap a harvest of those lies. But if we wield the Word like a sword coming from our mouths, we will eventually reap victory over the devil! The devil has been defeated by Jesus, the Word!

Beat your plowshares into swords and your pruning hooks into spears; Let the weak say, 'I am strong.' "

Joel 3:10 NKJV

In *The Beautiful Dream*, Jesus set me free from all bondage the moment I received Him. But when I woke up I didn't *feel* whole. Scene three tells us that we must *be seated* in the truth of what Jesus did for us in scene one. He paid for our salvation and freedom on the cross and there is hope for our present and our future if we keep trusting the Word.

God, who gives life to the dead and calls those things which do not exist as though they did;

Romans 4:17b NKJV

Jesus is the Word and we know Him! *Dance with the Word* and follow His lead. He will protect you and provide for you because He loves you. Be seated at His Table, which is high above the mindset of this world. His Word is fire and light, burning away impurities and allowing us to be seated with God in the light. Darkness cannot stay in the light. *Pay close attention* and the Word Himself will set you free! Share the Gospel and the Word will be planted in others like a seed. We are going to be amazed by the good harvest in these end times, just by sharing the Word in the power of the Spirit!

See Notes: #8 The Written Word

Declaration

**THE WORD OF GOD IS FILLING ME
WITH LIGHT, LIFE AND LOVE!**

27

Kingdom Prayer

[Jesus said] This, then, is how you should pray: Our Father in heaven, hallowed be your name, your kingdom come, your will be done, on earth as it is in heaven. Give us today our daily bread. And forgive us our debts, as we also have forgiven our debtors. And lead us not into temptation, but deliver us from the evil one. For yours is the kingdom and the power and the glory forever. Amen.

Matthew 6:9-13 NIV

Jesus was so clear about praying intimately to our Father from a Kingdom perspective! When we pray *submitted to God*, we are spiritually seated with God the Father, Son and Spirit in His Kingdom. We can be confident that we are sons and daughters of our Father, and at the same time *be in awe* of God's greatness! Abba desires His will to be done in the earthly realm as it is in Heaven. That can happen if we are *paying attention to God in the Spirit*. He wants to be our Provider, but He wants us to ask, because asking is Father-to-child *relationship*.

Our prayers are filled with gratitude when we Love Jesus for the way He touched our lives. In that gratitude, we forgive others as our Father does. We have to ask our Shepherd to lead us away from the danger of temptation and to deliver us when we stray. We cannot lead ourselves or deliver ourselves. Our life in God's Kingdom has begun. And when we are seated with God, His will can be accomplished through us for His glory! When the Body of Christ aligns with the Spirit in prayer, our lives on earth begin to look and feel more like Heaven!

Prayer is two-way communication with God *from the heart*. Whether with spoken words or a silent inner voice, prayer is *intentional interaction* with God. You can pray *privately* or *together with others*. You can pray for yourself and for others. Prayer happens as you worship and praise Him in song. It can happen spirit to Spirit as you marvel at the beauty of the starry sky, or the crashing waves of on the seashore. Prayer happens when you are overwhelmed with Love for your newborn baby and you realize *that* download of immense Love didn't come from you. It came from your Father and you speechlessly give Him thanks through tears and emotion. Prayer happens when you are brokenhearted and don't know what to do except sit in His presence and let Him Love you. Prayer happens when you receive a dream or vision from God and talk with Him about it.

Prayer is not a ritual. It is a relationship. God is *always* ready to hear from you and speak to you, but He can't if you aren't *paying attention* or if you are *afraid* of what He might ask of you. Prayer at His Table is submissive because you know *He is Love*.

Now it was at this time that He went off to the mountain to pray, and He spent the whole night in prayer with God.
Luke 6:12 NASB

Perhaps Jesus chose to pray on a mountain as a symbol of the heavenly realms. In that place, I believe Abba's Love *restored His soul* and *prepared Him* for the upcoming day.

But when you pray, go away by yourself, shut the door behind you, and pray to your Father in private. Then your Father, who sees everything, will reward you.
Matthew 6:6 NLT

When we pray alone, we don't have the temptation to impress anyone with our words. Praying with others is powerful, but if we don't ever meet with God alone in a *secret place*, our relationship with Him is not genuine. Private prayer *prepares us* to have powerful group prayer. But prayer is also timeless, just like the heavenly realms where we are seated. We don't really stop and start prayer. We are seated with God at all times!

Samuel was only a boy when he heard the Lord calling his name for the first time. He didn't know the Lord was speaking, but with help from Eli, the high priest, Samuel went back to bed and answered the Lord's call.

Then the LORD came and stood, and called as at the other times: "Samuel! Samuel!" And Samuel said, "Speak, for Your servant is listening."

1 Samuel 3:10 NASB

"Speak, your servant is listening" is a humble prayer that opens the door to hearing from God! Have you ever been trying to speak to someone and they kept ignoring you? In scene three of *The Beautiful Dream* I was ignoring the Spirit as He spoke! Thinking *about* the Lord is *very good*, but it's not necessarily prayer. Prayer is a *spirit to Spirit exchange with God*, sometimes using spoken words.

My sheep hear My voice, and I know them, and they follow Me. And I give them eternal life, and they shall never perish; neither shall anyone snatch them out of My hand. My Father, who has given them to Me, is greater than all; and no one is able to snatch them out of My Father's hand. I and My Father are one.

John 10:27-30 NKJV

If we follow our Good Shepherd and *listen* to His voice, nothing can snatch us out of His care. But wandering off, bleating carelessly away from the flock draws attention to *lions and bears.* So stay close and *bleat* in response to the Shepherd's voice. He keeps us safe and provides for us!

This is the confidence we have in approaching God: that if we ask anything according to his will, he hears us. And if we know that he hears us—whatever we ask—we know that we have what we asked of him.

1 John 5:14-15 NIV

3

Reading the Word helps us understand what *God's will* is. Then we can *confidently* ask God for what we need!

Which of you, if your son asks for bread, will give him a stone? Or if he asks for a fish, will give him a snake? If you, then, though you are evil, know how to give good gifts to your children, how much more will your Father in heaven give good gifts to those who ask him!

Matthew 7:9-11 NIV

Your Father who owns everything Loves you! He is pleased when you ask Him for *good gifts!*

One day Jesus told his disciples a story to show that they should always pray and never give up. "There was a judge in a certain city," he said, "who neither feared God nor cared about people. A widow of that city came to him repeatedly, saying, 'Give me justice in this dispute with my enemy.' The judge ignored her for a while, but finally he said to himself, 'I don't fear God or care about people, but this woman is driving me crazy. I'm going to see that she gets justice, because she is wearing me out with her constant requests!'" Then the Lord said, "Learn a lesson from this unjust judge. Even he rendered a just decision in the end. So don't you think God will surely give justice to his chosen people who cry out to him day and night? Will he keep putting them off? I tell you, he will grant justice to them quickly! But when the Son of Man returns, how many will he find on the earth who have faith?"

Luke 18:1-8 NLT

Sometimes we pray about a need and the answer doesn't come right away, even if we are praying the will of God. Those who *humbly keep on praying* keep their faith in a Loving God whose grace flows freely. We cannot *earn* answered prayer, so guard your heart from doing things to try to *convince God* that you are worthy to receive His favor. We already have His favor through Jesus. God invites us into *intimacy* and wants us to come to Him because *we are His children.* Holding anything against God or others will affect your ability to keep praying by faith in His favor. Agape Love is the atmosphere of prayer.

Are any of you suffering hardships? You should pray. Are any of you happy? You should sing praises. Are any of you sick? You should call for the elders of the church to come and pray over you, anointing you with oil in the name of the Lord. Such a prayer offered in faith will heal the sick, and the Lord will make you well. And if you have committed any sins, you will be forgiven. Confess your sins to each other and pray for each other so that you may be healed. The earnest prayer of a righteous person has great power and produces wonderful results. Elijah was as human as we are, and yet when he prayed earnestly that no rain would fall, none fell for three and a half years! Then, when he prayed again, the sky sent down rain and the earth began to yield its crops.

James 5:13-18 NLT

Sin pulls us into darkness and causes our faith in God to be distorted. God does not block prayer, but our rebellion can. It can open the door to illness and other strongholds. But humility and repentance brings us back into faith and relationship with God. God's mercies are new every morning!

You ask and do not receive, because you ask with the wrong motives, so that you may spend what you request on your pleasures.

James 4:3 NASB

Selfish motives can stand in the way of our prayers. But unanswered prayer is not always because of sin. If Holy Spirit hasn't revealed sin in your heart, don't allow the devil to twist your mind against yourself, the Lord, or others. Pray *free of blame*—from a heart of praise!

Rejoice always, pray continually, give thanks in all circumstances; for this is God's will for you in Christ Jesus.

1 Thessalonians 5:16-18 NIV

Sincerely praising God is like releasing bombs against the enemy in the spirit realm. Miracles can happen when you pray seated with God, even when you are facing the greatest trials of your life. When you pray in faith, you are making a difference in God's Kingdom — and God is making a difference in you!

For if you have the ability to speak in tongues, you will be talking only to God, since people won't be able to understand you. You will be speaking by the power of the Spirit, but it will all be mysterious.

1 Corinthians 14:2 NLT

Holy Spirit makes it possible for you to pray in a heavenly language, sometimes known as *praying in the Spirit* or *speaking in tongues*. When you pray this way, God's Spirit is praying for you and through you. It is one of the most unselfish, faith-filled ways to pray because there is no way for you to know who is being blessed by it, unless the Lord interprets it for you!

God's voice is often faint, so that you have to *draw close to Him*. He speaks through dreams, visions, numbers, sounds, physical sensations, smells, nature, other people and in so many amazing ways! Keep your heart *attentive* to *His* heart. Just like humans communicate without saying a word, we can do the same with God. Our attitude, heart-thoughts and body language speak loudly in the spirit realm! God also Loves the creative ways *you* communicate with Him such as dance and art! Prayer without Love is unfruitful, but He has placed His Love in you without measure. So fall in Love with God and allow your heart to dance adoringly in awe of Him through prayer. Be seated with God at His Table and talk with Him *heart to heart!*

Declaration

GOD AND I TALK WITH EACH OTHER ~ A LOT!

28

Be Seated in Worship

Jesus was traveling through Samaria. The Samaritans were shunned by the Jews at that time because of their spiritual compromise and disobedience to God. Jesus stopped there and sat beside a well, very tired and thirsty from His long journey. But this was part of the Father's plan!

Soon a Samaritan woman came to draw water, and Jesus said to her, "Please give me a drink." He was alone at the time because his disciples had gone into the village to buy some food. The woman was surprised, for Jews refuse to have anything to do with Samaritans. She said to Jesus, "You are a Jew, and I am a Samaritan woman. Why are you asking me for a drink?"

Jesus replied, "If you only knew the gift God has for you and who you are speaking to, you would ask me, and I would give you living water." "But sir, you don't have a rope or a bucket," she said, "and this well is very deep. Where would you get this living water? And besides, do you think you're greater than our ancestor Jacob, who gave us this well? How can you offer better water than he and his sons and his animals enjoyed?" Jesus replied, "Anyone who drinks this water will soon become thirsty again. But those who drink the water I give will never be thirsty again. It becomes a fresh, bubbling spring within them, giving them eternal life."

"Please, sir," the woman said, "give me this water! Then I'll never be thirsty again, and I won't have to come here to get

*water." "Go and get your husband," Jesus told her. "I don't
have a husband," the woman replied. Jesus said, "You're right!
You don't have a husband—for you have had five husbands,
and you aren't even married to the man you're living with now.
You certainly spoke the truth!" "Sir," the woman said, "you
must be a prophet. So tell me, why is it that you Jews insist
that Jerusalem is the only place of worship, while we
Samaritans claim it is here at Mount Gerizim, where our
ancestors worshiped?" Jesus replied, "Believe me, dear woman,
the time is coming when it will no longer matter whether you
worship the Father on this mountain or in Jerusalem. You
Samaritans know very little about the one you worship, while
we Jews know all about him, for salvation comes through the
Jews. But the time is coming—indeed it's here now—when true
worshipers will worship the Father in spirit and in truth. The
Father is looking for those who will worship him that way. For
God is Spirit, so those who worship him must worship in spirit
and in truth."*

*The woman said, "I know the Messiah is coming—the one who
is called Christ. When he comes, he will explain everything to
us." Then Jesus told her, "I AM the Messiah!" Just then his
disciples came back. They were shocked to find him talking to a
woman, but none of them had the nerve to ask, "What do you
want with her?" or "Why are you talking to her?" The woman
left her water jar beside the well and ran back to the village,
telling everyone, "Come and see a man who told me everything
I ever did! Could he possibly be the Messiah?" So the people
came streaming from the village to see him.*

John 4:7-30 NLT

Everything she had believed all her life was flipped upside-
down when she met the Messiah. Jesus freed her from sin and
from the stigmas of being a woman *and* a Samaritan. Jesus, the
Living Water, was washing her clean as He spoke *truth* to her.

Jesus had told the woman to *bring her husband* to Him. But after
He lovingly exposed the truth about her whole life story and
introduced Himself as her Savior, she ran to town and brought

everybody! She experienced the powerful grace and Love of Jesus for herself and could not keep the Messiah a secret! Everybody had to know the One who was *Truth*. She *adored* Jesus worshiping unashamedly!

If you love me, keep my commands. And I will ask the Father, and he will give you another advocate to help you and be with you forever— the Spirit of truth. The world cannot accept him, because it neither sees him nor knows him. But you know him, for he lives with you and will be in you.

John 14:15-17 NIV

Before Jesus came to earth, God's people could worship Him from their hearts, but they couldn't be *born again by the Holy Spirit*. The Spirit would minister to them and do mighty works through them, but He did not live *in* them to transform and teach them from the heavenly realms. They depended heavily on priests, kings and prophets for their spiritual well being. Unfortunately, some of the religious leaders lost their Love for God and led people astray.

But now we who are *born again* have the Spirit of Truth inside us! The woman at the well *was seated with Jesus*. He taught her what she needed to know and ministered to her. *Spending time with Jesus transformed her life* and will transform our lives as well! And when the eyes of our hearts are opened more and more to see *who Jesus really is*, we will drink from His well and will be able to worship Him *in Spirit and in Truth.*

These things I have written to you concerning those who are trying to deceive you. And as for you, the anointing which you received from Him remains in you, and you have no need for anyone to teach you; but as His anointing teaches you about all things, and is true and is not a lie, and just as it has taught you, you remain in Him.

1 John 2:26-27 NASB

Though we need to be ministered to by the Body of Christ, it is never spiritually healthy to *follow people* and *ignore the Lord*. If you don't *sit and talk to Jesus personally* and *learn from His Word*, how will you know that you are being led in the right direction? Worshiping in Spirit and Truth can only happen if you *know God personally* and *seek His Truth* for yourself. We worship God, not people. We bow before His truth, not the ideas, arguments and doctrines of man.

The devil led him [Jesus] up to a high place and showed him in an instant all the kingdoms of the world. And he said to him, "I will give you all their authority and splendor; it has been given to me, and I can give it to anyone I want to. If you worship me, it will all be yours." Jesus answered, "It is written: 'Worship the Lord your God and serve him only.'
Luke 4:5-8 NIV

The devil will tempt you to set your eyes on what the world has to offer instead of on what the Spirit is saying which is always true. The devil is always a liar. What realm are you *paying attention* to—the earthly realm that will lead you astray, or the heavenly realms where you are seated with Jesus, the Truth?

If you worship me, the LORD your God, I will bless you with food and water and take away all your sicknesses. In your land no woman will have a miscarriage or be without children. I will give you long lives.
Exodus 23: 25-26 GNT

This scripture promise was written to the nation of Israel. These and all the promises of God apply to us in the Body of Christ and to every nation whose people voluntarily choose to worship the Lord. Blessings flow when we are united in Christ's Love and worship in Spirit and in Truth.

You hypocrites! Isaiah was right when he prophesied about you: "These people honor me with their lips, but their hearts are far from me. They worship me in vain; their teachings are merely human rules."
Matthew 15:7-9 NIV

King David of Israel brought the ark of God back to Jerusalem after it had been captured. The ark contained God's presence! As the ark returned, trumpets sounded and the people shouted before the Lord in worship.

Now as the ark of the LORD came into the City of David, Michal, Saul's daughter, [David's wife] looked through a window and saw King David leaping and whirling before the LORD; and she despised him in her heart.

Then David returned to bless his household. And Michal the daughter of Saul came out to meet David, and said, "How glorious was the king of Israel today, uncovering himself today in the eyes of the maids of his servants, as one of the base fellows shamelessly uncovers himself!"

So David said to Michal, "It was before the LORD, who chose me instead of your father and all his house, to appoint me ruler over the people of the LORD, over Israel. Therefore I will play music before the LORD. And I will be even more undignified than this, and will be humble in my own sight. But as for the maidservants of whom you have spoken, by them I will be held in honor." Therefore Michal the daughter of Saul had no children to the day of her death.

2 Samuel 6:16, 20-23 NKJV

Michal's worldly pride caused her to *despise* the outward passionate humility of her husband's worship! In scene two of *The Beautiful Dream*, my husband, Mark, and I were unified in our adoration of Jesus. When the Body of Christ comes together in unity to worship the Lord from the heavenly realms, His presence is amplified! Worship is not sounding or looking a certain outward acceptable way at church while you sing. Worship is *shame-free* inward devotion and adoration—lived, spoken and expressed to God from the heart *in many different ways!* If every believer took time to worship God alone in Spirit and in Truth, our worship *together* would be so full of God's tangible glory!

Give to the Lord the glory he deserves! Bring your offering and come into his presence. Worship the Lord in all his holy splendor.

1 Chronicles 16:29 NLT

God created music and song as one of the most powerful portals into the heavenly realms! If our flesh gets in the way, worship through music can become earthly and religious. But if our worship happens seated at God's Table, the Spirit will flow freely around us and in us. He will speak revelations of truth to our spirit that may or may not even be in the song we are singing. That only causes us to worship more joyfully! The songs of the Kingdom are Love gifts from Holy Spirit presented to us through the Body of Christ!

In Heaven, every being is worshiping God because they are so filled with awe and *deeply affected by His Love.* When we are seated with God at His Table, we begin to enter the same *atmosphere of Heaven* and worship becomes deeply intimate and joyful. The Spirit reveals truth so we can see the glory of our King and who He created us to be! The lies of the earthly realm start falling to the ground!

So drink deeply of the songs of the Kingdom, prophetically declaring His goodness! Let your heart dance intimately with Jesus in passionate worship. Be amazed, awestruck, enamored and elated by His Words of truth as you engage with *Agape Love Himself.* Your encounters seated with Jesus at the Well will send you out running to tell the Good News, "I've met the Messiah — and He is wonderful!"

Declaration

I WORSHIP GOD IN HIS SPIRIT AND IN HIS TRUTH!

29

Amazing Grace

Then I will pour out a spirit of grace and prayer on the family of David and on the people of Jerusalem. They will look on me whom they have pierced and mourn for him as for an only son. They will grieve bitterly for him as for a firstborn son who has died.

Zechariah 12:10 NLT

Holy Spirit will open the eyes of the beautiful Jewish people so they can see that *Jesus really was their Messiah!* They will grieve in repentance, and many will accept God's amazing grace! This prophecy is happening right now!

This righteousness is given through faith in Jesus Christ to all who believe. There is no difference between Jew and Gentile for all have sinned and fall short of the glory of God, and all are justified freely by his grace through the redemption that came by Christ Jesus.

Romans 3:22-24 NIV

Grace is *God's gift of righteousness* through Jesus that cancels all accusations against us and gives us life! All of us have sinned, but because of God's amazing grace, we are guilt-free!

But there is a great difference between Adam's sin and God's gracious gift. For the sin of this one man, Adam, brought death to many. But even greater is God's wonderful grace and his gift of forgiveness to many through this other man, Jesus Christ. And the result of God's gracious gift is very different from the result of that one man's sin. For Adam's sin led to condemnation, but God's free gift leads to our being made right with God, even though we are guilty of many sins. For the sin of this one man, Adam, caused death to rule over many. But even greater is God's wonderful grace and his gift of righteousness, for all who receive it will live in triumph over sin and death through this one man, Jesus Christ.

Romans 5:15-17 NLT

The word *grace,* in the Greek language, means *kindness, favor* and *blessing.* Grace comes from a root word meaning *thanks* and *joy* because it is a *gift!* We don't earn God's grace and we don't deserve it. Jesus gives us God's *kindness, favor* and *blessing* when we say *yes* to the generous offer He paid for on the cross! In the dream, Jesus gave me grace that felt like I was in Heaven! If this amazing grace is the *kindness, favor* and *blessing* of God, it sounds to me like we're supposed to have faith in God's Love — the Agape Love of God that I experienced in the dream!

Peter replied, "Repent and be baptized, every one of you, in the name of Jesus Christ for the forgiveness of your sins. And you will receive the gift of the Holy Spirit."

Acts 2:38 NIV

When we say *yes* to Jesus, the *gift of Holy Spirit* comes inside us with the *gift of grace* to help us grow in Christ.

... the gospel which has come to you, just as in all the world also it is bearing fruit and increasing, even as it has been doing in you also since the day you heard it and understood the grace of God in truth;

Colossians 1:5b-6 NASB

If we don't understand that God's grace is the Spirit in us filling us with God's Love and supernatural life, we will believe lies like, *"God is far away,"* or *"I don't feel saved so maybe I'm not,"* or *"I am powerless to do anything about this problem."*

May grace and peace be lavished on you as you grow in the rich knowledge of God and of Jesus our Lord!

2 Peter 1:2 NET

Holy Spirit doesn't come into your life to lay down and take a nap until you go to Heaven. He is there to *keep you advancing* in Jesus and *empower* you for God's glory! God's grace can't flow unless we are connecting ourselves to the One who gives grace. Spending time with God in the heavenly realms makes this possible because it is there that God reveals His supernatural Love to us. Agape Love, or amazing grace, comes to us through relationship with God the Father, Son and Holy Spirit.

There is no shame for any child of God who is struggling but staying in the dance with Jesus. His grace covers us as we are growing in our faith — in the good times and in our worst trials. God's grace will not fail you! But we have to place all our hope in God's Love and the grace He has poured out on us!

Therefore, with minds that are alert and fully sober, set your hope on the grace to be brought to you when Jesus Christ is revealed at his coming.

1 Peter 1:13 NIV

Until we see Him face to face, it is important to *keep our hearts and minds fixed on Jesus* who brought us the *gift* of God's kindness, favor, and blessing — God's grace!

But grow in the grace and knowledge of our Lord and Savior Jesus Christ. To him be glory both now and forever! Amen.

2 Peter 3:18 NIV

When we were *born again,* we received grace because we *believed* in Jesus. We need to receive God's grace *every day* as much as we need to eat food and breathe air or as much as a garden needs rain and sunshine. It takes time to mature. But the intimacy that develops between us as we depend on God, helps us to stay *thankful* and *joyful.* The power of grace helps us not go back into sin again.

For the grace of God has appeared that offers salvation to all people. It teaches us to say "No" to ungodliness and worldly passions, and to live self-controlled, upright and godly lives in this present age, while we wait for the blessed hope—the appearing of the glory of our great God and Savior, Jesus Christ, who gave himself for us to redeem us from all wickedness and to purify for himself a people that are his very own, eager to do what is good.

Titus 2:11-14 NIV

Holy Spirit's grace *empowers us to stay out of sin*. Self-control is a fruit of Holy Spirit. Sin will eventually drive a person into deep darkness. So God has *blessed* us with the ability to *stay in His Agape Love* through His amazing grace!

And you know that Jesus came to take away our sins, and there is no sin in him. Anyone who continues to live in him will not sin. But anyone who keeps on sinning does not know him or understand who he is.

1 John 3:5-6 NLT

If you *misunderstood God's grace* and you want to *repent* of a sinful lifestyle, the Spirit is there to help you. Jesus wants you in His light, close to Himself because He Loves you!

Some claim to know Jesus yet think it's okay to deliberately sin. But there are also the opposites that live in fear and anxiety, hoping to *get* God's grace by being perfect. God's grace and favor are *free* through Jesus — *never earned!*

For if you are trying to make yourselves right with God by keeping the law, you have been cut off from Christ! You have fallen away from God's grace.

Galatians 5:4 NLT

Trying to *earn* God's grace makes a person anxious because they *fear* being rejected by God. If you have accepted Jesus, God has accepted you! He Loves you! This is the *foundation* of your faith! *You are accepted!* Your heavy burden to perform has been lifted so you can *enjoy* fulfilling your purpose in the Family.

The Holy Spirit gives each of us special *gifts of grace* to do supernatural works for His glory! God's Spirit unifies us as the Body so we can be a blessing in God's Kingdom.

For there is one body and one Spirit, just as you have been called to one glorious hope for the future. There is one Lord, one faith, one baptism, one God and Father of all, who is over all, in all, and living through all. However, he has given each one of us a special gift through the generosity of Christ. That is why the Scriptures say, "When he ascended to the heights, he led a crowd of captives and gave gifts to his people."
Ephesians 4:4-8 NLT

God's Spirit gives us grace to do supernatural things because Jesus has *ascended to the heights.* Seated at God's Table, we can receive His power to heal the sick, and do many other miraculous things just like Jesus did on earth. When He shows you how He wants to work through you, keep your heart humble and give *Him* all the credit!

Because you Love Jesus, the grace of God empowers you to be your best at school or work, to raise your children, and to do anything you need to do. He can *empower you to make grace-filled decisions,* to bless you and to bless those around you. You are filled with God's Agape Love—God's amazing grace!

And the child [Jesus] grew and became strong; he was filled with wisdom, and the grace of God was on him.
Luke 2:40 NIV

Jesus had the grace of God but He didn't need grace to be *forgiven.* That's because He never sinned! So, grace doesn't *only* mean forgiveness of sin. Grace is the *kindness, favor* and *blessing* of the Father to us because we know Jesus, His Son! The grace of God is ours *through Jesus* if we believe.

The Jewish people of the old covenant understood the power of a *prayer-blessing* from their earthly fathers that would allow them to live productive and joyful lives. The Holy Spirit will pour out the Father's kindness, favor and blessing as you lay your hands on your children and bless them in prayer.

The LORD bless you and keep you; the LORD make his face shine on you and be gracious to you; the LORD turn his face toward you and give you peace.

Numbers 6:24-26 NIV

If you never received a blessing from your earthly father, the Body of Christ can bless you and pray over you. But if you believe Jesus died for you and you know Him personally, your Father God has adopted you as His own. He has seated you next to Himself and will give you His blessing through the Holy Spirit. Your Abba is with you to bless you with His grace!

Your Father's *grace* flows freely because you are always seated in His presence! Be seated next to your Abba's heart and *allow Him* to pour out His kindness, favor and blessing on you. He will fill you every day with His *amazing grace* through Jesus Christ so you are able to pour it out on others! His grace looks and feels like perfect Love!

Declaration

I AM SEATED IN THE AMAZING GRACE OF GOD!

30

Be Seated in Humility

In *The Beautiful Dream*, scene two, my husband and I were sitting on the first step of a concrete stadium. This can represent positioning ourselves *low in humility* before the Lord and each other. In our spiritual walk with Jesus, we must keep our hearts in a place of humility, *resting our faith in God's grace* and seeing each other through Jesus' eyes, *perfect and beautiful.* Jesus is the *Foundation* of every part of our lives. Every step we take upward is done by God's grace. If we want to *be seated high* in the heavenly realms, we must first *be seated low* in humility before God on earth.

Pride goes before destruction, and a haughty spirit before a fall.
Proverbs 16:18 NKJV

Pride was Lucifer's downfall—*literally.* Satan tries to tempt us with *pride* so we will fall like he did. But in God's Kingdom, we live by the standard of *humility.*

Then the mother of Zebedee's sons came to Jesus with her sons and, kneeling down, asked a favor of him." What is it you want?" he asked. She said, "Grant that one of these two sons of mine may sit at your right and the other at your left in your kingdom." "You don't know what you are asking," Jesus said to them. "Can you drink the cup I am going to drink?" "We can," they answered. Jesus said to them, "You will indeed drink from my cup, but to sit at my right or left is not for me to grant. These places belong to those for whom they have been prepared by my Father." When the ten heard about this, they were indignant with the two brothers.

Jesus called them together and said, "You know that the rulers of the Gentiles lord it over them, and their high officials exercise authority over them. Not so with you. Instead, whoever wants to become great among you must be your servant, and whoever wants to be first must be your slave—just as the Son of Man did not come to be served, but to serve, and to give his life as a ransom for many."

Matthew 20:20-28 NIV

Humiliation and shame are from the devil. But the Lord says if you get rid of your pride and *humble yourself* to think of others before yourself, He will lift you up! When you *know* you are of royal Blood in Christ, seated with the King in the heavenly realms, it seems silly to boast about earthly things. *Rich* or *poor* in the earthly realm, we have everything that matters, seated at God's Table.

When Jesus noticed that all who had come to the dinner were trying to sit in the seats of honor near the head of the table, he gave them this advice. "When you are invited to a wedding feast, don't sit in the seat of honor. What if someone who is more distinguished than you has also been invited? The host will come and say, 'Give this person your seat.' Then you will be embarrassed, and you will have to take whatever seat is left at the foot of the table!

Instead, take the lowest place at the foot of the table. Then when your host sees you, he will come and say, 'Friend, we have a better place for you!' Then you will be honored in front of all the other guests. For those who exalt themselves will be humbled, and those who humble themselves will be exalted."

Luke 14:7-11 NLT

In *The Beautiful Dream*, I was given the best seat at God's Table but failed to sit down! Everyone *humbled themselves* to give me another chance. When we take a seat of humility on earth by showering Agape Love on others in the power of the Spirit, that's when God can give us a seat of honor at His Table in the heavenly realms.

You adulterers! Don't you realize that friendship with the world makes you an enemy of God? I say it again: If you want to be a friend of the world, you make yourself an enemy of God. Do you think the Scriptures have no meaning? They say that God is passionate that the spirit he has placed within us should be faithful to him. And he gives grace generously. As the Scriptures say, "God opposes the proud but gives grace to the humble."

Go humble yourselves before God. Resist the devil, and he will flee from you. Come close to God, and God will come close to you. Wash your hands, you sinners; purify your hearts, for your loyalty is divided between God and the world. Let there be tears for what you have done. Let there be sorrow and deep grief. Let there be sadness instead of laughter, and gloom instead of joy. Humble yourselves before the Lord, and he will lift you up in honor.

James 4:4-10 NLT

Humbling yourself before the Lord will cause you to lose friends who don't Love Jesus. But the person who knows God will desire *the face of Jesus* above all others!

If I shut up the heavens so that there is no rain, or if I command the locust to devour the land, or if I send a plague among My people, and My people who are called by My name humble themselves, and pray and seek My face, and turn from their wicked ways, then I will hear from heaven, and I will forgive their sin and will heal their land. Now My eyes will be open and My ears attentive to the prayer offered in this place.

2 Chronicles 7:13-15 NASB

A nation's hope can be restored when God's people *humbly seek the face of Jesus* in repentance, and faith in His grace.

Watch out! Don't do your good deeds publicly, to be admired by others, for you will lose the reward from your Father in heaven. When you give to someone in need, don't do as the hypocrites do—blowing trumpets in the synagogues and streets to call attention to their acts of charity! I tell you the truth, they have received all the reward they will ever get. But when you give to someone in need, don't let your left hand know what your right hand is doing. Give your gifts in private, and your Father, who sees everything, will reward you.

When you pray, don't be like the hypocrites who love to pray publicly on street corners and in the synagogues where everyone can see them. I tell you the truth, that is all the reward they will ever get. But when you pray, go away by yourself, shut the door behind you, and pray to your Father in private. Then your Father, who sees everything, will reward you. When you pray, don't babble on and on as the Gentiles do. They think their prayers are answered merely by repeating their words again and again. Don't be like them, for your Father knows exactly what you need even before you ask him!

Matthew 6:1-8 NLT

When the *prideful* do "good deeds," they expect a hand of applause. The *humble* serve because they truly Love!

But as the scripture says, "Whoever wants to boast must boast about what the Lord has done."

2 Corinthians 10:17 GNT

Earthly fame is like poverty to a royal son or daughter who serves the King of kings and the Lord of lords. The secret of the humble is that they live from a much higher realm.

God blesses those who are poor and realize their need for him, for the Kingdom of Heaven is theirs. God blesses those who mourn, for they will be comforted. God blesses those who are humble, for they will inherit the whole earth. God blesses those who hunger and thirst for justice, for they will be satisfied. God blesses those who are merciful, for they will be shown mercy. God blesses those whose hearts are pure, for they will see God.

God blesses those who work for peace, for they will be called the children of God. God blesses those who are persecuted for doing right, for the Kingdom of Heaven is theirs.

Matthew 5:3-10 NLT

True humility grows out of a relationship with the God of Agape Love. It produces a heart that God can use to bring the treasures of Heaven to earth!

Elijah, the prophet, had prophesied there would be no rain for several years. As a result there was a famine. The Lord told Elijah that He had instructed a woman in Zarephath to give him something to eat.

So he went to Zarephath. As he arrived at the gates of the village, he saw a widow gathering sticks, and he asked her, "Would you please bring me a little water in a cup?" As she was going to get it, he called to her, "Bring me a bite of bread, too." But she said, "I swear by the LORD your God that I don't have a single piece of bread in the house. And I have only a handful of flour left in the jar and a little cooking oil in the bottom of the jug. I was just gathering a few sticks to cook this last meal, and then my son and I will die."

But Elijah said to her, "Don't be afraid! Go ahead and do just what you've said, but make a little bread for me first. Then use what's left to prepare a meal for yourself and your son. For this is what the LORD, the God of Israel, says: There will always be flour and olive oil left in your containers until the time when the LORD sends rain and the crops grow again!" So she did as Elijah said, and she and Elijah and her family continued to eat for many days. There was always enough flour and olive oil left in the containers, just as the LORD had promised through Elijah.

1 Kings 17:10-16 NLT

This woman was *so humble before God* that she gave away her last meal. The blessings that followed were astounding! The flour and oil never ran out! Later her son died from an illness but God, through Elijah, brought him back to life!

Her greatest humility was her *faith*. Elijah spoke God's Word to her, that she would not run out of food, and she humbled herself to *believe* and *obey* God!

God does not view things the way people do. People look on the outward appearance, but the Lord looks at the heart.
1 Samuel 16:7b NET

God knew the widow's poverty, but *He also knew her heart.* Of all the people in the region, God chose her because she was humbly obedient. God saw this as an opportunity to bless her, and as a bonus she had the honor of seating one of the greatest prophets in all of history *at her table!*

Humbly believing God will often seem *contrary to human reasoning*, but in the end, the blessings of God will overflow! Be willing to *be seated on the lowest step* here on earth, and you will find yourself seated in a place of honor at God's Table!

Declaration

**I HUMBLE MYSELF ON EARTH
SO I CAN BE SEATED AT GOD'S TABLE!**

31

The Promised Land

The Beautiful Dream was divided into three scenes, similar to the exodus of the children of Israel. They left Egypt, stayed in the wilderness for a season, and then moved into the Promised Land. I hope you can follow the symbolism of the Exodus story in the dream.

Scene One

This scene in the dream represents *salvation*. Jesus is the *Lamb* whose blood conquers death. We follow His lead into *the sea of baptism*, freeing us from the slavery of sin!

The Israelites had become *slaves* in the land of Egypt. There was *no way out* of their bondage, but God heard their cries and *came* to rescue them. Through *signs, wonders, and plagues on the Egyptians*, God proved His Love for the Israelites and humiliated the kingdom of darkness. Filled with hope, the Israelites obeyed God and packed to leave. Their sentence of death was overruled when they applied the blood of a lamb around the doors of their homes that night. The next morning *they left Egypt!*

As the Israelites were leaving, the Egyptians showered them with gifts of all kinds — even gold. *God's presence* guided the Israelites in the form of a cloud during the day and a pillar of fire at night. Their journey took them to a body of water. *This was their baptism!* They walked toward the sea *by faith* realizing that they were *facing death*. The Egyptian army trapped them from behind, but as they stepped forward, God split the sea in two, making a wide, dry path to the other side! When God's people reached the shore, *they looked back and saw their past was dead!* The Egyptians that had whipped them into submission drowned that day in the sea of baptism!

Then Moses and the Israelites sang this song to the LORD: I will sing to the LORD, for he is highly exalted. Both horse and driver he has hurled into the sea. The LORD is my strength and my defense; he has become my salvation. He is my God, and I will praise him, my father's God, and I will exalt him. The LORD is a warrior; the LORD is his name. Pharaoh's chariots and his army he has hurled into the sea. The best of Pharaoh's officers are drowned in the Red Sea. The deep waters have covered them; they sank to the depths like a stone.

Your right hand, LORD, was majestic in power. Your right hand, LORD, shattered the enemy. Who among the gods is like you, LORD? Who is like you — majestic in holiness, awesome in glory, working wonders? You stretch out your right hand, and the earth swallows your enemies. In your unfailing love you will lead the people you have redeemed. In your strength you will guide them to your holy dwelling. The nations will hear and tremble; anguish will grip the people of Philistia. The chiefs of Edom will be terrified, the leaders of Moab will be seized with trembling, the people of Canaan will melt away; terror and dread will fall on them. By the power of your arm they will be as still as a stone — until your people pass by, LORD, until the people you bought pass by.

You will bring them in and plant them on the mountain of your inheritance — the place, LORD, you made for your dwelling, the sanctuary, Lord, your hands established. "The LORD reigns for ever and ever."

Exodus 15:1-18 NIV

Scene Two

Scene two of the dream represents the season when our faith is established. We rejoice and tell the world how Jesus saved us! This is *a time of testing* to see if the Word planted in us will grow and produce fruit, or wither and die. Trials are there to prove where our faith lies. But if we take our eyes off Jesus, darkness can creep back in, steal our faith and keep us from *our destiny in Christ*. The wilderness period is a time to *grow strong* by becoming *more dependent* on God's Love. Israel's song of deliverance, sung prophetically by the power of the Holy Spirit, laid out the three stages of God's plan. They sang of how *God Himself* would carry them through every phase of the journey. But would their faith stay strong?

God miraculously provided water and a bread called manna for them in the desert, but many of them were not thankful.

We remember the fish which we ate freely in Egypt, the cucumbers, the melons, the leeks, the onions, and the garlic; but now our whole being is dried up; there is nothing at all except this manna before our eyes!

Numbers 11:5-6 NKJV

The Israelites didn't believe that the God who miraculously rescued them from the Egyptians would sustain their bodies with manna. They made a golden calf to worship and partied sinfully as they had done in Egypt. The Lord wanted to train them for battle by teaching them humility, courage, righteousness and complete trust in Him. But most of them *failed every test* because of their pride.

Jesus is the *Bread of Life*. His body was broken so we could be given life—forgiven, healed, delivered, protected, provided for and empowered for service in His Kingdom. The people of Israel were thirsty in the desert, but God always provided water. Once God told Moses to speak to a rock and suddenly a spring of water flowed from the rock. Jesus is the Rock who gives us *Living Water* every day! He wants us to speak with Him, seated at His Table. God is offering His life to us every day, but He won't *make us* eat and drink. Jesus is reaching out His hand ready to show His extravagant Love, but many prefer to live from the earthly realm. They want all the riches of grace, but they don't want a close relationship with the source of life.

There were a few like Joshua and Caleb, who Loved God and remembered the wonderful things He had done for them. Joshua and Caleb saw God's Love in everything He did! They were *united* and *believed* the Lord would continue to drive out the kingdoms of darkness in front of them. But they had to *wait on the Lord* for 40 years until the *doubters* and *complainers* died off! During that time, Joshua and Caleb's faith in God's Love grew strong. *The old slaves* whose crusty hearts had rejoiced on the shore for only a moment, *chose to reject their faith* in a powerful Loving God. These critical ones never entered the Promised Land where they could have settled down in freedom and enjoyed the fruit of their labors.

Come, let us worship and bow down. Let us kneel before the LORD *our maker, for he is our God. We are the people he watches over, the flock under his care. If only you would listen to his voice today! The* LORD *says, "Don't harden your hearts as Israel did at Meribah, as they did at Massah in the wilderness. For there your ancestors tested and tried my patience, even though they saw everything I did. For forty years I was angry with them, and I said, 'They are a people whose hearts turn away from me. They refuse to do what I tell them.' So in my anger I took an oath: 'They will never enter my place of rest.'"*

Psalm 95:6-11 NLT

Instead of *letting God test them* in the trial period of the wilderness, many of them *tested and tried God!* Only a few kept the song of Moses fresh and alive in their hearts!

Scene Three
In scene three, Jesus escorted me to the heavenly realms where I was asked to be seated with God. In this place, God's Family lives in unity. It is *the high point* where battles against Satan on earth are won, and God's children can take hold of their promised destiny for God's glory.

Inside the Tent of Meeting, the LORD *would speak to Moses face to face, as one speaks to a friend. Afterward Moses would return to the camp, but the young man who assisted him, Joshua son of Nun, would remain behind in the Tent of Meeting.*

One day Moses said to the LORD, "You have been telling me, 'Take these people up to the Promised Land.' But you haven't told me whom you will send with me. You have told me, 'I know you by name, and I look favorably on you.' If it is true that you look favorably on me, let me know your ways so I may understand you more fully and continue to enjoy your favor. And remember that this nation is your very own people." The LORD replied, "I will personally go with you, Moses, and I will give you rest — everything will be fine for you."

Then Moses said, "If you don't personally go with us, don't make us leave this place. How will anyone know that you look favorably on me — on me and on your people — if you don't go with us? For your presence among us sets your people and me apart from all other people on the earth." The LORD replied to Moses, "I will indeed do what you have asked, for I look favorably on you, and I know you by name."

Exodus 33:11-17 NLT

Moses spoke face to face with God, like a friend. He knew there was no point in going anywhere without the Lord. It was God who led them out of Egypt, opened the sea for them to cross over, fed them and kept their shoes from wearing out for forty years in the desert. Moses cherished meeting with the Lord and so did Joshua, Moses' assistant, who *lingered with God* in the *Tent of Meeting* after Moses left.

Moses and Joshua *knew the Lord personally.* They had encountered His Love and life-giving power. Their passion for God's presence kept their faith strong. For them, life without a *Love relationship with God* would be no life at all! Our bodies are *the Tent of Meeting,* with the Holy Spirit inside us. We can linger and fellowship with God continually no matter what our circumstances are.

I have learned in whatever state I am, to be content.
Philippians 4:11 NKJV

After the complainers died, the people of Israel became *unified* and *obedient, trusting in the Lord.* God held back the Jordan River and they crossed over into their Promised Land! The Jordan River represents a second baptism, the baptism of the Holy Spirit's fire!

Rejoice in the Lord — *even in your wilderness season.* You have been set free from the slavery of sin and death! You have been given the Holy Spirit to guide you and provide for your needs. If you are seeking the Lord and times are tough, *He is not punishing you!* He is urging us all to crush the idols and slay fleshly attitudes, because in the Promised Land there are giants only our faith in God can conquer. If we Love God, obey Him and give grace to one another, the Lord will go ahead of us and we will defeat the enemy!

Be seated at God's Table and *linger in the Tent of Meeting* like Joshua! And like Moses, *know Jesus so well* that you will only go if you can follow His lead. The Promised Land is not for the faint at heart, but for *joyful and courageous warriors* who know the Lord and trust in His unfailing Love. God fights for us! Be *planted on the mountain of your inheritance* with the Spirit! There will be battles to fight, but seated in *unity* with God and our Family, we will reign victoriously — in this life and for eternity! *Sing joyfully to the Lord! Our God is highly exalted!*

Declaration

I LOVE TO LINGER IN THE TENT OF MEETING!

32

Table Talk: *Warriors Dream*

In actual life, my husband, Mark, one of our grandchildren and I went to a high school football game the night before this "Warriors" dream. We cheered for the Warriors who proudly wore their red and black colors. There were several people there that we knew, including a wonderful young man from our church that I will rename *John* just for this chapter. The Warriors won 51 to 0!

During the game I felt sorry for the other team and prayed that God would help them score at least one touchdown. But as the game went on, I prayed, "Nevertheless Lord, not my will but Yours be done." I asked God to help me see the people around me through His eyes.

Right about then one of the Warriors football players ran off the field right below where we were seated and took off his helmet. On his cheek was painted a black cross! My heart felt so proud for him even though I didn't know him. He was my Brother! I realized there were even more believers under those shiny helmets.

The next morning I woke up to a dream about Warriors! God was just setting the stage for it the night before!

The Warrior Dream: I was in "our house" when some young people showed up. The young man I will call *John* asked me for something *red* to paint his knuckles with. He was so *happy* about getting painted up for the *game!* I thought about what I had in my house that was red and suggested a red *Sharpie* since *it wouldn't wear off.* I was in the process of looking for the red Sharpie when I woke up.

We overcome by *the Blood of the Lamb* and the word of our testimony! We are God's Warriors! The Blood of Jesus is an all-powerful *sharp weapon* that defeats the devil. *John* was preparing for war by *applying the Blood* to his knuckles!

That is why I run straight for the finish line; that is why I am like a boxer who does not waste his punches. I harden my body with blows and bring it under complete control, to keep myself from being disqualified after having called others to the contest.
1 Corinthians 9:26-27 GNT

The *Blood of Jesus* from *His Cross* has already given the devil a deadly blow to the head. When Satan's troops stagger toward us to harm us, we get to *punch them out* with the Blood of the Lamb! The Blood will never lose it's power!

... knowing that you were not redeemed with corruptible things, like silver or gold, from your aimless conduct received by tradition from your fathers, but with the precious blood of Christ, as of a lamb without blemish and without spot.
1 Peter 1:18-19 NKJV

I love the way John, in the *warrior dream,* was so happy about the game. That's because he knew his team were winners! And I also love the way in real life, the Warriors won 51 to 0! God's grace is more than enough!

At the end of time, the devil will *not* have won *anything* from God's children. We will receive our full inheritance! In fact, we are receiving our inheritance right now, seated with God in the heavenly realms. Those who cover their lives in the Blood of Jesus are never losers. So paint your knuckles red and rejoice! We've already won by the Blood of the spotless Lamb of God!

33

Dancing in Praise

Blessed be the God and Father of our Lord Jesus Christ, who has blessed us with every spiritual blessing in the heavenly places in Christ,

Ephesians 1:3 NASB

In *The Beautiful Dream* I was *overwhelmed* with Jesus. I couldn't stop telling Mark about what He had done for me! God wants us to never lose the wonder of His Love, but we don't have to just stare at the ceiling daydreaming about Him. God wants us to *be seated with Jesus* so we can look straight into His eyes and praise Him face to face!

Therefore, let us offer through Jesus a continual sacrifice of praise to God, proclaiming our allegiance to his name.

Hebrews 13:15 NLT

Praise is a portal to God's presence in the heavenly realms! If we aren't *paying attention* to our relationship with God in the Spirit, our soul in the natural realm can block us from genuine praise. In several of his Psalms, David *commanded* his soul to praise the Lord! We can't afford to wait until we *feel good*, or until *something good happens* to praise the Lord. The devil is always prowling around hoping to bring a spirit of despair on God's people. But genuine praise becomes a powerful weapon to dismantle the plans of the enemy! Praise can help us to *be seated* with God!

When Jehoshaphat was king of Judah, his enemies came to fight against him. Jehoshaphat gathered the people of Judah, calling for fasting and prayer. He prayed *humbly* before the people. As he prayed, the Spirit of the Lord came on a Levite named Jahaziel who prophesied the Word of the Lord.

Jahaziel said *not* to be afraid or discouraged because of the vast army coming against them. Then Jahaziel told them exactly where the enemy would be the next day. But he said God's people would *not* have to fight the battle because *the Lord would be with them!* Everyone fell with their faces to the ground worshiping God. And then, some of them got back up and started shouting praises to the Lord! The next morning Judah set out in the direction of the enemy.

After consulting the people, Jehoshaphat appointed men to sing to the LORD *and to praise him for the splendor of his holiness as they went out at the head of the army, saying: "Give thanks to the* LORD, *for his love endures forever."*

As they began to sing and praise, the LORD *set ambushes against the men of Ammon and Moab and Mount Seir who were invading Judah, and they were defeated. The Ammonites and Moabites rose up against the men from Mount Seir to destroy and annihilate them. After they finished slaughtering the men from Seir, they helped to destroy one another. When the men of Judah came to the place that overlooks the desert and looked toward the vast army, they saw only dead bodies lying on the ground; no one had escaped.*

2 Chronicles 20:21-24 NIV

The men of Judah didn't have to fight! They only walked and praised the Lord, *and the Lord fought for them!* God confused the enemy so that they killed each other! Judah spent three days collecting all the plunder they wanted from the enemy. But that's not all!

On the fourth day they gathered in the Valley of Blessing, which got its name that day because the people praised and thanked the LORD *there. It is still called the Valley of Blessing today. Then all the men returned to Jerusalem, with Jehoshaphat leading them, overjoyed that the LORD had given them victory over their enemies. They marched into Jerusalem to the music of harps, lyres, and trumpets, and they proceeded to the Temple of the LORD. When all the surrounding kingdoms heard that the LORD himself had fought against the enemies of Israel, the fear of God came over them. So, Jehoshaphat's kingdom was at peace, for his God had given him rest on every side.*

2 Chronicles 20:26-30 NLT

There were many battles Israel had to fight with swords, *but not this one!* What powerful truth can we apply to our lives as individuals, families, churches and our nation from this true story? What happened there?

The people of God *experienced a crisis* and came together in *fasting and prayer.* They were *not complaining* to each other or critical of their leadership. Instead, *there was unity.* They were not trying to figure out what they could do in their own strength. *The Lord was their source* and all they wanted was to *pray and hear from God.* Then, *the Holy Spirit gave them a Word* from God and *they believed it.* Immediately, they began *worshiping and praising the Lord.* They didn't wait until the battle had been won. They praised God *before, during* and *after* the battle because *they believed the Word of God!*

What was the Word given to them? *The Lord would be with them.* That's all it took for them to praise and walk confidently into battle! As followers of Jesus, each one of us have Holy Spirit within us. But for some reason that Word doesn't *move* most Christians to praise and faith. I believe when we get a true revelation beyond head knowledge that the Lord is not only *with us* but *inside us,* we will not be able to stop praising Him! Demons will become terrified and thrown into confusion. They will begin attacking each other instead of God's children, and we will walk home in victory, praising the Lord! All the nations of the earth will be in awe of the glory of the Lord!

The only hard work Judah's warriors had to do was to go through the plunder and haul it home! Their battlefield became *the Valley of Blessing* because they believed the Lord was with them and for them, and that caused them to praise the Lord! After gathering the plunder they got together and praised the Lord *again! They were so happy!*

No doubt, they were tired when they got back to Jerusalem. But the warriors of Judah got their instruments and went straight to the Temple of the Lord to praise Him *again* — not because they had to, but because *they wanted to!* When God's Word, Jesus, is in our hearts and praise is on our lips, the battle belongs to the Lord!

Blessed be the LORD my Rock, who trains my hands for war, and my fingers for battle — my lovingkindness and my fortress, my high tower and my deliverer, my shield and the One in whom I take refuge, who subdues my people under me.
Psalm 144:1-2 NKJV

The Lord is the Word! He is our Rock, our Trainer, our Loving God, our Fortress, our Stronghold, our Deliverer, our Shield, our Refuge and our Mighty Warrior! He is such a *personal God* and worthy of our praise! He is with us and in us!

We know that some people are full of evil. But the enemy manipulating them is Satan who deceives hearts and works his terror through humans. Our fight is *in the spiritual realm* against many demonic ranks. We can live in victory through praise. We can also be a vessel for the Holy Spirit *to bring praise into the lives of others!*

Peter and John went to the Temple one afternoon to take part in the three o'clock prayer service. As they approached the Temple, a man lame from birth was being carried in. Each day he was put beside the Temple gate, the one called the Beautiful Gate, so he could beg from the people going into the Temple. When he saw Peter and John about to enter, he asked them for some money.

Peter and John looked at him intently, and Peter said, "Look at us!" The lame man looked at them eagerly, expecting some money. But Peter said, "I don't have any silver or gold for you. But I'll give you what I have. In the name of Jesus Christ the Nazarene, get up and walk!" Then Peter took the lame man by the right hand and helped him up. And as he did, the man's feet and ankles were instantly healed and strengthened. He jumped up, stood on his feet, and began to walk!

Then, walking, leaping, and praising God, he went into the Temple with them. All the people saw him walking and heard him praising God. When they realized he was the lame beggar they had seen so often at the Beautiful Gate, they were absolutely astounded!

Acts 3:1-10 NLT

Miracles like this will happen when we live at God's Table. The Spirit empowers us to destroy the works of the devil—just like Jesus and His disciples did. We can pray for the sick and bring great praise to God as they are healed!

Don't lose faith when you praise and pray and do everything you know to do and still lose a battle. Your faith is not in *your ability* to figure out what went wrong. Your faith is in Jesus Himself. Remain seated and keep your eyes on Him. It is in times of pain that we can lift up a *beautiful sacrifice of praise!* So acknowledge that the King is good, even if you are *wounded from battle.* God Loves you and has not abandoned you! He will pull you close in sorrow and heal your wounds.

Praise the LORD! For it is good to sing praises to our God; for it is pleasant and praise is beautiful. He heals the brokenhearted and binds up their wounds.

Psalm 147:1&3 NASB

In *The Beautiful Dream,* I said *yes* to the dance, but I was immediately afraid and ashamed of what Jesus would think of me when He noticed my flaws. He knew my flaws and danced with me anyway! He saved me and set me free *immediately!* My dance had several dips in it, representing my spiritual misunderstandings and mistakes. But I never let go of Jesus and He never let go of me! I followed His lead and my salvation just kept flowing. It was His Love that kept me holding on to His hands. I was ecstatic with praise! But in scene three, I allowed my mistake to make me *fearful* and *ashamed* again. Holy Spirit was showing me the root of my issues so I could let go of them and be seated with God.

God is not looking at your flaws! He's looking at the motives of your heart. Do you want to dance with Jesus? Will you follow His lead no matter the cost because you Love Him? If so, He removes your guilt so you can let go of fear and shame! You will dip and sway in your journey with Jesus, but no matter what anyone else thinks, you are holding on to Jesus and He is still holding on to you! The Father sees you complete through the Blood of Jesus and that's something to praise God about!

When we praise the Lord, we join our Brothers and Sisters from all over the world, and even the angels *in the spiritual realm!* What a blessing it must be to God when we are all praising Him together — hearts dancing for joy in His Love!

Praise the LORD! Praise God in His sanctuary; praise Him in His mighty expanse. Praise Him for His mighty deeds; praise Him according to His excellent greatness. Praise Him with trumpet sound; praise Him with harp and lyre. Praise Him with tambourine and dancing; praise Him with stringed instruments and flute. Praise Him with loud cymbals; praise Him with resounding cymbals. Everything that has breath shall praise the LORD. Praise the LORD!

Psalm 150:1-6 NASB

Declaration

SOUL, LISTEN TO ME! PRAISE THE LORD!

34

Faith over Fear

Dancing with Jesus represents our *intimately personal Love relationship with Him* that drives out fear. Faith is *trusting* wholeheartedly in Jesus — not changing what He has said to fit our own experience, desires or unbelief. Faith is believing in God's gift of grace through Jesus Christ. Faith is believing in God's Love!

To have faith is to be sure of the things we hope for, to be certain of the things we cannot see.

Hebrews 11:1 GNT

The Paralyzed Man
Several men carried their paralyzed friend on a cot hoping to see Jesus. Jesus was teaching in a house full of people and they couldn't maneuver the cot through the crowd. *Unashamed* and *unafraid*, they made a hole in the roof and lowered their friend down next to Jesus. Jesus healed the man and forgave him of his sins. What a beautiful picture of *believers bringing others to faith* and physical healing! They believed in Jesus' Love!

When Jesus saw their faith, he said, "Friend, your sins are forgiven."

Luke 5:20 NIV

The Storm
One day Jesus and the disciples were crossing the Sea of Galilee together in a boat. Jesus fell asleep on a cushion in the stern. A sudden storm came and scared the disciples so much that they

woke Jesus up saying, "...Don't you care if we drown!?"

Then He arose and rebuked the wind, and said to the sea, "Peace, be still!" And the wind ceased and there was a great calm. But He said to them, "Why are you so fearful? How is it that you have no faith?"

Mark 4:39-40 NKJV

The disciples were *afraid* that they were going to drown. Faith is *confidence* in our Loving God even in difficult circumstances. There is *no fear* when a person is *convinced* that God Loves them and is "in the boat with them." *Fear* can stand in the way of our *faith*. And on a side note, Jesus was showing us that we have authority over bad weather. We can silence storms like Jesus did — in His name. God protects us when we have faith in His Love and believe the truth He has revealed to us in His Word.

The Fig Tree
Jesus used a fig tree as an object lesson for the disciples. As they were walking along the road, Jesus was hungry and decided to eat some figs from a fig tree. Figs were not in season so this tree was producing no fruit. But Jesus spoke to it and decreed that no one would ever eat from it again. The next morning as they walked by the tree, they saw that it was withered up from the roots. The disciples were astonished and asked Jesus about it.

Jesus said to them, "Have faith in God. I tell you the truth, if someone says to this mountain, 'Be lifted up and thrown into the sea,' and does not doubt in his heart but believes that what he says will happen, it will be done for him. For this reason I tell you, whatever you pray and ask for, believe that you have received it, and it will be yours. Whenever you stand praying, if you have anything against anyone, forgive him, so that your Father in heaven will also forgive you your sins."

Mark 11:22-25 NET

Jesus was showing us the power of faith that comes from a pure heart. Jesus could have moved an actual mountain as His object lesson that day, but He chose a fig tree instead. I believe the

Lord is telling us that He has given us authority to speak to things in the earthly realm from a heavenly realms perspective. For instance, you can say to financial poverty that has grown up into a tree in your heart and say in Jesus name, "Poverty, you will never bear fruit again!" or, "Intimidation, you will never bear fruit again!" As you keep walking with Jesus, you will see that tree wither up from the roots! Hallelujah! If we don't speak to the trees that the devil has planted in our way, they will keep bearing fruit and become bigger strongholds.

But Jesus ended the lesson of faith by talking about faith and forgiveness. Holding a grudge will cause your faith to die because *our faith is in the Love of God*. If we believe in the Love of God, we will produce the fruit of Agape Love and give the fruit of grace away continually! God's grace through Jesus is for *every person* on earth. Comparing ourselves to others and thinking that we're better or worse than another person implies that we can *earn* our salvation. We can't *earn* anything from God including answered prayer. Every good gift comes to us because our *faith is in God's Loving grace.*

If a person is *hurt, offended or angry* and refuses to forgive, it means they believe that God's grace should extend only to the ones *they* approve of. They have set themselves up as a god. We can't have faith in God's grace for ourselves and not desire God's grace for others. Because Holy Spirit lives in us, we must humble ourselves to let go of every offense. Those sins have already been nailed to the cross. It is our lifestyle to embrace the Love God has for them even if they never change.

The devil wants us to carry offences against other believers. Sometimes Satan plants an offense or skepticism against another believer because that person *carries a gift of blessing for us!* If we can't see them as a child of God growing up and carrying the Spirit's power, we won't be able to receive the Love-gift they have to offer the Body of Christ. The infection of offense will block our blessing and can poison those around us.

My dear brothers and sisters, take note of this: Everyone should be quick to listen, slow to speak and slow to become angry, because human anger does not produce the righteousness that God desires.

James 1:19-20 NIV

Human anger does not lead others to believe in God's Love. It leads others to fear that they are not Loved. *Human anger* is *earthly* and of the *flesh,* not of the Spirit.

Fearing people is a dangerous trap, but trusting the LORD means safety.

Proverbs 29:25 NLT

When someone doesn't forgive, it's because they *fear.* Maybe they fear that justice will not be done, and so they want *revenge.* Maybe they fear that someone will *blame* them and *shame* them. Having *faith* that God is *our* Judge and *their* Judge will take the burden off us and set us free to Love. Fear will make us *suspicious* of our Brothers and Sisters so that we are unable to be seated at the Table of grace. But forgiveness covers the shame of others in the grace of Jesus. By resisting the spirit of offense, *our faith in God's Love and grace* is covering our shame as well!

The Boy with Seizures
Jesus' disciples healed the sick and drove out demons *in His name.* But one day they tried to drive a demon from a boy who had *terrible seizures* and they couldn't do it. Later they asked Jesus why they were unsuccessful. Jesus said it was because *they didn't have enough faith.* Maybe Jesus was saying that it doesn't take much faith to move a mountain if the heart is filled with God's Love and *not corrupted by fear.*

Jesus said, "You faithless and corrupt people! How long must I be with you? How long must I put up with you? Bring the boy here to me." Then Jesus rebuked the demon in the boy, and it left him. From that moment the boy was well. Afterward the disciples asked Jesus privately, "Why couldn't we cast out that demon?" "You don't have enough faith," Jesus told them. "I tell you the truth, if you had faith even as small as a mustard seed,

you could say to this mountain, 'Move from here to there,' and it would move. Nothing would be impossible."
Matthew 17:17-20 NLT

Walking on Water

One night the disciples were in a boat in very bad weather when Jesus approached them walking on the water. They thought He was a ghost! Jesus called out to them telling them *not to be afraid*. Peter asked if he could walk out on the water to meet Him, so Jesus told Peter to *come on!* Peter actually walked on the water for a little while...

But seeing the wind, he became frightened, and when he began to sink, he cried out, saying, "Lord, save me!" Immediately Jesus reached out with His hand and took hold of him, and said to him, "You of little faith, why did you doubt?" When they got into the boat, the wind stopped. And those who were in the boat worshiped Him, saying, "You are truly God's Son!"
Matthew 14:30-33 NASB

Fear hindered Peter's *faith*. But when Peter cried out to Jesus, He didn't let him drown. Instead, Jesus immediately reached out His hand and caught him! The Lord rebuked Peter for his little faith *after* saving him because He wanted Peter to *grow in faith*. Jesus proved His Love to Peter that night by saving him.

During the three years the 12 disciples were being taught by Jesus, Jesus had to tell them several times that their faith was not where it needed to be. If they had become offended at the Lord, we wouldn't have the Good News of Jesus today. Let's be humble and not offended when Jesus asks the question, *"Why did you doubt me?"* When Jesus asks us that question, it's because there is something blocking our faith in God's kindness, favor and blessing. He wants to free us of it!

God doesn't condemn us when we step out in faith and the breakthrough doesn't come. There is *no condemnation* for those who are in Christ Jesus. Peter *didn't blame Jesus* for his own lack of faith. He cried out to Jesus, *"Lord save me!"* And Jesus did.

Whether our faith lets us walk on water, or our lack of faith causes us to sink, our response should always be to *trust in the Loving grace of God!* He is our Savior!

We know how much God loves us, and we have put our trust in his love. God is love, and all who live in love live in God, and God lives in them. And as we live in God, our love grows more perfect. So we will not be afraid on the day of judgment, but we can face him with confidence because we live like Jesus here in this world. Such love has no fear, because perfect love expels all fear. If we are afraid, it is for fear of punishment, and this shows that we have not fully experienced his perfect love. We love each other because he loved us first.

1 John 4:16-19 NLT

Our trust is in God's Love! If you *sincerely repented*, but you still think God is going to punish you, it will be hard for you to get rid of your *fear* and build your *faith*. Jesus was punished in your place so you can live free from the *fear of punishment*.

If you only want God's grace for your selfish desires, it's not faith and it's not Love. Faith in God's perfect Love drives out fear and produces *good fruit* that will nourish the faith of others!

Just like *The Beautiful Dream*, true faith will embrace Jesus who drives out *all fear* and transforms you with His Agape power. You are not running after sin anymore because you are dancing with Love Himself, and Love doesn't sin. Even in the storms of life you will be able to rest in the Helm of God's grace! Your simple faith in the God of Love will move mountains and calm storms for His glory!

Declaration

GOD'S PERFECT LOVE DRIVES OUT ALL MY FEARS!

35

Have Faith and Believe

*Then he [Abraham] believed in the L*ORD*; and He credited it to him as righteousness.*

Genesis 15:6 NASB

Abraham lived nearly 2,000 years before Jesus came and died on the cross, but even he received righteousness by faith. Grace has always been given to those who repented of their sin and *believed* that God was full of grace.

For if we are faithful to the end, trusting God just as firmly as when we first believed, we will share in all that belongs to Christ.

Hebrews 3:14 NLT

Believing in Jesus means committing wholeheartedly to Him *for life,* like a child growing up in a family.

For though by this time you ought to be teachers, you have need again for someone to teach you the elementary principles of the actual words of God, and you have come to need milk and not solid food.

Hebrews 5:12 NASB

Just because someone has been a Christian for a long time doesn't mean they are *mature* in their faith.

And without faith it is impossible to please Him, for the one who comes to God must believe that He exists, and that He

proves to be One who rewards those who seek Him.
Hebrews 11:6 NASB

Some want the *perks* that come with grace but they don't seek the God of Love Himself. That's not faith.

A church leader must not be a new believer, because he might become proud, and the devil would cause him to fall.
1 Timothy 3:6 NLT

New believers should *grow in Christ* and be given time to prove that their faith and humility in Jesus is established before being given *leadership positions in ministry.* However, a new believer who is faithfully growing in the Lord can heal the sick, drive out demons and do miracles because the Spirit lives in them. This is *basic discipleship,* not just leadership. For three years, Jesus trained His disciples this way as part of their *early spiritual growth experience.* The Word of God tells us this is true for every believer.

Later Jesus appeared to the Eleven as they were eating; he rebuked them for their lack of faith and their stubborn refusal to believe those who had seen him after he had risen. He said to them, "Go into all the world and preach the gospel to all creation. Whoever believes and is baptized will be saved, but whoever does not believe will be condemned.

And these signs will accompany those who believe: In my name they will drive out demons; they will speak in new tongues; they will pick up snakes with their hands; and when they drink deadly poison, it will not hurt them at all; they will place their hands on sick people, and they will get well."
Mark 16:14-18 NIV

These signs of God's supernatural and tangible Love can flow through us by the Holy Spirit. We can *grow* in faith by spending time with God, *hearing* testimonies, *seeing* miracles and *reading* about them in the Bible. Jesus left faith-stories for us, not for entertainment, but *so the Spirit can build our faith.* We also grow in faith by just doing what Jesus did. Don't be discouraged if you don't see results right away. You are planting seeds and watering them every time you Love people enough to pray for them in Jesus' name. When we think that *He might not...* we lose faith because we aren't seeing correctly. When we remember the cross and that *He already has...* then our faith has a chance to grow.

As Jesus went on from there, two blind men followed him, calling out, "Have mercy on us, Son of David!" When he had gone indoors, the blind men came to him, and he asked them, "Do you believe that I am able to do this?" "Yes, Lord," they replied. Then he touched their eyes and said, "According to your faith let it be done to you"; and their sight was restored. Jesus warned them sternly, "See that no one knows about this." But they went out and spread the news about him all over that region.

Matthew 9:27-31 NASB

News about miracles goes viral! After Jesus fed 5,000 people with 5 small barley loaves and 2 fish, word spread fast! Some believed, but others just wanted the *power* Jesus possessed for their own glory. They didn't want *Him.*

When they found him on the other side of the lake, they asked him, "Rabbi, when did you get here?" Jesus replied, "I tell you the truth, you want to be with me because I fed you, not because you understood the miraculous signs. But don't be so concerned about perishable things like food. Spend your energy seeking the eternal life that the Son of Man can give you. For God the Father has given me the seal of his approval."

They replied, "We want to perform God's works, too. What should we do?" Jesus told them, "This is the only work God wants from you: Believe in the one he has sent." They answered, "Show us a miraculous sign if you want us to believe in you. What can you do? After all, our ancestors ate manna while they journeyed through the wilderness! The Scriptures say, 'Moses gave them bread from heaven to eat.'" Jesus said, "I tell you the truth, Moses didn't give you bread from heaven. My Father did. And now he offers you the true bread from heaven. The true bread of God is the one who comes down from heaven and gives life to the world." "Sir," they said, "give us that bread every day."

Jesus replied, "I am the bread of life. Whoever comes to me will never be hungry again. Whoever believes in me will never be thirsty. But you haven't believed in me even though you have seen me. However, those the Father has given me will come to me, and I will never reject them. For I have come down from heaven to do the will of God who sent me, not to do my own will. And this is the will of God, that I should not lose even one of all those he has given me, but that I should raise them up at the last day. For it is my Father's will that all who see his Son and believe in him should have eternal life. I will raise them up at the last day."

John 6:25-40 NLT

Those men then started *grumbling and arguing with Jesus* just like their ancestors did when God miraculously gave them manna in the wilderness! They missed a perfect opportunity to *believe* in Jesus and experience God's grace! Believing in Jesus is *receiving Him*—like eating bread. Miracles like God multiplying food through us are beautiful signs of God's Love and grace through Jesus. They are not works to earn our salvation or to take glory away from the cross. They are the Father's works through us!

Moses was a hundred and twenty years old when he died; he was as strong as ever, and his eyesight was still good.

Deuteronomy 34:7 GNT

Why was Moses so healthy and strong at 120 years of age? Some people would say that God made him strong and healthy so he could fulfill his purpose and calling. I agree with that statement. But the same people don't believe that statement applies to them. They don't believe that their purpose and calling is as important as Moses' was, therefore they don't believe they are important. These are lies from the enemy. So, what made Moses different? He encountered God, therefore he *believed* God and *followed His lead* no matter the cost! Moses kept meeting with God in the Tent of Meeting for the rest of his life. Now that we are filled with the Holy Spirit, we can meet with God just as intimately as Moses did! His glory will rise in us and on us as we meet with Him every day. Our faith will grow. We can find out what our purpose and calling is and allow God to work through us. Living in God's presence produces life!

It was now winter, and Jesus was in Jerusalem at the time of Hanukkah, the Festival of Dedication. He was in the Temple, walking through the section known as Solomon's Colonnade. The people surrounded him and asked, "How long are you going to keep us in suspense? If you are the Messiah, tell us plainly." Jesus replied, "I have already told you, and you don't believe me. The proof is the work I do in my Father's name. But you don't believe me because you are not my sheep. My sheep listen to my voice; I know them, and they follow me.

The Father and I are one." Once again the people picked up stones to kill him. Jesus said, "At my Father's direction I have done many good works. For which one are you going to stone me?" They replied, "We're stoning you not for any good work, but for blasphemy! You, a mere man, claim to be God."

Don't believe me unless I carry out my Father's work. But if I do his work, believe in the evidence of the miraculous works I have done, even if you don't believe me. Then you will know and understand that the Father is in me, and I am in the Father." Once again they tried to arrest him, but he got away and left them.

John 10:22-27, 30-33, 37-39 NLT

Jesus said, *"The proof is the work I do in my Father's name."* Not everyone will believe the message of Jesus, but *some will be encouraged to believe* when their pain leaves or when you go out of your way to help them. For many, it will be the power of the Spirit's Love working through you that will convince them that the Gospel is real! Jesus taught His disciples to share God's Love this way, and we can begin learning that beautiful dance as well!

Jesus Christ is the same yesterday, today, and forever.
Hebrews 13:8 NKJV

Our faith cannot be kept a secret because our faith is directly connected to Jesus *who lives in us*. Some will reject Jesus, but others will receive Him with joy!

[I pray] that they all may be one, as You, Father, are in Me, and I in You; that they also may be one in Us, that the world may believe that You sent Me.
John 17:21 NKJV

The Beautiful Dream urges us to become *one with God* at His Table in the heavenly realms so others will *believe* in Jesus!

For we walk by faith, not by sight. 2 Corinthians 5:7 NKJV

We can't see Jesus in human form like His first disciples did, but *we believe* in Him. One day we will see Jesus in Heaven. But for now, we are *seated with Jesus at His Table* eating His Bread because we have faith and we believe!

Jesus said to him, "Thomas, because you have seen Me, you have believed. Blessed are those who have not seen and yet have believed."
John 20:29 NKJV

Declaration

I BELIEVE YOU, JESUS!

36

We Are Covered!

Covered in Jesus

The *fear* and *shame* that mankind feels today is traced all the way back to the first sin. But that guilt has been atoned for (paid for) by the precious blood of Jesus Christ on the cross. We are covered by the Lamb of God!

Also for Adam and his wife the LORD God made tunics of skin, and clothed them.

Genesis 3:21 NKJV

The *clothing* God made for Adam and Eve after they sinned represents Jesus' sacrifice that covered our sin. Saying *yes* to the covering of Jesus is a *legal transaction* against the devil's claim on our lives. Our debt is paid in full! But it's much more than a transaction. It was, and still is the great expression of His immense Love to rescue us and bring us close to His side!

Those who look to him are radiant; their faces are never covered with shame.

Psalm 34:5 NIV

Jesus covers your guilt, so you are free of accusation, condemnation, shame, blame and punishment! He did it because *He Loves us so much and wants us free and joyful!* The devil will try to disgrace you, but he is a liar! You are no longer exposed or ashamed — *Jesus has covered you!*

So in Christ Jesus you are all children of God through faith, for all of you who were baptized into Christ have clothed yourselves with Christ.

Galatians 3:26-27 NIV

Our sins are washed away in the baptism and death of *our old self.* We have been made new and clothed in the righteousness of Christ! What if you sin? Grieve over your sin, repent, receive God's grace, rejoice and sin no more. God delights in seeing His kids enjoying their new clothes!

You turned my wailing into dancing; you removed my sackcloth and clothed me with joy, that my heart may sing your praises and not be silent. LORD my God, I will praise you forever.

Psalm 30:11-12 NIV

It was Jesus who came to you and turned your depression into joy! It wasn't just *understanding the transaction* He made on the cross that gave you joy. It was Jesus Himself! He is our joy! We are covered in Jesus! Hallelujah!

I will rejoice greatly in the LORD, my soul will be joyful in my God; for He has clothed me with garments of salvation, He has wrapped me with a robe of righteousness, as a groom puts on a turban, and as a bride adorns herself with her jewels.

Isaiah 61:10 NASB

It is *His perfection* that we are covered in, *not our own!* Jesus was the sinless, spotless Lamb of God, who died for the sins of the world. *His righteous Blood* has provided our garments of salvation! *He covers us!*

When it snows, she has no fear for her household; for all of them are clothed in scarlet [red].

Proverbs 31:21 NIV

The Bride of Christ can be confident when bitterly cold seasons in this world surround us. We are covered by the Blood of Jesus! We do not have to fear for those under our care because

208

we can also cover our family and friends in the Blood of Jesus through prayer.

She makes bedspreads and wears clothes of fine purple linen.
Proverbs 31:22 GNT

In scripture, *the bed* can represent spiritual intimacy with God. Even our *secret place of intimate prayer in the heavenly realms* is draped and covered by the Spirit of Jesus so we can continually receive His grace.

In God's Kingdom all His children have been made priests *and* kings. The garments of linen represent our priestly garments, and purple represents our royal robes as sons and daughters of God. God covers us in the *royal* and *priestly* garments of Christ our King of kings and High Priest. We are clothed as warriors and ministers in God's Kingdom. *In Christ* we are Loved, honored and commissioned by God to carry out His will for His glory! We confidently wear the garments of the Kingdom of God!

Strength and dignity are her clothing, and she smiles at the future.
Proverbs 31:25 NASB

We, the Bride of Christ, are clothed in God's strength and integrity because we know that we have been made perfect by the blood of Jesus and His Spirit of grace. Even if the world falls apart, the Lord is wrapped around us like a garment, and we are *safe in Him*. Rejoice and stay seated in the Spirit—in relationship with God! *Be dressed* and ready to serve wherever God places you in His Kingdom.

Be dressed for service and keep your lamps burning, as though you were waiting for your master to return from the wedding feast. Then you will be ready to open the door and let him in the moment he arrives and knocks. The servants who are ready and waiting for his return will be rewarded. I tell you the truth, he himself will seat them, put on an apron, and serve them as they sit and eat! He may come in the middle of the night or just before dawn. But whenever he comes, he will reward the servants who are ready.

Understand this: If a homeowner knew exactly when a burglar was coming, he would not permit his house to be broken into. You also must be ready all the time, for the Son of Man will come when least expected.

Luke 12:35-40 NLT

The Lord wants us to *stay dressed* in the garments He purchased for us. He wants us to do His will by keeping His House *clean* and *functioning at full capacity* until His return—in His Love. Jesus is coming one day to take us home to Heaven! Be *dressed in Him* by staying in Love with Him, serving Him by Loving others and looking for Him!

How amazing it is to know that Jesus already served us through His death on the cross. But one day, *our King will dress Himself again as a servant* and serve us at His Table in Heaven! His Love is overwhelming!

Covered by His Shadow

The Lord gives us a picture of a parent eagle whose nestling has taken flight for the first time. The adult eagle watches and soars majestically over the eaglet as it clumsily learns to navigate with its immature wings.

Keep me as the apple of Your eye; hide me under the shadow of Your wings,

Psalm 17:8 NKJV

The Lord's majestic shadow covers us! He is watching over us, so there is no need to fear!

Whoever dwells in the shelter of the Most High will rest in the shadow of the Almighty.

Psalm 91:1 NIV

Unlike the young eagle, we must *always dwell* in the shelter of the Most High to be safe. God's presence doesn't leave us, and we shouldn't leave Him either. If we're doing what *we* want without the counsel of Holy Spirit, we will find ourselves in a state of vulnerability. But if we yield to the covering of God's Spirit, we will *learn to soar* beautifully in the heavenly realms!

How priceless is your unfailing love, O God! People take refuge in the shadow of your wings.

Psalm 36:7 NIV

Disasters will happen in the world, especially in these end times. People will fail us and unexpected problems will arise. But if we remain underneath the shadow of His unfailing Agape Love, we will not fall apart!

For You have been my help, and in the shadow of Your wings I sing for joy.

Psalm 63:7 NASB

When fear, illness or trials try to steal your joy, *rise up above them and praise the Lord.* He has been and will be your Helper in blessing and trouble. Soar with Him even if your soaring is clumsy and weak. *His shadow will protect you!*

I look up towards the hills. From where does my help come? My help comes from the LORD, the Creator of heaven and earth. May he not allow your foot to slip. May your Protector not sleep. Look! Israel's Protector does not sleep or slumber. The LORD is your protector; the LORD is the shade at your right hand. The sun will not harm you by day, or the moon by night. The LORD will protect you from all harm; he will protect your life. The LORD will protect you in all you do, now and forevermore.

Psalm 121:1-8 NET

In *The Beautiful Dream*, Jesus took *all* my sin, sickness and strongholds upon Himself so I could be clothed in His righteousness, health, protection and provision! We are no longer naked, ashamed, condemned, blamed or waiting for our punishment. The Lord is our shade—our covering of protection! Our nest is secure, high up on *the Rock*, Jesus! People may blame you, shame you and condemn you, but if you are *in Christ*, you are *free from all accusations*. You are safe!

The clothing you wear was purchased by Love Himself and it looks amazing on you! You are clothed in the fruit of the Holy Spirit. You are full of God's Love and able to view others from His Heavenly perspective—covered by grace!

Even if you are in a jail cell, but you are covered by the blood of Jesus, God does not hold your sin against you! You are a saint! You are free to soar like a young eagle underneath the shadow of God's wings. Wear your priestly and royal garments in confidence. You are a totally new person—a child of God!

You have been *seated with God at His Table* where every blessing in Christ is being served to you. Rejoice! You look amazing because *you are amazing*—covered in the righteous robe of Jesus Christ!

Declaration

I AM COVERED BY THE BLOOD OF JESUS!
I AM COVERED BY GOD'S SHADOW!

37

In Christ

But because of his great love for us, God, who is rich in mercy, made us alive with Christ even when we were dead in transgressions—it is by grace you have been saved. And God raised us up with Christ and seated us with him in the heavenly realms in Christ Jesus, in order that in the coming ages he might show the incomparable riches of his grace, expressed in his kindness to us in Christ Jesus.

For it is by grace you have been saved, through faith—and this is not from yourselves, it is the gift of God—not by works, so that no one can boast. For we are God's handiwork, created in Christ Jesus to do good works, which God prepared in advance for us to do.

Ephesians 2:4-9 NIV

If you understand that you are *in Christ Jesus,* you have taken a big step in your spiritual growth. The moment you said *yes* to Jesus, you became *one with Life Himself!*

For in Him we live and move and exist [that is, in Him we actually have our being], as even some of your own poets have said, 'For we also are His children.'

Acts 17:28 AMP

Jesus has brought you *into Himself,* making you a child of God. Everyone who believes in the grace of Jesus are your Brothers and Sisters *in Christ.* You were born again into a *huge* Loving family, the Family of God! You are not who you once were. In

213

Christ you are a brand new person with God as your Father!

Therefore, if anyone is in Christ, he is a new creation; old things have passed away; behold, all things have become new. Now all things are of God, who has reconciled us to Himself through Jesus Christ, and has given us the ministry of reconciliation...
2 Corinthians 5:17-18 NKJV

In Christ, our relationship with God has been *perfectly restored!* We have the honor of bringing others to Jesus so that they can be reconciled with God as well. All of us come in contact with people who need Jesus — some of us more than others. We don't have to be influential, smart, or rich. We just have to care about people.

Remember, dear brothers and sisters, that few of you were wise in the world's eyes or powerful or wealthy when God called you. Instead, God chose things the world considers foolish in order to shame those who think they are wise. And he chose things that are powerless to shame those who are powerful. God chose things despised by the world, things counted as nothing at all, and used them to bring to nothing what the world considers important. As a result, no one can ever boast in the presence of God.

God has united you with Christ Jesus. For our benefit God made him to be wisdom itself. Christ made us right with God; he made us pure and holy, and he freed us from sin. Therefore, as the Scriptures say, "If you want to boast, boast only about the LORD.*"*
1 Corinthians 1:26-31 NLT

People that don't know Jesus yet have developed their own *worldly wisdom.* When they hear about Jesus it takes a lot of humility to let go of their old beliefs and lifestyle to follow Jesus. But when we meet Jesus and our life is changed, we realize that He has become *everything* to us! We can only boast *in God* and in *His wisdom.* The world's wisdom leads to death. Choosing to *stay humble* helps us grow *in Christ* and remain in an amazing life-long journey with Him.

Brothers and sisters, I could not address you as people who live by the Spirit but as people who are still worldly—mere infants in Christ. I gave you milk, not solid food, for you were not yet ready for it. Indeed, you are still not ready. You are still worldly. For since there is jealousy and quarreling among you, are you not worldly? Are you not acting like mere humans?

1 Corinthians 3:1-3 NIV

"I'm just human," is not an excuse to live a defeated, sinful life. You are *in Christ!* In the third scene of *The Beautiful Dream*, Jesus took me to the heavenly realms. The Holy Spirit asked me to *be seated*, but I didn't hear Him. I was daydreaming about Jesus and doing my own thing. This is a picture of someone who loves Jesus but is not functioning in the power and blessing of God by yielding to Holy Spirit. The person is *in* Christ, but not even looking *at* Christ. This is not good! The only way to mature *in Christ* is to sit down and really *engage with God.* Only the Holy Spirit can show you if there is anything like *jealousy* still lingering in your heart and only His power can remove it!

As surely as God is faithful, our word to you does not waver between "Yes" and "No." For Jesus Christ, the Son of God, does not waver between "Yes" and "No." He is the one whom Silas, Timothy, and I preached to you, and as God's ultimate "Yes," he always does what he says. For all of God's promises have been fulfilled in Christ with a resounding "Yes!" And through Christ, our "Amen" (which means "Yes") ascends to God for his glory. It is God who enables us, along with you, to stand firm for Christ. He has commissioned us, and he has identified us as his own by placing the Holy Spirit in our hearts as the first installment that guarantees everything he has promised us.

2 Corinthians 1:18-22 NLT

In *The Beautiful Dream*, Jesus touched me and *every* promise of God for me was instantly fulfilled! Living in the earth and being flooded with sounds of the world's wisdom can cloud our minds so we have trouble seeing by the Spirit that we are *in*

Christ Jesus. That is one reason the Holy Spirit said to *be seated* up there and not down here!

Sometimes Christians say *in so many words,* "Well, God doesn't always keep His promises." That's not true! *God is faithful,* and His promises are *already fulfilled* for us in Christ. But so often, Christians do not see themselves *in Christ* and they live from the earthly realm. *In Christ,* we can *yield to His righteousness* and experience the fullness of our inheritance.

It's not that we've lost God if we don't experience *all* His promises right away. The Lord is very aware that we are *growing up in Christ.* A good father doesn't shame his toddler for chasing a ball toward a busy street. The father warns him of the dangers and continues teaching his son as he grows up. His expectations increase as the son gets older, but he never discards him or stops loving him when he doesn't understand. The father keeps teaching his son until the son starts thinking and acting like Him. The relationship and the Love between them grows as the years go by.

One day the boy will inherit financial blessings from his father. But the biggest blessings of all were the time spent, the good memories, the adventures, the wisdom, the encouragement and the Love. Those blessings are priceless. In the same way, our Father delights in every stage of our faith. Abba will never die. Our inheritance has already been reserved for us *in Christ Jesus* and it will never run out. We can draw from God's riches of grace every day! As the Spirit is developing our character and faith *in Christ* on earth, we are safe, and His promises do belong to us!

Therefore, there is now no condemnation for those who are in Christ Jesus, because through Christ Jesus the law of the Spirit who gives life has set you free from the law of sin and death.
Romans 8:1-2 NIV

If you have *repented* and are *following Jesus,* you are *in Christ!* God promises that He sees you pure in Christ! Don't let the devil condemn you. Satan will accuse you even after you have been made right with God! The Father knows that the devil is going to try to wreak havoc in your life. He promises to be with you in trouble, help you and deliver you. God is so very pleased you belong to Him!

...nor height, nor depth, nor any other created thing, will be able to separate us from the [unlimited] love of God, which is in Christ Jesus our Lord.

Romans 8:39 AMP

Jesus didn't die so you would live life *wondering* if His Blood applies to you. He died on the cross for the sin of the whole world! *Be seated* and *rest in Christ's Love and grace!*

This righteousness is given through faith in Jesus Christ to all who believe. There is no difference between Jew and Gentile, for all have sinned and fall short of the glory of God, and all are justified freely by his grace through the redemption that came by Christ Jesus.

Romans 3:22-24 NIV

Some believers have matured *in Christ* more than others, but we are all Loved perfectly as a part of the Family. No matter how immature you may feel spiritually, when you follow Jesus, you have been made *worthy*. In Christ, you are amazing to God. He is so pleased with you simply because you said *yes* to Jesus and are not ashamed of Him. You Love Him and follow His lead. God isn't trying to decide if He Loves you. He Loves you because you belong to Him! Well, He loved you even before you said *yes* to Jesus. But now you are Home and the Father's heart is full! He has wonderful plans for you — to pour out His kindness, favor and blessing on you and through you.

Because you are in Christ, God has given *you* a special way of blessing the Family that no other person has. Perhaps you can see the Body of Christ like a jigsaw puzzle. Each piece is just as important as the others though each piece is different. Together we create a beautiful picture that displays God's glory. Don't wish you were a different piece and please don't hide under the Table! We all need you and what you have to offer *in Christ*. We are only complete *with you!*

...so in Christ we, though many, form one body, and each member belongs to all the others.

Romans 12:5 NIV

Outside of Jesus we were hopeless, but *in Him* we bring great glory to the cross! Look what the Lord has done!

And my God shall supply all your need according to His riches in glory by Christ Jesus.

Philippians 4:19 NKJV

When Jesus rose from the dead and ascended into Heaven, He sat down at the Father's right hand. When we died to our old life, Jesus raised us up to the heavenly realms to be seated with God in the Spirit. We could not go there except that we are trusting in *His* Love and grace. Abba is pleased with Jesus, and therefore He is pleased with us!

If you ever become anxious or afraid, close your eyes and remind yourself that *you are hidden in Christ*. You are safe! Holy Spirit is in you and will supply you with spiritual counsel, physical strength, health, mental stability, financial wisdom and every supernatural gift available *in Christ*.

But your first priority *in Christ* is to receive and give His Love through the power of His Spirit. The promises of God are always "yes" and "amen," and they are ours *in Christ Jesus!* Let's be seated as a Loving Family and grow up together *in Christ!*

Declaration

I AM SAFE AND BLESSED IN CHRIST!

38

Dance with the Judge

The Lord is Judge. We step into darkness when we try to *judge others*. That's the Lord's business. God will judge every person at the end of time.

As for me, it matters very little how I might be evaluated by you or by any human authority. I don't even trust my own judgment on this point. My conscience is clear, but that doesn't prove I'm right. It is the Lord himself who will examine me and decide. So don't make judgments about anyone ahead of time— before the Lord returns. For he will bring our darkest secrets to light and will reveal our private motives. Then God will give to each one whatever praise is due.
1 Corinthians 4:3-5 NLT

Paul was one of the most Loving human beings *after He met the Lord!* He was analyzed, judged, *and* idolized to a fault by fellow Christians. But Paul knew that if he took his critics and fans to heart, he would cross over from trusting the Lord to fearing man. He kept his conscience clear by *staying close to Jesus,* yet he didn't claim to have reached personal perfection. Jesus helped Paul not worry about what others thought of him and that's amazing!

Fear of man will prove to be a snare, but whoever trusts in the LORD is kept safe.
Proverbs 29:25 NIV

Fearing people is a trap. We don't fear because we are filled

219

with God's Love. We Love. Our *faith in God's grace* sets us free from fearing what other people think or may say about us. What our Father thinks about us is all that matters!

When hard pressed, I cried to the LORD; he brought me into a spacious place. The LORD is with me; I will not be afraid. What can mere mortals do to me? The LORD is with me; he is my helper. I look in triumph on my enemies. It is better to take refuge in the LORD than to trust in humans.

Psalm 118:5-8 NIV

When you start worrying about what people are saying or thinking about you, you open the door to fear. You know who you are in Christ. Your worth and value are not in question. Besides, *wondering what others think about you* is the first step toward judging their hearts. That kind of dark imagination is not from God and it will harm you.

There may be times that the Spirit will ask you to *correct* a Christian because of a sin. Only do it because the Spirit of grace asked you to, and because you care about them. Remind them that their sinful behavior is not who they are in Christ. Don't look for faults in others so you can accuse them. If it is a serious sin against you and they reject your Godly counsel, Jesus taught us what to do next.

"If your brother or sister sins, go and point out their fault, just between the two of you. If they listen to you, you have won them over. But if they will not listen, take one or two others along, so that 'every matter may be established by the testimony of two or three witnesses.' If they still refuse to listen, tell it to the church; and if they refuse to listen even to the church, treat them as you would a pagan or a tax collector [Tax collectors in that day cheated people]."

Matthew 18:15-17 NIV

Do not use this scripture as your chance to *humiliate* a Brother over a *trivial matter*. And by "tell it to the church" I suggest you tell a pastor privately rather than *shaming* the person in public. I believe "Treat them as you would a pagan" means recognize that they are walking in darkness. Pray for them to find their way back to the Father's Love.

... love is not happy with evil, but is happy with the truth.
1 Corinthians 13:6 GNT

The world's love embraces the sin of others, but God's Love wants them to be safe in the righteousness of Jesus Christ. You can pray for them, but unless the Spirit very *clearly* leads you to minister to them, *release them to God.*

Since you judge others for doing these things [blatant sin], why do you think you can avoid God's judgment when you do the same things? Don't you see how wonderfully kind, tolerant, and patient God is with you? Does this mean nothing to you? Can't you see that his kindness is intended to turn you from your sin? But because you are stubborn and refuse to turn from your sin, you are storing up terrible punishment for yourself.

For a day of anger is coming, when God's righteous judgment will be revealed. He will judge everyone according to what they have done. He will give eternal life to those who keep on doing good, seeking after the glory and honor and immortality that God offers. But he will pour out his anger and wrath on those who live for themselves, who refuse to obey the truth and instead live lives of wickedness.
Romans 2:3-8 NLT

Avoid correcting and rebuking others unless the Spirit specifically leads you to. Jesus warned us not to try to take a *speck* out of someone's eye when we have a *log* in our own. If we live from the earthly realm, we tend to point out the faults of others because our light has grown dim. The eyes of our hearts can't see clearly when we're not seated in the light.

"Don't judge" doesn't mean we abandon legal systems and allow evil to reign on earth. According to the Word, it is God's will that governments enforce *Biblically based moral laws* to keep the peace and protect the innocent. I *appreciate, respect* and *applaud* those whose job it is to do so! If everyone lived by the Spirit of God there would be no need for laws, courts, police, jails and military. But they don't.

If every believer lived perfectly by the Spirit, there would be no need for church leaders to correct or rebuke anyone. *But we're all still growing!* The Word encourages pastors to set very basic moral guidelines for church leaders. It is important for pastors to be *led by the Spirit* when making these decisions to avoid becoming legalistic. The goal for ministers is to bring people to Jesus and then teach them to *follow the correction of the Spirit* so that they don't live by a list of rules for the rest of their lives. Knowing the Judge intimately will set an atmosphere of grace so that when correction is needed, it is an act of Agape Love.

Don't use foul or abusive language. Let everything you say be good and helpful, so that your words will be an encouragement to those who hear them. And do not bring sorrow to God's Holy Spirit by the way you live. Remember, he has identified you as his own, guaranteeing that you will be saved on the day of redemption. Get rid of all bitterness, rage, anger, harsh words, and slander, as well as all types of evil behavior. Instead, be kind to each other, tenderhearted, forgiving one another, just as God through Christ has forgiven you.
Ephesians 4:29-32 NLT

Living from the earthly realm will make you offended, distrusting and cynical—unable to receive Love from others. You are still *afraid* someone might *shame* you. But if you live from the Table in the heavenly realms, nobody can take God's perfect Love away from you! Even if they throw dirt at you, the *Living Water* is always cleansing you!

For if you forgive other people when they sin against you, your heavenly Father will also forgive you. But if you do not forgive others their sins, your Father will not forgive your sins.
Matthew 6:14-15 NIV

Satan is called *the accuser of the Brothers*. We can't let him do his dirty work through us. *In Christ*, we are forgivers and Agape Lovers! We are called to build one another up.

Do not judge, and you will not be judged. Do not condemn, and you will not be condemned. Forgive, and you will be forgiven. Give, and it will be given to you. A good measure, pressed down, shaken together and running over, will be poured into your lap. For with the measure you use, it will be measured to you.

Luke 6:37-38 NIV

If you see a Brother or Sister facing a trial and you *assume* that they must have done something wrong to deserve it, that is a law-driven mindset, a judgmental spirit, not the Agape Spirit. How you treat other people is the way the Judge will treat you on Judgment Day. Follow the Spirit of grace by treating people with Love, respect, generosity, mercy and forgiveness, and God will do the same for you when you get to His Court Room at the end of time.

Beloved, do not believe every spirit, but test the spirits, whether they are of God; because many false prophets have gone out into the world. By this you know the Spirit of God: Every spirit that confesses that Jesus Christ has come in the flesh is of God, and every spirit that does not confess that Jesus Christ has come in the flesh is not of God. And this is the spirit of the Antichrist, which you have heard was coming, and is now already in the world.

1 John 4:1-3 NKJV

Testing a spirit is different from *judging* a person. Holy Spirit will tell you if someone is a false prophet so you won't follow their teaching. If you are seated with God at His Table in the heavenly realms it means you know the Lord and His Word. You have grown in the ways of the Spirit, and you will be able to *discern* whether they preach the true Gospel. But if you are dancing your own dance through life, not seated with God, you will be vulnerable to what everybody around you is saying.

Arguing, accusing, belittling and judging the intentions of the hearts of others does not happen at the Judges Table because *strife is earthly and demonic.* It creates evil chaos in lives, homes, churches, communities and nations.

In *The Beautiful Dream,* Jesus took all my guilt away and filled me with God's Love! It is not our own ability to stay strong and live right that keeps us seated in confidence at the Judge's Table. Our good works don't undo the sin we have committed. Saying *yes* to the Judge's Son and knowing Him intimately places us in good graces with the Judge! Jesus is the one who paid the ultimate price to bring us to Abba for adoption! Our Father, the Judge, has reviewed our case, cleared us of all wrongdoing, checked the adoption papers, signed them, and welcomed us with joy into His arms! There is no safer place to be seated than next to the Judge's heart!

You are a child of the Judge of Heaven who has *generously removed your penalty* and has poured out blessings beyond measure! Don't take the gavel out of the Judges hand! Trust Holy Spirit to take care of your issues on earth and enjoy dancing with your King, *free of judgment and condemnation.* Be seated at *His Loving Table.* Leave the judging to God and enjoy the wonderful life He has given you!

See Notes: #9 Forgiveness Questions & Answers

Declaration

I'M SEATED WITH THE JUDGE!

39

Be Seated and Rest in Grace

This world tells us we have to *work* for the approval, position, love, acceptance of others and that we have to *pay for our mistakes*. But in the Kingdom of God, it is not our work, but *faith* in God's *grace* (kindness, favor and blessing) through Jesus that makes us accepted by God.

For a believer, *fear of accusation, punishment and shame* are some of the most crippling and exhausting lies from the enemy. In scene two of *The Beautiful Dream* I was *seated* on concrete bleachers talking with my husband about the grace of Jesus. We were full of joy! God wants us to *be seated* and *rest* in grace!

Come to me, all you who are weary and burdened, and I will give you rest. Take my yoke upon you and learn from me, for I am gentle and humble in heart, and you will find rest for your souls. For my yoke is easy and my burden is light.
Matthew 11:28-30 NIV

Working hard to measure up to the expectations of others is like being tethered to a bull. It's impossible! It will leave your *soul* broken and carrying a heavy load. When we *stop stressing and trust in God's grace*, then our soul will find rest. But in order to find this rest, we must be *yoked*, or *tied*, to Jesus, *allowing Him to do the impossible for us*. It's like dancing with Jesus!

The path Jesus leads us on is narrow. It's not the "easy" path that everyone seems to be taking where you can do whatever you want to. You are *yoked* and you *follow* Jesus, not the world.

And the *supernatural power of His grace* will lighten your heart giving you mental, spiritual and physical well-being! Paul knew what it was like to be yoked to Jesus. He depended on God's power!

So when I came to you, I was weak and trembled all over with fear, and my teaching and message were not delivered with skillful words of human wisdom, but with convincing proof of the power of God's Spirit. Your faith, then, does not rest on human wisdom but on God's power.

1 Corinthians 2:3-5 GNT

That power will come on us when we *set our hearts at rest* in God's grace, *following the Spirit.* When we *work hard* to figure everything out through *our own reasoning and efforts,* we bypass the Spirit and cannot *rest* in His grace.

As Jesus and his disciples were on their way, he came to a village where a woman named Martha opened her home to him. She had a sister named Mary, who sat at the Lord's feet listening to what he said.

But Martha was distracted by all the preparations that had to be made. She came to him and asked, "Lord, don't you care that my sister has left me to do the work by myself? Tell her to help me!" "Martha, Martha," the Lord answered, "you are worried and upset about many things, but few things are needed — or indeed only one. Mary has chosen what is better, and it will not be taken away from her."

Luke 10: 38-42 NIV

Martha invited Jesus into her house but then *she left His presence to work* in the kitchen. She was stressed, bossy, angry and resentful. Mary, however, sat at Jesus' feet to learn from Him. Her *heart* was in the right place.

We have Jesus in our house too — in our hearts. Will we be drawn away from His presence by earthly things? Many of God's children are doing things out of pride, obligation or fear.

The Father certainly has things for us to do. But first, He wants us to sit at Jesus' feet, *rest in His grace*, listen to His voice, worship Him and soak up His Words. When we are saturated with God's Love and grace, *then* we're ready to do His work! A person whose heart is *at rest in the grace of Jesus* will not criticize, shame and demand things to be done their way like Martha. They would rather heat up some good leftovers than to serve condemnation to others!

This is how we know that we belong to the truth and how we set our hearts at rest in his presence: If our hearts condemn us, we know that God is greater than our hearts, and he knows everything. Dear friends, if our hearts do not condemn us, we have confidence before God and receive from him anything we ask, because we keep his commands and do what pleases him.

And this is his command: to believe in the name of his Son, Jesus Christ, and to love one another as he commanded us. The one who keeps God's commands lives in him, and he in them. And this is how we know that he lives in us: We know it by the Spirit he gave us.

1 John 3:19-24 NIV

Resting in God is not a lack of productivity. The Holy Spirit will cause us to *bear much fruit* when we are *resting* in Him. The Spirit can do more through us in one minute than we can do for Him in a lifetime by our own strength. Actually, that's not true. We can do *nothing of eternal value* without His power flowing through us!

Shift your heart from wearing yourself out to impress God, to *resting in His grace* and presence. You can even *rest in His grace* as you are working, playing, cooking or whatever you do. But nothing is as sweet as sitting with God at His Table and allowing your spirit to commune with His. He will melt your stress and worries away.

Let's look at the Exodus story again. God worked so many *huge miracles* to get them out of Egypt, across the sea and into the desert.   The Lord miraculously provided everything they needed yet many of them *grumbled* and *complained*, over and over again! Their lack of faith in God's Loving grace kept that generation from entering into their *resting place*.   So they wandered around in the desert for another 40 years *until the next generation grew up*. Joshua *trusted God*, led them in and they took the Promised Land!

So, as the Holy Spirit says: "Today, if you hear his voice, do not harden your hearts as you did in the rebellion, during the time of testing in the wilderness, where your ancestors tested and tried me, though for forty years they saw what I did. That is why I was angry with that generation; I said, 'Their hearts are always going astray, and they have not known my ways.' So I declared on oath in my anger, 'They shall never enter my rest.'"

Hebrews 3:7-11 NIV

The Israelites were completely free from Egyptian slavery, but they behaved as if they were not! They refused to have faith in God for the next part of their journey. They were *so addicted to hard labor* that they ignored the obvious: The God who brought them out of Egypt and provided for them in the wilderness *Loved them!* If they had learned to trust God's favor they would have inherited the Promised Land.   But they were rebellious complainers, *proud* of their hard work. Their faith didn't *rest in God's grace* for their future, but in what they had learned from the culture of their past.   They trusted in the earthly realm instead of resting their faith in God's kindness, favor and blessing.

So there is a special rest still waiting for the people of God. For all who have entered into God's rest have rested from their labors, just as God did after creating the world. So let us do our best to enter that rest. But if we disobey God, as the people of Israel did, we will fall.

Hebrews 4:9-11 NLT

Resting in grace doesn't mean being lazy. Working to support your family is a noble and good thing! Working is a Godly trait when you are motivated by Agape Love!

... and to make it your ambition to lead a quiet life and attend to your own business and work with your hands, just as we instructed you, so that you will behave properly toward outsiders and not be in any need.

1 Thessalonians 4:11-12 NASB

Having a good work ethic is a healthy and Godly way to live — even if your work is staying home to raise your children or to care for an elderly parent. If you want to work a job and are unable to for some reason, God wants you to *rest in His grace.* He understands what you are going through and is proud of you for trusting in His unfailing Love!

But stressing over your work because *you have to have the approval and praise of someone else* could be a sign that you still don't know who you are in Christ. Trying to *earn God's Love and approval* does not please God. You already have His Love and approval! Isn't that wonderful!? You can rest assured that God is very proud that you are His son or daughter. The Lord knows who you are better than you know your own self, and He thinks you are way more amazing than you think you are!

It's okay for people to say nice things about you and honor you. The Word of God teaches us to do that for one another. But to *feel worthless* if you didn't get "Teacher Of The Month" or "Top Sales," etc., is a lie from the devil! *You are so valuable* that God's Son left beautiful Heaven to come to earth and die for your sins! Your performance doesn't cause you to be valuable. You are valuable because you are God's child. Rest your faith on Abba's heart. He approves of you and is cheering you on!

Live on earth and do the work God has for you to do, but as you do, *be seated restfully at the Table of Grace.* Trust the chair God has given you. His grace will not let you down.

Like Joshua, place all your faith in God's kindness and walk confidently toward the promises of God! You will encounter opposition, but *God's grace* will cover you as you take the territory He has assigned to you. You are such a blessing in the Kingdom of God! You may not believe in your worth like God does, but as you get to know Him, He will reveal how amazing He made you to be.

In *The Beautiful Dream*, God and my Brothers and Sisters stood up for me. They gave me another chance to be seated because they knew what it meant to *rest* in God's grace. They Loved me and wanted me to experience it as well. They were following the Holy Spirit's lead. That's not what would have happened on earth! We have become so accustomed to the finger pointing, the sarcastic belittlement and the shame that we expect it to happen, even when it doesn't. We're on edge. *Fear* and *shame* don't belong in us anymore. In the heavenly realms, we live in the atmosphere of grace. When that truth becomes a reality to you, people on this earth can accuse and put you down, but your heart will be free. You know where you are seated and you wouldn't trade that seat for the world!

Choose what is *better* and be seated at the feet of Jesus. Yoke up to Jesus and let your soul *rest in His power.* When your motivation in life is Agape Love and grace, you will not be overwhelmed!

Truly my soul finds rest in God; my salvation comes from him. Truly he is my rock and my salvation; he is my fortress, I will never be shaken.

Psalm 62:1-2 NIV

Declaration

~ I AM SEATED ~ RESTING IN GOD'S GRACE ~

40

Dance Through Your Trials

Consider it all joy, my brothers and sisters, when you encounter various trials, knowing that the testing of your faith produces endurance. And let endurance have its perfect result, so that you may be perfect and complete, lacking in nothing.

James 1:2-4 NASB

Our natural response to trials is to think that we did something wrong to deserve it, but that's not always true. Sometimes we do experience trials because of our own sin and we can receive forgiveness. The Lord will help us face the consequences and offer His miraculous help through the trial. But other times *it seems* that we have been doing everything right and the trial of our lives comes anyway. Whatever the case may be, the Lord wants us to trust His Loving-kindness. He will help us through *every trial* and make us *stronger* than we were before. God *will* allow us to go through trials to build our faith, but He *won't* let us be tempted beyond our ability to resist sin.

The temptations in your life are no different from what others experience. And God is faithful. He will not allow the temptation to be more than you can stand. When you are tempted, he will show you a way out so that you can endure.

1 Corinthians 10:13 NLT

Holy Spirit will deliver you from addictions and sin, and He will give you self-control to resist temptation.

In all this you greatly rejoice, though now for a little while you

231

may have had to suffer grief in all kinds of trials. These have come so that the proven genuineness of your faith—of greater worth than gold, which perishes even though refined by fire—may result in praise, glory and honor when Jesus Christ is revealed.

1 Peter 1:6-7 NIV

When gold is refined, it is heated up until it becomes liquid. The impurities rise to the top so they can be skimmed off until only pure gold remains. Trials *heat up* the impurities that are still lingering deep down in our hearts and minds so we can give them over to God. Difficult circumstances may expose character traits in us that don't look like Jesus. View those difficult times as opportunities to grow in God's Love. Without trials we really don't know where our faith rests.

Job did not give up seeking God in his greatest testing of faith. Job's trial ended in huge blessings from God!

There was a man in the land of Uz whose name was Job; and that man was blameless, upright, fearing God and turning away from evil.

Job 1:1 NASB

Job loved his family and was blessed with land and possessions. Job's children were ungodly, so Job went to God regularly, sacrificing burnt offerings on behalf of each of them. Even though Job was a very good man, loved God and was well respected, he was attacked by Satan.

Job's farm was raided. The farmhands were killed and all the cattle stolen. The sheep and shepherds died in a fire. Job's children were having one of their wild parties when something like a tornado came through, destroying the house and killing them.

Job stood up and tore his robe in grief. Then he shaved his head and fell to the ground to worship. He said, "I came naked from my mother's womb, and I will be naked when I leave. The LORD gave me what I had, and the LORD has taken it away. Praise the name of the LORD!" In all of this, Job did not sin by blaming God.

Job 1:20-22 NLT

Wow! Job knew that God was good and didn't blame Him for what had happened.   Satan was furious and got God's permission to attack Job *again*, this time with painful boils all over his body. As if that wasn't enough, Job's wife began to criticize him for his faithfulness to God.

Then Job took a piece of broken pottery and scraped himself with it as he sat among the ashes. His wife said to him, "Are you still maintaining your integrity? Curse God and die!"

Job 2:8-9 NIV

Job's friends showed up and just sat with him in silence for seven days. Job's pain was so bad that he *cursed* the day he was born and said that *what he feared* had become a reality. Then everything got even worse. One by one, three of his friends *analyzed* Job's situation, *accusing* him of sinning. They *judged* Job's integrity with long religious speeches. Job must have felt like an abused dog backed into a corner with no way to escape. His friends seemed entertained by the lengthy conversations as if Job's life was a riddle to be solved.

Job finally felt like he had to defend himself. He talked about the goodness of God on his life and all of the blessings he had enjoyed. Then Job began to talk about all that had gone wrong. As he did, he became angry with God and wished he could *take God to court and argue his case.* A fourth *good friend* spoke up reminding Job of God's greatness and goodness. He advised Job not to accuse God, but instead, to ask Him for wisdom.

God met with Job to speak with him in person. In a way, God answered Job's request and *took him to court.*

Then the LORD spoke to Job out of the storm. He said: "Who is this that obscures my plans with words without knowledge?

233

Brace yourself like a man; I will question you, and you shall answer me.

Job 38:1-3 NIV

God began to ask Job all about creation—question after question. Job could not even begin to answer Him. Job was *in awe* of God! But the Lord continued…

Then the LORD said to Job, "Do you still want to argue with the Almighty? You are God's critic, but do you have the answers?" Then Job replied to the LORD. "I am nothing—how could I ever find the answers? I will cover my mouth with my hand. I have said too much already. I have nothing more to say."

Job 40:1-5 NLT

God continues speaking, asking Job questions he cannot answer. I believe God's presence filled Job with infinite Love but terrified him with His pure holiness and majesty. Job responds in complete humility and submission.

I had only heard about you before, but now I have seen you with my own eyes. I take back everything I said, and I sit in dust and ashes to show my repentance.

Job 42:5-6 NLT

Job had spent many hours *debating* with his friends by *using human reasoning*. He became more and more confused and angry with God, believing he *deserved* God's favor because of *his own good works*. God wanted to save Job from *religious pride* that was hidden deep in his soul. Job had not *known God intimately*, but when he finally spoke directly with Jesus, he experienced Agape Love! God wants *relationship!* If we are *seated with God in His Court*, trials can bring us into a wonderful intimate relationship with Him.

The Lord rebuked Job's friends for their behavior and Job was asked to pray for them. After Job humbled himself to believe in God's grace he was healed! God *multiplied* Job's possessions and gave him seven sons and three gorgeous daughters. Job may not have done everything right during the *trial* of his life, but he wanted to *talk with God*. When he finally did, that powerful encounter with Jesus ended Job's terrible trial and opened up the door to blessings in his life.

I hope your trials are *never* as severe as Job's were. Everyone will experience trials but we don't have to fail. In fact, because Holy Spirit lives inside us, *we have everything we need* to endure and make it safely through!

By his divine power, God has given us everything we need for living a godly life. We have received all of this by coming to know him, the one who called us to himself by means of his marvelous glory and excellence. And because of his glory and excellence, he has given us great and precious promises. These are the promises that enable you to share his divine nature and escape the world's corruption caused by human desires.

In view of all this, make every effort to respond to God's promises. Supplement your faith with a generous provision of moral excellence, and moral excellence with knowledge, and knowledge with self-control, and self-control with patient endurance, and patient endurance with godliness, and godliness with brotherly affection, and brotherly affection with love for everyone. The more you grow like this, the more productive and useful you will be in your knowledge of our Lord Jesus Christ.

But those who fail to develop in this way are shortsighted or blind, forgetting that they have been cleansed from their old sins. So, dear brothers and sisters, work hard to prove that you really are among those God has called and chosen. Do these things, and you will never fall away. Then God will give you a grand entrance into the eternal Kingdom of our Lord and Savior Jesus Christ.

2 Peter 1:3-11 NLT

The Beautiful Dream was God's incredible blessing for me in the trial of my life! It was filled with His Love and grace to keep me pursuing Jesus. Every encounter with Him is lifting me up!

The end result of our trials is drawing closer in to God's heart—His Agape Love! Jesus said that if we bear fruit, the Father *prunes us back so we can yield even more fruit.* Pruning involves trimming away the old and that can be very uncomfortable! But then we will be ready to walk into God's next assignment that can bring a greater yield for God's Kingdom! So stay seated in the fire and you will come through your trials shining like pure gold!

Happy is the one who endures testing, because when he has proven to be genuine, he will receive the crown of life that God promised to those who love him.

James 1:12 NET

Declaration

**I CHOOSE TO LET THESE TRIALS
DRIVE ME CLOSER IN TO GOD'S LOVE!**

41

TABLE TALK: *Little Girl Dream*

One night I asked God why certain spiritual obstacles were so stubborn in my life. That night I had a simple dream:

It was dark so I couldn't see anything well, but I was standing, looking downward at the top of a little girl's head. I heard others talking to my right, but I could not understand what they were saying. The little girl spoke with a baby-like voice, indicating she was extremely young — probably 2 or 3 years old. With a sorrowful and despairing tone, she said slowly and convincingly in her quiet and high-pitched little voice, "Nobody loves me." I woke up immediately with *the sadness of her words* ringing in my soul.

I knew the little girl in the dream was *me*. My family or others were to my *right*, most likely meaning that they were "in the right," not intentionally trying to hurt me by their words or actions. But my little heart believed that I was not loved by anyone so early in life that I don't remember saying this.

The little girl represented *my soul* and a deceptive belief hidden deep inside my heart. The Lord showed me that this *lie from the devil* affected my identity and my view of others. I didn't realize it was there, so I didn't know I needed to get rid of it! This was the enemy's way of stealing much of the goodness that the Lord had for my life.

I share this with you because I believe *many* Christians carry this same belief and don't realize it. But if you recognize it and take it to the Lord, He can remove the lie and bring healing, restoration and Love to your heart. *In Christ* you are Loved, Loveable and able to genuinely Love!

The dream about the little girl was an encounter in the Spirit. In that sense, I was seated with God in the heavenly realms listening, even though I was asleep. His motive behind every dream He gives us is Agape Love, even if it doesn't look that way on the surface. Dreams invite us to *intimate conversations with Jesus,* and amazing things always happen seated with Him at His Table!

Some of the famous dreamers of the Bible are: Jacob, Joseph, Solomon, Daniel, Jesus' adoptive father, Joseph, and the "wise men from the east" who brought gifts to Jesus when He was born.

God speaks to His children in dreams and we would be wise to *pay attention.* Through dreams, Holy Spirit counsels and directs us. He gives us prophetic dreams to prepare us for the future, show us how to pray and help us make important decisions. He also gives us dreams to encourage the Body of Christ.

The Lord may want to speak to you through your dreams. Get your pen and notebook ready. Find a *good, rock-solid Christian resource* to help you understand the basics of dream interpretation, but rely on the Holy Spirit above all. Always use *the Word of God* as your compass. Pray and ask God to speak to you through dreams — and dream away! Your *Table Talk with God* will be elevated to another level!

42

Dancing with the Healer

Then Moses led Israel from the Red Sea and they went into the Desert of Shur. For three days they traveled in the desert without finding water. When they came to Marah, they could not drink its water because it was bitter. (That is why the place is called Marah.) So the people grumbled against Moses, saying, "What are we to drink?"

Then Moses cried out to the LORD, and the LORD showed him a piece of wood. He threw it into the water, and the water became fit to drink. There the LORD issued a ruling and instruction for them and put them to the test. He said, "If you listen carefully to the LORD your God and do what is right in his eyes, if you pay attention to his commands and keep all his decrees, I will not bring on you any of the diseases I brought on the Egyptians, for I am the LORD, who heals you."

Exodus 15:22-26 NIV

It is no coincidence that the Lord told Moses to *throw a piece of wood* into the water. The wood represents the cross! The Savior of the cross *changes* our source of water from the earthly realm to Living Water in the heavenly realm. Jesus is the Healer! What God told Moses after the water was purified sounds very familiar to me. Some of the key phrases are also in *The Beautiful Dream*. The Lord basically told God's people to *pay attention* to Him, *follow His lead* and He would be their Healer.

Listening and obeying the Lord is not a self-righteous mindset. It's a Love mindset! We experience His Love and grace for

239

ourselves and we grow to know Him intimately. We want to stay close! Even though He is God, Creator, King and Lord and Judge — His Love for us is so extravagant! Why would we not want to follow His lead?

... and He Himself brought our sins in His body up on the cross, so that we might die to sin and live for righteousness; by His wounds you were healed.

1 Peter 2:24 NASB

The children of Israel saw the bitter waters made sweet by the grace of God and a piece of wood. It is the cross of Jesus that brings us *out of bitterness into God's Love*. Jesus can turn your bitter waters into an oasis of healing!

To have a fool for a child brings grief; there is no joy for the parent of a godless fool. A cheerful heart is good medicine, but a crushed spirit dries up the bones.

Proverbs 17:21-22 NIV

How does our Loving Father feel when He offers help but we only *complain* and try to solve our own problems? What joy it must bring Him when we place all our hope in Jesus!

My son, pay attention to what I say; turn your ear to my words. Do not let them out of your sight, keep them within your heart; for they are life to those who find them and health to one's whole body.

Proverbs 4:20-22 NIV

Paying close attention to God's Word and God's Love brings *life* to our whole being. You can pray for an *unbeliever* who doesn't know scripture and they can be healed. But some of us adopted beliefs that limit our faith for healing. What we *say* gives us clues about *what we truly believe* in our hearts.

If you *constantly* explain why you will just have to live with illness, that's what you believe. But if you want to *believe in the impossible*, God's Word can build your faith. Our faith is in God who Loves us, and He is our Healer!

Jesus answered and said to them, "Those who are well have no need of a physician, but those who are sick."
Luke 5:31 NKJV

Jesus used an *earthly* example to tell a *spiritual truth*. He was also letting us know that God's grace has blessed us with medical professionals. They and others save many lives in the natural realm every day. Always obey the Spirit if He tells you to seek medical help. But there is even more for us from God. Luke, the Gospel writer, was a physician but he only boasted about *Jesus healing the sick supernaturally,* not about his own work. Luke knew Jesus was The Healer and he was amazed!

For bodily exercise profits a little, but godliness is profitable for all things, having promise of the life that now is and of that which is to come.
1 Timothy 4:8 NKJV

God certainly wants us to take care of our bodies in the natural realm *with the Spirit's guidance.* Not everybody can be helped by human effort, but when we are, it is also a gift from God. But where there is good in the earthly realm there is the danger of making it your god. Strongholds of fear and illness can develop when our faith is rooted in the earthly realm. That is why we must wake up and be seated with God in the heavenly realms. We do that by *paying attention* to the Holy Spirit and the Word as we rest in His Love and grace. *The Beautiful Dream* and *scripture* show us that our healing comes from Jesus.

He heals the brokenhearted and binds up their wounds.
Psalm 147:3 NASB

When a believer has lost heart over illness, guard against *lecturing* them about their faith. There is a time to teach and a time to refrain from teaching. Jesus gathers our tears in His bottle, so *be compassionate in the Holy Spirit.* Listen and encourage them with your concern and Love. And certainly offer to lay hands on them and pray for their healing.

Jesus was going about in all of Galilee, teaching in their synagogues and proclaiming the gospel of the kingdom, and healing every disease and every sickness among the people. And the news about Him spread throughout Syria; and they brought to Him all who were ill, those suffering with various diseases and severe pain, demon-possessed, people with epilepsy, and people who were paralyzed; and He healed them.
Matthew 4:23-24 NASB

Jesus shows us that *divine healing* is part of the Good News of His Kingdom! But not everyone is receptive to that message. One time Jesus went to His hometown and the people there rejected His ministry. Because of their *unbelief* He only healed a few who had faith and then He left town. Jesus told His disciples that when this happened to them they were to leave the town they were in and find another town with faith. The soil there is just not ready for planting.

Let all that I am praise the LORD; with my whole heart, I will praise his holy name. Let all that I am praise the LORD; may I never forget the good things he does for me. He forgives all my sins and heals all my diseases. He redeems me from death and crowns me with love and tender mercies.
Psalm 103:1-4 NLT

In *The Beautiful Dream,* Jesus took *all disease* out and put His Agape Love Spirit in. I was whole—*body, soul and spirit!* All three scenes of the dream took place *in this life,* so God was not referring to me dying and going to Heaven. Jesus purchased our healing and it was His joy to suffer so we wouldn't have to. He told us that we would suffer persecution for sharing the Gospel, but *He never told us to accept disease as God's will.* Because of *The Beautiful Dream,* I believe a deep revelation of God's Love is the first step to being able to receive healing grace—or any of the incomparable gifts of grace!

I certainly don't look down on anyone who is suffering with

pain or illness. The Lord has been taking me through a process of healing for many years. I have compassion for anyone who is sick. And although I have received a steady increase in healing from God, I personally will not settle for "almost whole" and I hope you won't either. Sometimes healing is instant. Other times it is gradual, released in our intimate journey with the Healer. I have had healing come to me both ways!

Jesus summoned His twelve disciples and gave them authority over unclean spirits, to cast them out, and to heal every disease and every sickness.... And as you go, preach, saying, 'The kingdom of heaven has come near.' Heal the sick, raise the dead, cleanse those with leprosy, cast out demons. Freely you received, freely give.

Matthew 10:1, 7-8 NASB

We have received God's Spirit of grace and *Jesus gave us authority* to give grace away to others! Sometimes healing comes by asking God for it. We can also *command* pain and disease to leave because we are *speaking* in Jesus' name.

On a Sabbath Jesus was teaching in one of the synagogues, and a woman was there who had been crippled by a spirit for eighteen years. She was bent over and could not straighten up at all. When Jesus saw her, he called her forward and said to her, "Woman, you are set free from your infirmity." When he put his hands on her, and immediately she straightened up and praised God.

Luke 13:10-13 NIV

Jesus *said* the woman was healed even *before* she was healed! I believe that is what Jesus is saying in *The Beautiful Dream*. In the spiritual realm, we are already healed. When we decide to *be seated in God's truth*, then He can touch us, and it *becomes a reality* in the earthly realm as well.

"And now, O Lord, hear their threats, and give us, your servants [all the believers], great boldness in preaching your word. Stretch out your hand with healing power; may

miraculous signs and wonders be done through the name of your holy servant Jesus." After this prayer, the meeting place shook, and they were all filled with the Holy Spirit. Then they preached the word of God with boldness. All the believers were united in heart and mind. And they felt that what they owned was not their own, so they shared everything they had.

Meanwhile, Peter traveled from place to place, and he came down to visit the believers in the town of Lydda. There he met a man named Aeneas, who had been paralyzed and bedridden for eight years. Peter said to him, "Aeneas, Jesus Christ heals you! Get up, and roll up your sleeping mat!" And he was healed instantly. Then the whole population of Lydda and Sharon saw Aeneas walking around, and they turned to the Lord.

Acts 4:29-35 NLT

One man was healed and *two towns* turned to the Lord! We need the Spirit's Agape Love to ignite our prayers and shake the house with His power to share the Gospel of the cross of Jesus that makes us whole — spirit, soul and body! Be seated at the Table with God and healing scriptures. Drink the Living Water for yourself and then share it with others!

But he was pierced for our transgressions, he was crushed for our iniquities; the punishment that brought us peace was on him, and by his wounds we are healed.

Isaiah 53:5 NIV

Declaration

HE HEALS ALL MY DISEASES!

43

The Bride of Christ

God spoke to the people of Israel telling them to see Him as a groom, full of joyful Love for his bride!

Your children will commit themselves to you, O Jerusalem, just as a young man commits himself to his bride. Then God will rejoice over you as a bridegroom rejoices over his bride.

Isaiah 62:5 NLT

In the same way, we who follow Jesus are called *the Bride of Christ*. This is a *spiritual covenant* that is beautifully symbolic. We know it is symbolic because Jesus has told us that humans do not marry in Heaven as they do on earth. The Love Jesus has for us is the unmatched Agape Love of God, not the earthly physical love that unites a man and woman in marriage.

Jesus rejoices over us like a groom rejoices over his bride on their wedding day! But His rejoicing never fades. His passionate Love does not die out with our mistakes and failures. His intimate Love removes them! Jesus always sees us as perfect and beautiful—because we always say *yes,* and *embrace Him* in His dance!

I will make you my wife forever, showing you righteousness and justice, unfailing love and compassion. I will be faithful to you and make you mine, and you will finally know me as the LORD.

Hosea 2:19-20 NLT

The picture of the *Bride of Christ* is so astounding! It unveils a depth of faithful and passionate Love that can't be explained with words. It shows us God's never-ending pursuit for our hearts. This *covenant* with Jesus Christ causes us to be united with Him in *His* righteousness and justice. He stays faithful to His Bride!

The Song of Solomon is a song about the marriage of an earthly king, but woven throughout its story is the prophetic romance of Jesus for His Bride. In *The Beautiful Dream*, I experienced this indescribable, romantic, spiritual Love Jesus has for us!

You have stolen my heart, my sister, my bride; you have stolen my heart with one glance of your eyes, with one jewel of your necklace. How delightful is your love, my sister, my bride! How much more pleasing is your love than wine, and the fragrance of your perfume more than any spice!

Song Of Solomon 4:9-10 NIV

The Love Jesus had for me in *The Beautiful Dream* was so *powerfully romantic* that I can't possibly describe it! He wants us all to *cherish the zeal and passion He has for us.* Jesus is not trying to decide whether He likes you or not. He is totally and completely in Love with you, His Bride!

The Father has reserved a very special chair of honor just for the Bride of His Beloved Son!

"I, Jesus, have sent my angel to give you this testimony for the churches. I am the Root and the Offspring of David, and the bright Morning Star." The Spirit and the bride say, "Come!" And let the one who hears say, "Come!" Let the one who is thirsty come; and let the one who wishes take the free gift of the water of life.

Revelation 22:16-17 NIV

If you're thirsty, come to the Water and drink! The Bride of Christ has become one with Jesus through the Spirit! They bear the fruit of Holy Spirit in their lives. The Bride of Christ longs to be with Jesus because of His *immense Love* for her. She has *died to all other passions*, gods and the sins that once enslaved her. Now she clings to the King who *Loved her and rescued* her from the kingdom of darkness.

Do not worship any other god, for the Lord, whose name is Jealous, is a jealous God.

Exodus 34:14 NIV

The Lord is *jealous* for us with a holy jealousy! If we *leave His dance*, He does everything He can to woo us back into His arms without taking away our right to *choose*. If we turn our passions toward the pleasures of this world and worship earthly things, we have rejected the one true Savior and Lover who gave His life to save us. It astounds me and comforts me that *Jesus is jealous for us* and always wants us in His arms and seated at His Table!

One day, all of God's faithful ones will actually be in Heaven together. On that day, the greatest celebration ever will occur — *the wedding supper of the Lamb!* Jesus is called the spotless Lamb of God because He became the sinless blood-sacrifice for our sins. We, His Bride, will finally be with Him face to face, forever! Our trials will be over! Can you imagine the beauty and majesty of the wedding supper Table and the joy on that day!?

"Let us rejoice and be glad and give him glory! For the wedding of the Lamb has come, and his bride has made herself ready. Fine linen, bright and clean, was given her to wear." (Fine linen stands for the righteous acts of God's holy people.) Then the angel said to me, "Write this: Blessed are those who are invited to the wedding supper of the Lamb!" And he added, "These are the true words of God."

Revelation 19:7-9 NIV

We're so blessed because we've been invited! We need to get ready for the wedding by dressing ourselves with the Holy Spirit's acts of Love and grace. But we don't make those

247

sacrifices out of *fear* or *obligation*. We are the Bride and *Love* is
the whole reason for the wedding!

But I have this against you, that you have left your first love.
Therefore, remember from where you have fallen, and repent,
and do the deeds you did at first; or else I am coming to you and
I will remove your lampstand from its place—unless you
repent.

Revelation 2:4-5 NASB

The fire of His presence at His Table purifies us, making us *red*
hot with spiritual passion and totally surrendered.

You are the most handsome of all. Gracious words stream from
your lips. God himself has blessed you forever. Put on your
sword, O mighty warrior! You are so glorious, so majestic! In
your majesty, ride out to victory, defending truth, humility, and
justice. Go forth to perform awe-inspiring deeds! Your arrows
are sharp, piercing your enemies' hearts. The nations fall
beneath your feet. Your throne, O God, endures forever and ever.

You rule with a scepter of justice. You love justice and hate evil.
Therefore God, your God, has anointed you, pouring out the oil
of joy on you more than on anyone else. Myrrh, aloes, and
cassia perfume your robes. In ivory palaces the music of strings
entertains you. Kings' daughters are among your noble women.
At your right side stands the queen, wearing jewelry of finest
gold from Ophir!

Psalm 45:2-9 NLT

We adore Jesus, our King! His Words are full of grace! Jesus is the
Mighty Warrior winning battles for us, His Bride! He is glorious and
majestic ruling over all, and His Kingdom never ends.

Jesus is so full of joy because of the anointing oil that God, His Father,
placed upon Him to rescue His Bride from her sins. His robes are
drenched with the fragrance of salvation. Jesus listens from His royal
chair in the ivory palaces as the songs of the Bride are sung from
hearts filled with awe and adoration! The atmosphere is full of Agape

Love! And the beautiful Holy Spirit, to the right of the Son, stands to welcome the Bride of Christ and to give her wisdom and advice!

Listen, daughter, and pay careful attention: Forget your people and your father's house. Let the king be enthralled by your beauty; honor him, for he is your lord. The city of Tyre will come with a gift, people of wealth will seek your favor. All glorious is the princess within her chamber; her gown is interwoven with gold. In embroidered garments she is led to the king; her virgin companions follow her— those brought to be with her.

Led in with joy and gladness, they enter the palace of the king. Your sons will take the place of your fathers; you will make them princes throughout the land. I will perpetuate your memory through all generations; therefore the nations will praise you forever and ever.

Psalm 45:10-17 NIV

The Lord is telling you to forget about everything that has weighed you down here on earth. Your past is gone and Jesus has given you a new start with a new Family! Allow your Lord to be enthralled by your beauty by being seated with Him and honoring Him! His glory will rest upon you in such a way that people will be blessed by you. They will come to you, bringing gifts and seeking the same grace and favor God has given you. He has provided you with His righteous garments of praise, embroidered in refined gold.

His angels accompany you as you come into the King's presence full of joy! Those you bring into His Kingdom will be like princes in the land. Old and young will exalt the Name of Jesus and the Gospel will spread to the nations bringing great praise to the Lord! This is who you are as the Bride of Christ and who we are together – in Love with Jesus our King!

Our King has so much to tell us, food from His Word to feed us, Living Water to give us, the wine of the Spirit to fill us with joy, anointing oil to empower us, and Love to express through us if we will just be seated at His Table in the ivory palaces! We get to partner with Him by spreading the fragrance of the Good News of joy. Justice has been served through the cross. The sins of the whole world have been atoned for and King Jesus is inviting everyone who will say *yes* to receive His generous gift of grace!

There are invitations to be given out for *the Wedding Supper Of The Lamb!* The Bride's chair has been chosen—across from her Groom and next to her Father's heart. The Bride is Loving and compassionate just like her King. She doesn't want anyone to die outside of Christ. The Bride wants everyone to receive their invitation!

We, the Bride of Christ, freely give our King all of our Love, devotion, obedience and praise! We are so in Love—with eyes only for Jesus!

He escorts me to the banquet hall; it's obvious how much he loves me.

Song of Solomon 2:4 NLT

Declaration

IT'S OBVIOUS HOW MUCH JESUS LOVES ME!

44

Your Maker is Your Husband

In the second scene of *The Beautiful Dream*, my husband and I were in perfect unity as we spoke to one another about our relationship with Jesus. Your personal relationship with Jesus *is* the life and health of your marriage! He is the reason you can have healthy relationships with others.

As you encounter Jesus intimately, His life-giving Agape Love will spill over to the people in your life. This is also true in marriage. Nothing can keep a Godly Christian marriage on track better than a genuine fiery-hot relationship with Jesus Himself! You are the Bride of Christ—*first!*

For your Maker is your husband— the LORD Almighty is his name—the Holy One of Israel is your Redeemer; he is called the God of all the earth. The LORD will call you back as if you were a wife deserted and distressed in spirit—a wife who married young, only to be rejected," says your God.

Isaiah 54:5-6 NIV

"Your Maker is your husband" is not a scripture just for women. Anyone redeemed by the blood of Jesus is *His Bride*. So whether you are single or married, male or female, you can look to the Lord as your *Husband* in the spiritual sense. The Lord is the *Husband* who will sign a *spiritual covenant of marriage* with you and will never abandon you. Jesus signed this covenant with His precious blood when He died on the cross. No matter how badly you have been treated by parents, siblings, friends, teachers, strangers, bosses or your own spouse, the Lord, your

251

Husband, will never treat you that way. Jesus Loves you very deeply and *His Love* gives you grace for others!

Jesus sees you as *perfect and amazing* because He Himself washed your sins away! His Love and grace flow like a river to those who Love Him back. Yes, Jesus will warn you of danger and correct you when your eyes wander, but that's because He Loves you! He will transform you into a confident and forgiving person, just like He is. Your relationship with Jesus will grow closer with every heart encounter! Paul wrote to new Christians in Corinth, warning them to stay true to Jesus.

For I am jealous for you with the jealousy of God himself. I promised you as a pure bride to one husband — Christ.
2 Corinthians 11:2 NLT

Christians often follow the world's lead instead of Jesus when it comes to relationships. Your Maker sees the whole picture from His Table in the heavenly realms. He will show you *(and your spouse if you have one)* how to spend your money so that you are financially blessed. God will help you resolve conflicts with your children. Abba will be *the other parent* for your children when a spouse is not physically or emotionally present. *Jesus* will make up the difference if you will let Him be the Love and Authority of your life.

Good relationships with your Brothers and Sisters often improve when you decide as an individual to have a close relationship with God. If you build your life's foundation on people, your world will surely fall apart. When you become *one with God*, and you continue in that intimate relationship every day, Jesus becomes your spiritual, physical, and emotional *foundation*. Instead of *demanding* Love from other people, you will have God's Love to give away. You will also be able to *receive Love* when it is given to you!

Owe nothing to anyone except to love one another; for the one who loves his neighbor has fulfilled the Law.
Romans 13:8 NASB

The friendships you choose in this life should allow you to live by the Holy Spirit and live righteously *as He leads.* If a relationship of any kind leaves you constantly feeling controlled manipulated and put down, seek Godly counsel.

Your identity is not in personal success, material things, pleasure, doing good things, *or in another person.* It is in *the Lord your Husband's* extravagant Love. These other things are not bad in themselves. They may even be blessings sent from God. But they *can* become Satan's distractions if you *trust in them* as your foundation. Jesus Himself is always our Savior, foundation and source of Love and life!

But then I will win her back once again. I will lead her into the desert and speak tenderly to her there. I will return her vineyards to her and transform the Valley of Trouble into a gateway of hope. She will give herself to me there, as she did long ago when she was young, when I freed her from her captivity in Egypt. When that day comes," says the LORD, "you will call me 'my husband' instead of 'my master.' O Israel, I will wipe the many names of Baal from your lips, and you will never mention them again.

Hosea 2:14-17 NLT

Jesus is calling His Bride away from the world into intimacy with Him again. The gods of this world that appeared so innocent will suddenly raise their evil heads. Their intent to steal, kill and destroy will be exposed and the wayward Bride, horrified, will run back to follow Jesus. She had wandered away from her first Love, but He will bring her into a desert. And there, *in the Valley of Trouble,* she will remember the way He rescued her in the beginning.

In the desert of intimacy she will place her hope in Jesus again and fall in Love! The vineyards that used to bear sweet fruit will be returned to her to look after again. Jesus will take what the enemy meant for evil and use it for good. The Bride that returns will give *hope* to others. She will never be lured away again! Her past is gone and she doesn't have to worry about it anymore. The Bride will finally realize that Jesus never desired to be her taskmaster. He always was her *Faithful, Loving Husband – Her King!*

Many marriages, friendships, work relationships, family relationships etc., focus on trivial disagreements—*who is wrong and who is right*. Every follower of Jesus has been made perfect in God's eyes. God expects us to *pull the beauty of Christ forward* in one another, not magnify flaws and weaknesses. How the Lord changes you on the inside will affect the true Bride of Christ in a dynamically positive way. You will be a blessing wherever you go.

There is no guarantee that your spouse or anyone else will respond positively to the goodness of God rising in your heart. But when your time on earth is up, *all that will matter then* is that you knew the Lord your Husband well, and blessed others with the Love He placed in your heart.

If you feel depleted of affection, your heart seems to collapse and you can't give or receive Love anymore. That's when God's Love comes to the rescue. In His presence, seated at His Table, He will *revive your heart* one encounter at a time. You will be able to give Love extravagantly, even if it is rejected by some.

God receives Love from His immature children every day, and He is blessed by us! We can become like God! We can learn to receive God's Love from our Brothers and Sisters, even if they aren't good at expressing it! We're growing up together!

Until our hearts are healed by the Lover of our soul, even the best advice can seem overwhelming—sometimes even offensive. Allow the Lord to take you on a journey of truth and healing, and never give up pursuing wholeness in His arms.

What if your spouse does not have a relationship with Jesus?

To the rest I say this (I, not the Lord): If any brother has a wife who is not a believer and she is willing to live with him, he must not divorce her. And if a woman has a husband who is not a believer and he is willing to live with her, she must not divorce him. For the unbelieving husband has been sanctified through his wife, and the unbelieving wife has been sanctified through her believing husband. Otherwise your children would be unclean, but as it is, they are holy. But if the unbeliever leaves, let it be so. The brother or the sister is not bound in such circumstances; God has called us to live in peace. How do you know, wife, whether you will save your husband? Or, how do you know, husband, whether you will save your wife?

1 Corinthians 7:12-16 NIV

The strong presence of Jesus flowing from one spouse can transform an entire family. In the same way, God's presence in you can affect the students at your school or change the atmosphere where you work. If you're satisfied and confident in your *Love relationship with Jesus*, you will be at peace in your heart with others, whether they choose to be at peace with you or not. You carry Jesus everywhere you go—into every room, business, street and ball field. Just His presence in and on you brings His light and Love into that space because you are seated with Him and the atmosphere of the heavenly realms goes with you!

Jesus will always be faithful to you! You will make decisions together, laugh and cry together, dance and sing together, dream and plan together, tell secrets and bless one other with praises. You will accomplish things together that you never imagined possible on your own. Your relationships with other believers will become amazing and powerful! When you learn to receive Agape Love from *your Maker, your Husband*, then you will be able to give and receive Love from your Brothers and Sisters in Christ. The power of agreement goes to another level!

Again I say to you that if two of you agree on earth concerning anything that they ask, it will be done for them by My Father in heaven. For where two or three are gathered together in My name, I am there in the midst of them.

Matthew 18:19-20 NKJV

In the second scene of *The Beautiful Dream*, my husband and I were seated in unity because the source of our faith and Love was Jesus Christ. We were so happy! We were not talking about getting a new house or taking a vacation, even though the Lord sometimes blesses us with nice things. Our earthly circumstances had not improved. We were one with each other and one in Christ and it was deeply felt!

When we walk hand in hand with Jesus, He *unites* us like beautiful harmony in a song. The power that flows from that kind of unity and Love is astounding! The Lord, *your Husband*, takes you to the heavenly realms so He can give you His wisdom, guidance, grace, protection, Love and favor. He wants you to be blessed so you can be a blessing everywhere you are.

Do not be dismayed when people treat you unkindly. Remember who you truly are and that you are seated with the Lord *in His House* high above the trials of this life. He is your defender when you are misjudged by others, so do not lose control and be shaken off your foundation in Christ.

Jesus is shaping your heart for eternity with *His affirmation* so you can walk confidently as you live out your destiny in the Kingdom. Be seated with the King at His Table. Adore, honor and follow *your Maker, your Husband*, in everything. If you do, the other table-relationships God brings into your life will be incredibly blessed!

Declaration

**JESUS TRANSFORMS MY VALLEY OF TROUBLE
INTO A GATEWAY OF HOPE!**

45

Dance in His Righteousness

God made him [Jesus] who had no sin to be sin for us, so that in him we might become the righteousness of God.

2 Corinthians 5:21 NIV

The righteousness of God is sinless perfection. We are righteous through Jesus Christ alone. Only Jesus can take us to be seated with our holy God. In Christ, God has made you *clean* and *set apart* from the world — holy! Get out of your mind that you are *bad*. Thinking like that will only make you sin again! *The old is gone — the new has come!*

My dear children, I write this to you so that you will not sin. But if anybody does sin, we have an advocate with the Father — Jesus Christ, the Righteous One. He is the atoning sacrifice for our sins, and not only for ours but also for the sins of the whole world.

We know that we have come to know him if we keep his commands. Whoever says, "I know him," but does not do what he commands is a liar, and the truth is not in that person. But if anyone obeys his word, love for God is truly made complete in them. This is how we know we are in him: Whoever claims to live in him must live as Jesus did.

1 John 2:1-6 NIV

A righteous person is someone who has been made *right* with God. We have met Jesus and become one with Him. We don't want to sin because we've experienced the cleansing power of

Jesus' Love and we want to stay close to Him

If someone trusts in their own works to bring them closer to God, they are *self-righteous*. They live as though they can become righteous by their own efforts. A self-righteous person may even believe that Jesus made them righteous when they were saved, but they believe that after meeting Jesus *it's up to them to work hard to stay righteous*. Their salvation experience may have been very genuine, and they may have been in Love with Jesus. They may still treasure their early experiences with the Lord. But a self-righteous person sometimes believes that the grace of Jesus *plus* their own effort to not sin will produce the righteousness that will get them into Heaven. They've forgotten what mercy and grace means.

Sometimes a person can *become self-righteous* because they experienced first-hand, the pain that sin can cause. They become *focused on not sinning*. They fear sin so much because sinful circumstances in their life caused them to feel *vulnerable and unloved*. They don't fully understand the righteousness of God that comes from a powerful Love-relationship with Jesus. Out of fear, they become the "sin police," trying to keep everyone from sinning so the environment will be spiritually clean and safe. They believe if they do that, everybody around them will feel happy and loved. But it is a lie from the devil. Only Jesus can make us righteous, safe and Loved!

God is pleased when we lean completely on *His power* to keep us righteous and away from sin. You can count on the devil to *falsely accuse* the children of God on a regular basis. Those who trust in the grace and mercy of God through Jesus can easily reject those lies. People who depend on their own *self-righteous* behavior to keep them right with God are targets for accusation. They will become *afraid* of making the slightest mistake. They will do all sorts of things to avoid *shame* – sometimes even accusing others. It is a law-driven mindset that produces *distasteful fruit* such as pride, gossip, comparison, jealousy, criticism, competition, cynicism, control and an overall feeling of failure and anxiety. It is a very deceptive trick of the enemy to make God's children lose faith in the grace of our Father—His kindness, favor and blessing. There is no joy in a law-driven mindset. But knowing God intimately keeps us in His Love and leads to a grace-filled lifestyle. Paul knew this very well!

I was so zealous [for God] that I harshly persecuted the church. And as for righteousness, I obeyed the law without fault. I once thought these things were valuable, but now I consider them worthless because of what Christ has done. Yes, everything else is worthless when compared with the infinite value of knowing Christ Jesus my Lord. For his sake I have discarded everything else, counting it all as garbage, so that I could gain Christ and become one with him.

I no longer count on my own righteousness through obeying the law; rather, I become righteous through faith in Christ. For God's way of making us right with himself depends on faith. I want to know Christ and experience the mighty power that raised him from the dead. I want to suffer with him, sharing in his death, so that one way or another I will experience the resurrection from the dead!

Philippians 3:6-11 NLT

Paul had been a professional in Jewish religious laws and thought that keeping them would save him from hell. He had kept all the religious rules and regulations, but *he still didn't know God*. When he met Jesus, he knew without a doubt that all his *self-righteous works* had been worthless to save him!

Paul experienced the rebuke and correction of Jesus, but more powerfully, *he experienced Jesus Himself!* He was cleansed, forgiven and filled with the healing Agape Love of God! Paul was so *overwhelmed* by God's Love and the *righteousness* he had received through Jesus, he couldn't stop telling people about it! Shortly after Paul met Jesus, he spent several years just focusing on his relationship with God in the heavenly realms! He was saturated with Jesus!

Some people believe that after they ask Jesus to forgive their sins they can keep sinning intentionally and stay in God's grace. A person who believes this is deceived. They don't want Jesus. They want a religion that allows them to serve the ruler of darkness but still get to Heaven one day. *Knowing Jesus and following Him is the only Way to Heaven!* Anyone who wants to go to Heaven must hate their old life of sin and follow Jesus to the heavenly realms. We *grow* in righteousness at God's Table!

Or do you not know that wrongdoers will not inherit the kingdom of God? Do not be deceived: Neither the sexually immoral nor idolaters nor adulterers nor men who have sex with men or thieves nor the greedy nor drunkards nor slanderers nor swindlers will inherit the kingdom of God. And that is what some of you were. But you were washed, you were sanctified [set apart], you were justified in the name of the Lord Jesus Christ and by the Spirit of our God.
1 Corinthians 6:9-11 NIV

You are not who you were! Praise God! You were *born* of the Spirit to *live* by the Spirit. But God will not force His will on us. We still have the gift of *choice* even after we meet our amazing Savior. Those who choose to pick up their life of sin again have forgotten who they are and who Jesus is.

Jesus had healed a lame man one day, but the man didn't know who had healed him. Jesus came to him *again!*

The man who was healed had no idea who it was, for Jesus had slipped away into the crowd that was there. Later Jesus found him at the temple and said to him, "See, you are well again. Stop sinning or something worse may happen to you."
John 5:13-14 NIV

God delights in healing our physical bodies, but there is one thing worse than illness and that's *rebelling against God* and spending eternity in hell. If a person realizes what they have done and *repents,* the Spirit will lead them back into the arms of Jesus. God's grace is big!

In *The Beautiful Dream*, Jesus asked if I would dance with Him and I said *yes*. I wasn't really sure what I was committing to, but when He touched me, all evil left me and *His* righteousness and Love entered me! I didn't *do* anything to make the evil leave and goodness come in. I just said *yes to the dance!* It was *not my effort* that saved me—it was *His righteousness* that cleansed me. It is *impossible* for us to save ourselves and it is *impossible* for us to live our lives in His Love without yielding to the Holy Spirit who does the impossible!

But Jesus looked at them and said to them, "With men this is impossible, but with God all things are possible."
Matthew 19:26 NKJV

The dance can represent our journey with Jesus. If we stay in the dance and trust His grace, His righteousness will keep flowing into our lives. We have nothing to fear! When we plant our tree next to His stream in the heavenly realms, we will always drink from His life-giving water. When we, as a branch, stay attached to the Vine, we will thrive with life-giving nourishment, producing good fruit! Living in relationship with God in the heavenly realms will, over time, cause us to *look more like Jesus* in the earthly realm.

Dear children, don't let anyone deceive you about this: When people do what is right, it shows that they are righteous, even as Christ is righteous. But when people keep on sinning, it shows that they belong to the devil, who has been sinning since the beginning.

But the Son of God came to destroy the works of the devil. Those who have been born into God's family do not make a practice of sinning, because God's life is in them. So they can't keep on sinning, because they are children of God. So now we can tell who are children of God and who are children of the devil. Anyone who does not live righteously and does not love other believers does not belong to God.
1 John 3:7-10 NLT

In scene three, I was daydreaming in the heavenly realms, thinking about *myself* and *my* relationship with Jesus. As a result, I was standing and everyone else was seated. That can symbolize *pride* that causes you to *look down on* others. I may have been thinking good thoughts, but I was not making an effort to be aware of *everyone else* in the room.

Fear and shame can make you feel so self-conscious that you think you can't be a blessing to anyone else. But that is a lie. Your shame has been erased and your Brothers and Sisters see you as *righteous in Christ*. They feel so honored to have you there and they want to include you in the conversation at the Table. Your part in the Kingdom is unique and vital, and they're excited to see what God has in store for you!

God Loved you and saw you as perfect even before He made the world. Stop striving to prove through your performance that you are perfect and amazing. That's a law driven mindset. When Jesus saved you, He made you perfect and amazing, and He accepts you as you are with His boundless Love! You will make mistakes as you grow, but you will become more like your Father every day! Stay close to your Father's heart!

We have such a good Father! He knows we don't have it all together here on this earth. But because we depend on Abba's grace through Jesus, *all of us are perfectly righteous* in His eyes— seated at His Table in the heavenly realms! Praise the Lord!

Even before he made the world, God loved us and chose us in Christ to be holy and without fault in his eyes.

Ephesians 1:4 NLT

Declaration

IN CHRIST I AM RIGHTEOUS AND VERY LOVED!

46

Wait for the Lord

Why do you say, O Jacob, and speak, O Israel: "My way is hidden from the LORD, and my just claim is passed over by my God"? Have you not known? Have you not heard? The everlasting God, the LORD, the Creator of the ends of the earth, neither faints nor is weary. His understanding is unsearchable.

He gives power to the weak, and to those who have no might He increases strength. Even the youths shall faint and be weary, and the young men shall utterly fall, but those who wait on the LORD shall renew their strength; they shall mount up with wings like eagles, they shall run and not be weary, they shall walk and not faint.

Isaiah 40:27-31 NKJV

The word *hope* in the Hebrew language also means *to wait*. Waiting on the Lord *is* placing all your hope in Him and letting *Him* be your source of power and strength.

In the morning, LORD, you hear my voice; in the morning I lay my requests before you and wait expectantly.

Psalm 5:3 NIV

The Lord cares about *every* need you have. Every morning He is waiting for you to wake up. God is eager to hear from you and minister to you! Talk with Him *anytime* about *everything*. *Confide* in Him. He cares! Be willing to listen to Him speak to you. Your answer may be in His words. Your answer may even be in the dream you had before you woke up. So, as you wait on the Lord, pay attention to His voice. He is speaking.

I remain confident of this: I will see the goodness of the LORD in the land of the living. Wait for the LORD; be strong and take heart and wait for the LORD.

Psalm 27:13-14 NIV

When the waiting turns from days to seasons or years, keep your hope in the One who made His home inside you. We will see His goodness while we are living here on earth!

"Now then, sons, listen to me [the Spirit of wisdom], for blessed are those who keep my ways. Listen to instruction and be wise, and do not neglect it. Blessed is the person who listens to me, watching daily at my gates, waiting at my doorposts. For one who finds me finds life, and obtains favor from the LORD. But one who sins against me injures himself; all those who hate me love death."

Proverbs 8:32-36 NASB

The *Spirit of wisdom* will instruct you as you are seated and wait at His Table. Listen patiently in prayer, and worship in Spirit and in truth. Read scripture desiring a revelation from Holy Spirit, and He will give you joy as you *wait.*

I waited patiently for the LORD; he turned to me and heard my cry. He lifted me out of the slimy pit, out of the mud and mire; he set my feet on a rock [Jesus] and gave me a firm place to stand. He put a new song in my mouth, a hymn of praise to our God. Many will see and fear the LORD and put their trust in him.

Psalm 40:1-3 NIV

Did you know you can wait patiently for the Lord and cry at the same time? Don't act tough like you don't need Him. God knows you are hurting and *He's full of compassion!* When you realize *it's impossible* for you to fix your problem on your own, then you are in the position to put all your hope in Him! You're ready to seek a deeper relationship with Him.

Don't say, "I will get even for this wrong." Wait for the LORD *to handle the matter.*

Proverbs 20:22 NLT

Sometimes when we have been wronged, our first impulse is to take matters into our own hands. Instead of living by fleshly desires, go to the Lord in prayer and *wait on His Spirit* to direct you. In many cases, God will take care of the whole problem. Occasionally, He wants us to get involved. In all cases, God wants us to forgive.

For since the world began, no ear has heard and no eye has seen a God like you, who works for those who wait for him!

Isaiah 64:4 NLT

Waiting and hoping in the Lord means *we believe the Lord will act.* We are convinced that He is faithful and Loving.

If You, LORD, *were to keep account of guilty deeds, Lord, who could stand? But there is forgiveness with You, so that You may be revered. I wait for the* LORD, *my soul waits, and I wait for His word. My soul waits in hope for the Lord more than the watchmen for the morning; yes, more than the watchmen for the morning. Israel, wait for the* LORD; *for with the* LORD *there is mercy, and with Him is abundant redemption.*

Psalm 130:3-7 NASB

What if everything fell apart because you ignored Him and followed your own way—instead of waiting on Him? The person who is deeply aware that they did wrong and asks God to forgive them, has a greater Love relationship with God than the person who thinks their sin is no big deal! Do not let your sin keep you from hoping in the Lord. Come to Him!

Therefore I tell you, her sins, which were many, are forgiven, thus she loved much; but the one who is forgiven little loves little.

Luke 7:47 NET

It's never too late to hope in the Lord. No matter what your situation is, Jesus is full of Love and grace for those who repent and follow His lead.

But Moses told the people, "Don't be afraid. Just stand still and watch the LORD rescue you today. The Egyptians you see today will never be seen again. The LORD himself will fight for you. Just stay calm."

Exodus 14:13-14 NLT

Even the most devoted child of God will experience serious attacks from the enemy. We can't rescue ourselves, but God's grace rescues us! As we *wait on the Lord,* we may discover spiritual strongholds that need to be torn down. Be seated, quiet your heart and *hope* in the Lord. As we hope, we can pray, praise, rebuke the devil and declare the Word in spiritual warfare, or just be still. God fights for us!

The whole assembly of the Israelites gathered at Shiloh and set up the tent of meeting there. The country was brought under their control, but there were still seven Israelite tribes who had not yet received their inheritance. So Joshua said to the Israelites: "How long will you wait before you begin to take possession of the land that the LORD, the God of your ancestors, has given you?

Joshua 18:1-3 NIV

The people of Israel, under Joshua, obeyed the Lord, packed up their belongings and moved by faith. They crossed the Jordan River with the help of a huge miracle from God. Miracles took place as they fought battles together. Finally, they conquered all the strongholds of the Promised Land! It was time for them to separate into tribes, settle down, and enjoy the peace and prosperity God had promised them. But 7 of the 12 tribes procrastinated. They didn't move into their assigned territories. There is a time to *wait* and there is a time to get up and *take possession* of what the Lord has purchased for you! Take courage in the Lord and move into your destiny!

On one occasion, while he was eating with them, he gave them this command: "Do not leave Jerusalem, but wait for the gift my Father promised, which you have heard me speak about. For John baptized with water, but in a few days you will be baptized with the Holy Spirit."

Acts 1:4-5 NIV

Jesus' disciples were already believers and the Holy Spirit lived in them. But Jesus was telling them to *wait for the Spirit's empowering baptism.* Waiting on God in prayer is like fasting *time.* Waiting says, "Nothing is more important than You, God. Everything else can wait. I need to be with You."

But you, dear friends, must build each other up in your most holy faith, pray in the power of the Holy Spirit, and await the mercy of our Lord Jesus Christ, who will bring you eternal life. In this way, you will keep yourselves safe in God's love.

Jude 1:20-21 NLT

The Holy Spirit will lead us to build one another up in faith as we wait for Jesus to return. The Spirit will help us pray seated in His Love at His Table! *Hoping* in the Lord keeps us *expectant* every day of our lives. We are able to see Him working in ways that others miss or call *a coincidence.*

Now faith is confidence in what we hope for and assurance about what we do not see.

Hebrews 11:1 NIV

When our *hope* and our *faith* join forces, the Lord becomes very evident in our lives. But people sometimes use the word *hope* as a filler word. They say, "I hope it doesn't rain today." But they only convey *what would make them happy* though they have no control over the outcome. That is not real *hope.* Hoping in the Lord is so very different from the world's hope. Our hope is attached to faith in the One who created the universe and also lives within us!

As the deer pants for the water brooks, so my soul pants for You, God. My soul thirsts for God, for the living God; when shall I come and appear before God? My tears have been my food day and night, while they say to me all day long, "Where is your God?" I remember these things and pour out my soul within me. For I used to go over with the multitude and walk them to the house of God, with a voice of joy and thanksgiving, a multitude celebrating a festival. Why are you in despair, my soul? And why are you restless within me? Wait for God, for I will again praise Him for the help of His presence, my God.

Psalm 42:1-5 NASB

God can't tell us everything that's happening in the universe because only He can handle it. We don't have all the answers and we have to be okay with that. But we can *rest assured* that He is *very attentive* to our prayers. God is not as interested in giving you a lot of information as He is in developing a trusting relationship. In coming to Him, we encounter His Love.

In *The Beautiful Dream*, I couldn't wait to be with Jesus again, so He took me to the heavenly realms. Jesus has made it possible for us to never be without Him! Even in the *waiting*, we are seated with our King who *Loves* us. In that atmosphere of Love and acceptance, that place of waiting and confident hope, the Lord reveals what we need to know—one day at a time.

The Spirit brings us closer to God's heart *by His power*, not ours. It's like an eagle that soars for miles with wings outstretched and perfectly still. We are moving forward as we wait with God! So, stretch your wings and soar in the wind of the Holy Spirit.

Declaration

~ I AM SEATED WITH GOD AS I WAIT ~

47

Dancing with Joy

With joy you will draw water from the wells of salvation.
Isaiah 12:3 NIV

The Living Water from the heavenly realms is the presence of the Holy Spirit that fills us with the joy of our salvation!

You will show me the way of life, granting me the joy of your presence and the pleasures of living with you forever.
Psalm 16:11 NLT

In *The Beautiful Dream*, I was filled with Love and joy the moment Jesus touched me! It was the *presence of God Himself* that drove out all sadness and depression! My past was gone!

But what happened in scene three? By daydreaming I made a mistake and suddenly my joy was gone! Fear and shame returned as if all the sins of my past were thrown in my face. God was not the one who reminded me of my guilt. He had *forgiven* my guilt. Fear and shame are lies from the enemy!

One of the worst things we can do after asking God to forgive us is to live in regret over our past sins, even the most recent ones. Regret is a sign that you don't really believe you are forgiven. It will cause you to lose the joy of your salvation. Regret keeps you from experiencing the fullness of the grace of God! So embrace the fact that the Lord has forgiven you, and give yourself permission to mature in Him. If you focus on all your insignificant faults or the sin of your past you will become fearful and embarrassed every time you make an honest mistake. Why does the Word of God command us to rejoice? It's because we are the product of His powerful grace—the beautiful fruit of the Love of Jesus Christ! He wants us to believe it and rejoice in His Love!

When your words came, I ate them; they were my joy and my heart's delight, for I bear your name, Lord God Almighty.
Jeremiah 15:16 NIV

If you're *in Love* with Jesus you will be *in Love* with His Word. His Words, the Bread of Life, become alive and active, nourishing us and filling us with His joy!

After the people of Israel returned from seventy years of captivity in Babylon, Ezra, the priest, read God's Word to them. They began to weep and mourn, but Nehemiah interrupted them. He told them to *stop mourning and rejoice* because the joy of the Lord was their strength!

Do not sorrow, for the joy of the LORD *is your strength.*
Nehemiah 8:10b NKJV

It is important to weep and mourn over sin. But *after repentance* there is forgiveness, restoration and joy! *Focusing on the past* is a trick of the enemy to keep you from enjoying the blessings of God and living out your destiny. The Lord wants you to *move forward and rejoice* in His grace! Your past is *forgiven* and God has great plans for your future!

You may ask, "But should we not mourn over our own loss and the loss of others?" The joy of the Lord is not the absence of compassion. Jesus felt grief and compassion. Not having compassion for someone who has experienced loss is a sign that you haven't received a full revelation of Holy Spirit's Love that lives inside you.

Rejoice with those who rejoice; mourn with those who mourn.
Romans 12:15 NIV

Jesus wept with Mary and Martha over the death of their brother Lazarus. God sees what we cannot see with our natural eyes or perceive with our natural soul. Staying close to Jesus keeps us in a place where *we do not give in to despair* but stay in the hope of Father's Love.

Precious in the sight of the LORD is the death of His saints.
Psalm 116:15 NKJV

God comforts us in times of grief and walks with us through *the valley of the shadow of death.* He honors those who Love deeply and mourn the loss of their beloved. Let us not forget that after Jesus wept, He brought Lazarus back to life. God is full of joy *and* compassion. And because of Jesus, there is hope for joy here on earth as we wait for our perfect joy in Heaven.

Jesus spoke His concern over the people of Israel, who for centuries had ignored the Word of the Lord and killed the prophets God had sent to them. Jesus knew He would also be killed by them for obeying His Father. Even so, He kept doing His Father's will because of the *joy* awaiting Him!

Therefore, since we are surrounded by such a great cloud of witnesses, let us throw off everything that hinders and the sin that so easily entangles. And let us run with perseverance the race marked out for us, fixing our eyes on Jesus, the pioneer and perfecter of faith.

For the joy set before him he endured the cross, scorning its shame, and sat down at the right hand of the throne of God. Consider him who endured such opposition from sinners, so that you will not grow weary and lose heart.
Hebrews 12:1-3 NIV

Jesus faced the cross because He *looked forward with joy to setting us free!* Like Jesus, we can *endure persecution with joy.* It will be worth it all one day when we see Jesus *face to face!*

Consider it all joy, my brothers and sisters, when you encounter various trials, knowing that the testing of your faith produces endurance. And let endurance have its perfect result, so that you may be perfect and complete, lacking in nothing.

James 1:2-4 NASB

Joy is *foundational* for overcoming trials and maturing in the Lord. We find joy *in the presence of the Lord*. Like Jesus, you can look forward to the end result of your trial. If you keep pursuing Jesus, you will become more aware of the joy of your salvation. *He* is the joy of our salvation.

Obey your spiritual leaders, and do what they say. Their work is to watch over your souls, and they are accountable to God. Give them reason to do this with joy and not with sorrow. That would certainly not be for your benefit.

Hebrews 13:17 NLT

The Lord asks us to cooperate with and support our spiritual leaders so that we don't become a source of frustration in their ministry, but a source of joy. Of course, you shouldn't support a leader if they ask you to *sin.* In that case, go straight to the pastor leading over them and explain what happened. *But don't lose your faith and joy* over another person's sin. Our faith and joy are in Jesus!

Even if the fig tree does not blossom, and there is no fruit on the vines, if the yield of the olive fails, and the fields produce no food, even if the flock disappears from the fold, and there are no cattle in the stalls, yet I will triumph in the LORD, I will rejoice in the God of my salvation.

Habakkuk 3:17-18 NASB

No matter what happens in this world, we can remain joyful in the Lord. Depression is from the devil. Our faith and joy are *in Jesus* our Savior, not in our circumstances. God will certainly rescue those who Love Him—either in this life or when He takes us to Heaven! We receive that kind of supernatural joy on earth from the place we are seated in the heavenly realms!

Rejoice in the Lord always; again I will say, rejoice!
Philippians 4:4 NASB

Rejoicing in the Lord is a portal that wakes us up at God's Table in the heavenly realms! That is why we must *rejoice in the Lord all the time!* The earthly realm is loud with sadness, depression, hopelessness, accusation, murder and all forms of evil. But our joy is louder, that is, if it comes from the place we are seated with God! It is like a weapon against the kingdom of darkness. People are in need of the joy and Love of the Lord and we carry the joy of the Lord everywhere we go!

The believers who were scattered went everywhere, preaching the message. Philip went to the principal city in Samaria and preached the Messiah to the people there. The crowds paid close attention to what Philip said, as they listened to him and saw the miracles that he performed. Evil spirits came out from many people with a loud cry, and many paralyzed and lame people were healed. So there was great joy in that city.
Acts 8:4-8 GNT

Everywhere Jesus is, there is joy! When Mary was pregnant with baby Jesus, she visited her cousin Elizabeth who was pregnant with John the Baptist. John would become the prophet who prepared the way for Jesus' ministry to begin. When Mary greeted Elizabeth, *the presence of the Holy Spirit* was so strong that baby John *leaped for joy!* Then, Elizabeth and Mary prophesied in the joy of the Holy Spirit!

A few days later Mary hurried to the hill country of Judea, to the town where Zechariah lived. She entered the house and greeted Elizabeth.

At the sound of Mary's greeting, Elizabeth's child leaped within her, and Elizabeth was filled with the Holy Spirit. Elizabeth gave a glad cry and exclaimed to Mary, "God has blessed you above all women, and your child is blessed. Why am I so honored, that the mother of my Lord should visit me? When I heard your greeting, the baby in my womb jumped for joy. You are blessed because you believed that the Lord would do what he said."

Mary responded, "Oh, how my soul praises the Lord. How my spirit rejoices in God my Savior! For he took notice of his lowly servant girl, and from now on all generations will call me blessed. For the Mighty One is holy, and he has done great things for me. He shows mercy from generation to generation to all who fear him.

Luke 1:39-50 NLT

Like Elizabeth, recognize the Spirit of Jesus in your Brothers and Sisters! Give a shout of joy and bless them! Praise the Lord and *rejoice in Him* together. The *Mighty One* is holy and has done great things for us. We are *blessed* and *favored* because of God's grace and mercies through Jesus Christ! We rejoice in Jesus!

Whatever *well* you drink from will determine the cup you serve to others. Renounce all regret and be seated with God at *His Table of joy!* Drink the *Living Water* from the fountain of salvation. You just might notice that your heart is smiling! You may from time to time be overcome with His laughter! The Spirit Loves to fill to overflowing so we can serve the cup of joy to others!

I will shout for joy as I play for you; with my whole being I will sing because you have saved me.

Psalm 71:23 GNT

Declaration

THE JOY OF THE LORD IS MY STRENGTH!

48

The Fear of the Lord

In the third scene of *The Beautiful Dream,* I wanted to ask Jesus when we could be alone again, but somehow I knew that it wasn't the appropriate time to ask that question. It was obvious that He had other plans as we walked toward the room with the Table. *I was still so completely in awe of Him!* Jesus was more than amazing! I felt so honored to be with Him that I followed Him and trusted Him without question.

Sadly, however, I didn't pay attention to what was happening at the Table. What was important to Jesus should have been important to me, but at that moment in the dream it wasn't. In the dream I thought the man was beyond wonderful, although I did not realize who he really was. In the same way, if we truly knew who God was, we would *pay attention* to Him. We would be in awe of His majestic glory! We would tremble at the revelation of His power and humbly bow low before our Creator and Judge!

By the LORD's decree the heavens were made, and by the breath of his mouth all the starry hosts. He piles up the water of the sea; he puts the oceans in storehouses. Let the whole earth fear the LORD. Let all who live in the world stand in awe of him. For he spoke, and it came into existence. He issued the decree, and it stood firm.

Psalm 33:6-9 NET

The fear of the Lord is admitting the truth—He knows *everything* and we don't. We must give Him our attention!

*The fear of the L*ORD *is the instruction of wisdom, and before honor is humility.*

Proverbs 15:33 NKJV

The Lord wants to honor us, but first, we *have* to humble ourselves to learn from Him and then obey Him.

*The fear of the L*ORD *is the beginning of wisdom; all who follow his precepts have good understanding. To him belongs eternal praise.*

Psalm 111:10 NIV

The fear of the Lord is following and *obeying* the wisdom of Holy Spirit instead of *our own earthly reasoning.* It is giving Him *all the praise for every good thing* that happens.

*He will be the sure foundation for your times, a rich store of salvation and wisdom and knowledge; the fear of the L*ORD *is the key to this treasure.*

Isaiah 33:6 NIV

Fearing the Lord brings stability and true riches!

*Praise the L*ORD*! How joyful are those who fear the L*ORD *and delight in obeying his commands. Their children will be successful everywhere; an entire generation of godly people will be blessed. They themselves will be wealthy, and their good deeds will last forever.*

Light shines in the darkness for the godly. They are generous, compassionate, and righteous. Good comes to those who lend money generously and conduct their business fairly. Such people will not be overcome by evil. Those who are righteous will be long remembered.

*They do not fear bad news; they confidently trust the L*ORD *to care for them. They are confident and fearless and can face their foes triumphantly. They share freely and give generously to* *those in need. Their good deeds will be remembered forever. They will have influence and honor. The wicked will see this and be infuriated. They will grind their teeth in anger; they will slink away, their hopes thwarted.*

Psalm 112:1-10 NLT

Those who fear the Lord are filled with His character and advance God's Kingdom on earth. Demons cringe at the Agape Love and confidence that believers bear as fruit!

But don't be afraid of those who threaten you. For the time is coming when everything that is covered will be revealed, and all that is secret will be made known to all. What I tell you now in the darkness, shout abroad when daybreak comes. What I whisper in your ear, shout from the housetops for all to hear!

Don't be afraid of those who want to kill your body; they cannot touch your soul. Fear only God, who can destroy both soul and body in hell.

What is the price of two sparrows — one copper coin? But not a single sparrow can fall to the ground without your Father knowing it. And the very hairs on your head are all numbered. So don't be afraid; you are more valuable to God than a whole flock of sparrows. Everyone who acknowledges me publicly here on earth, I will also acknowledge before my Father in heaven. But everyone who denies me here on earth, I will also deny before my Father in heaven.

Matthew 10:26-33 NLT

Those who *fear the Lord* have come to know Abba Father and know how much He Loves them. They are not afraid of being persecuted because the Lord is their life. They also realize He is Judge and will judge righteously, so they want to be on His side, following His Spirit!

I, Wisdom, live together with good judgment. I know where to discover knowledge and discernment. All who fear the LORD will hate evil. Therefore, I hate pride and arrogance, corruption and perverse speech. Common sense and success belong to me. Insight and strength are mine.

Proverbs 8:12-14 NLT

A person who *fears the Lord* grows in the wisdom of the Holy Spirit. They Love what God Loves and hate what God hates. They live a Kingdom lifestyle of honesty, insight and common sense through the power of the Spirit.

I will praise the LORD *at all times. I will constantly speak his praises. I will boast only in the* LORD*; let all who are helpless take heart. Come, let us tell of the* LORD*'s greatness; let us exalt his name together. I prayed to the* LORD*, and he answered me. He freed me from all my fears. Those who look to him for help will be radiant with joy; no shadow of shame will darken their faces.*

In my desperation I prayed, and the LORD *listened; he saved me from all my troubles. For the angel of the* LORD *is a guard; he surrounds and defends all who fear him. Taste and see that the* LORD *is good. Oh, the joys of those who take refuge in him!*

Fear the LORD*, you his godly people, for those who fear him will have all they need. Even strong young lions sometimes go hungry, but those who trust in the* LORD *will lack no good thing.*

Come, my children, and listen to me, and I will teach you to fear the LORD*. Does anyone want to live a life that is long and prosperous? Then keep your tongue from speaking evil and your lips from telling lies! Turn away from evil and do good. Search for peace, and work to maintain it. The eyes of the* LORD *watch over those who do right; his ears are open to their cries for help. But the* LORD *turns his face against those who do evil; he will erase their memory from the earth. The* LORD *hears his people when they call to him for help. He rescues them from all their troubles. The* LORD *is close to the brokenhearted; he rescues those whose spirits are crushed.*

The righteous person faces many troubles, but the LORD comes to the rescue each time. For the LORD protects the bones of the righteous; not one of them is broken! Calamity will surely destroy the wicked, and those who hate the righteous will be punished. But the LORD will redeem those who serve him. No one who takes refuge in him will be condemned.

Psalm 34:1-22 NLT

Fearing the Lord is taking refuge in Christ! It is believing that *God is who He says He is.* He is Almighty Judge who pours out mercy and grace to all who Love His Son. Those who blame the Lord for their problems do not fear Him because they do not believe in His Love. Those who fear the Lord grow more in *awe of His goodness and majesty* as time goes by. They Love the way He rules and reigns! They long to be closer to His glory no matter the cost, because to be closer to His glory is to know Him better.

We live in an earthly realm where God's presence is evident, even to those who have not said *yes* to Jesus. Darkness and Light both exist on this planet right now. Even the genuine, honest and good love that mankind experiences outside of Christ has been given to them by God. Everyone has experienced the goodness of God poured out in many ways—whether they give *Him* credit for it or not. But there will be a day of Judgment when *time will stop* and the opportunity to say *yes* to Jesus will be over.

At that point in eternity the King and Judge of His creation will separate those who *trusted* Jesus and followed His lead, from those who *rejected* Jesus and followed their own way. Hell will be *the total absence of God's Loving presence*—constant terror, pain and fear forever. There will be *no more sun by day and moon by night.* It won't be like the dark void with strands of light in scene one, where I was numb and was given a choice to repent.

The fear of the Lord will help you make the right decision and follow Jesus, not only to escape Hell, but to experience the glory of His presence for eternity. So if you aren't following Jesus yet, you still have a choice! Jesus, your Savior, invites you to say *yes!*

When Jesus touched me in scene one of *The Beautiful Dream,* I experienced what I believe Heaven will feel like. It was indescribable bliss and it lasted throughout all three scenes! There was no fear—only Love! *The fear of the Lord* does keep us aware of judgment day, but it is so much more! The fear of the Lord is being *so amazed by His Majesty* that we want to *pay attention* to who He is and what He is saying and doing! It is realizing that though He is awesome, all-powerful and Mighty, He lavishes His Bride with extravagant Agape Love!

Jesus is King of Kings and Lord of all lords, yet He has escorted *you* to His Father's House! God has given you a very high and prominent place at the Table in His Kingdom, though you didn't do anything to deserve it. The thought could become overwhelming—except you look across the Table into the eyes of the One who set you free, Jesus, and you know He Loves you *so very much.* He will never leave you! You belong to Jesus now and *there is absolutely nothing to be afraid of!*

Declaration

THE FEAR OF THE LORD IS THE BEGINNING OF WISDOM!

49

Be Seated in His Image

Then God said, "Let us make human beings in our image, to be like us. They will reign over the fish in the sea, the birds in the sky, the livestock, all the wild animals on the earth, and the small animals that scurry along the ground." So God created human beings in his own image. In the image of God he created them; male and female he created them.

Genesis 1:26-27 NLT

I was surprised that in the dream, the Lord depicted the Holy Spirit as a woman! God's Word does tell us that we, both men and women, are created *in His image*. It stands to reason that if the Father and the Son are the masculine forms of His image, the Holy Spirit represents the feminine form. Everything He created in the universe was good—that includes us!

God saw all that he had made, and it was very good.

Genesis 1:31a NIV

Imagine the perfect goodness Adam and Eve must have enjoyed in the beginning, walking and talking with God in the garden. The earth must have been amazingly beautiful and filled with the atmosphere of God's Love. But then sin entered Adam and Eve and distorted the perfect image of God in them. Mankind inherited that sinful nature and we have struggled with our identity ever since. But God did not leave us helpless. He sent Jesus and restored our identity. One day we'll walk and talk with God in Heaven, the perfect paradise free of temptation and evil. But for now, we can *be seated* with our Loving God and

Family while we live out our days here on earth.

God blessed them; and God said to them, "Be fruitful and multiply, and fill the earth, and subdue it; and rule over the fish of the sea and over the birds of the sky and over every living thing that moves on the earth."

Genesis 1:28 NASB

We were created for family—father, mother and children, and we were created *to reign with Him!* This was so clear in the third scene of *The Beautiful Dream*. I felt the beauty and comfort of the Loving structure of *authority* at the Table! The Father is not a wimp. He is all-powerful, strong and undefeatable, yet He delegated authority to His Son who passed it on to the Holy Spirit to give to all of His children! Perfect Agape Love is the atmosphere at His Table!

Marriage between a man and a woman is a blessing from God. In it's purest form, it *represents* the Father, Son and Holy Spirit. Jesus Loved us so much that He gave His life for His Bride. And every *born again* believer is a *child of God*, born because of the seed of the Word of God. Satan despises God's Family Table and is working hard to distort its image by destroying families *and* the family structure here on earth.

So many marriages and families have been torn apart by the wicked schemes of the devil! Some children grow up without loving protective fathers and nurturing mothers. If you have experienced pain from division in your family—there is deep healing available to you. Jesus did not come to condemn, but to save. He Loves you so much! Even if you believe you were the cause of the pain in your family, there is *complete forgiveness and healing* through Jesus! And if your family is experiencing trouble right now, the grace of Jesus is able to heal what has been broken.

Paul and Silas were thrown into prison for telling people about Jesus. In prison they prayed and sang praises to God and at about midnight, there was an earthquake, their chains fell off and the doors of the prison flew open! The jailer was about to kill himself for fear of the consequences when Paul stopped him and calmed him down.

The jailer called for lights and ran to the dungeon and fell down trembling before Paul and Silas. Then he brought them out and asked, "Sirs, what must I do to be saved?" They replied, "Believe in the Lord Jesus and you will be saved, along with everyone in your household." And they shared the word of the Lord with him and with all who lived in his household. Even at that hour of the night, the jailer cared for them and washed their wounds. Then he and everyone in his household were immediately baptized. He brought them into his house and set a meal before them, and he and his entire household rejoiced because they all believed in God.

Acts 16:29-34 NLT

The next morning Paul and Silas were released by the authorities and the jailer didn't get in trouble! Paul and Silas had been shackled to a dungeon wall but instead of complaining, *they stayed seated high with God at His Table in the heavenly realms*, praying and singing praises to God. Before the night passed they were sitting at *the jailer's family table* having a meal! Paul and Silas brought salvation to their jailer and his family because they displayed the image of God. The Spirit *reigned through them* with Agape Love!

Husbands, you have the awesome honor and joy of representing the immense and unconditional Love of Jesus toward your wife, just as Jesus Loves you, His Bride! No matter how immature or irritating she may seem to you, Jesus is jealous for her well-being. He Loves her without reservation and always shows it, regardless of her behavior.

Wives, you have the glorious privilege and blessing of representing the Bride of Christ toward your husband, just as the Bride shows her respect, honor and Love toward Jesus, her King. Jesus said whatever you do for those in need, you have done to me. Your husband *needs you* to encourage him, support him, help him and yes, make him look good instead of exposing his flaws.

Parents, give your children the blessing of the Spirit Loving through you! Drink of the Spirit and pour it out on them. They need your Love and support more than anything else in the world. The Holy Spirit will help you be a blessing to them!

If your marriage or your family is about to fall apart, don't give up. Find a Christian friend who will not just feel sorry for you, but will help you pray and believe the Lord for the healing of your family. You cannot force your family to change. But maybe, in time, they will experience the power of the Spirit's Love in you and desire the Lord as well!

God has created us biologically male or female with His purpose in mind. Many times, abuse, whether physical, verbal or something else, causes a person to wish they were *different* from who they really are. Satan is "the father of lies." *He hates the image of God* and wants to distort it by using every evil tactic imaginable. Some demonic attacks are subtle whispers, and some are brutally violent. Always guard the awesome image of God that you are! The Spirit gives you power to *reign over the lies!*

The devil doesn't want you to follow the Spirit into the Love of God. One way he does this is to make people despise their own biological gender. God chose your gender to reflect His glory. Your body is a temple of the Holy Spirit—God's dwelling place. God wants you to *see yourself through His eyes*, not through the eyes of those who abused or shamed you. Forgive them as Christ forgave you, and live free from the lies and curses that bound you.

A person doesn't have to struggle with gender identity to doubt their value and misunderstand their true identity. Many people hate themselves and don't even know why. Some hate others and look to blame whole groups of people for their own problems because they don't know who they were created to be.

Sin stripped the glory of the image of God in mankind, but *Jesus came to restore it!*

Only your Creator who Loved you even before He formed you can set you free from your past. God says that *in Christ*, you are *very good—even perfect!* You can be *born again* and start over! God will heal your broken heart and whisper Truth to you if you will say *yes* to Jesus! He knows you better than you know yourself! Don't be afraid.

O LORD, you have examined my heart and know everything about me. You know when I sit down or stand up. You know my thoughts even when I'm far away. You see me when I travel and when I rest at home. You know everything I do. You know what I am going to say even before I say it, LORD. You go before me and follow me. You place your hand of blessing on my head.

Such knowledge is too wonderful for me, too great for me to understand! I can never escape from your Spirit! I can never get away from your presence! If I go up to heaven, you are there; if I go down to the grave, you are there. If I ride the wings of the morning, if I dwell by the farthest oceans, even there your hand will guide me, and your strength will support me. I could ask the darkness to hide me and the light around me to become night—but even in darkness I cannot hide from you. To you the night shines as bright as day. Darkness and light are the same to you.

You made all the delicate, inner parts of my body and knit me together in my mother's womb. Thank you for making me so wonderfully complex! Your workmanship is marvelous—how well I know it. You watched me as I was being formed in utter seclusion, as I was woven together in the dark of the womb. You saw me before I was born.

Every day of my life was recorded in your book. Every moment was laid out before a single day had passed. How precious are your thoughts about me, O God. They cannot be numbered! I can't even count them; they outnumber the grains of sand! And when I wake up, you are still with me!

Psalm 139:1-18 NLT

God wrote down His plans for you in a book in Heaven—even before He formed you in your mother's womb. He is passionate about who He created you to be! Your Father knows your amazing potential! You can't hide from your Abba. He will keep pursuing you no matter how dark it is because He Loves you so much and wants you to be by His side! Only Jesus can take you to your Father, and He is so happy to do that for you! Jesus will *instantly* forgive you and restore your identity as a *born again* son or daughter of God. Then He will help you grow up strong by His Spirit.

You are not so broken that His grace cannot mend you! Your Creator can fix you and wants to, because He Loves you more than you can imagine! So, you have these moments in this life, to meet with God. It may take time, but Holy Spirit will set you free from lies about yourself.

You are God's child and Jesus has given you authority to *reign* over the power of the enemy so that you can live in victory. The Holy Spirit who Loves you will teach you these things and so much more. God will teach you who you really are in His image. You will live your life to the fullest measure as your Abba reads your book to you, seated with Him at His Table, one day at a time.

Declaration

I WAS MADE IN THE IMAGE OF GOD!

50

TABLE TALK: *Clip Art Vision*

Indeed God speaks once, or twice, yet no one notices it. In a dream, a vision of the night, when deep sleep falls on people, while they slumber in their beds,

Job 33:14-15 NASB

As I laid in bed I asked God to show me anything that needed to change in my life. With my eyes closed, I saw what looked like black and white clip art. It was a tall male executive in a black suit, white shirt and black tie. He was holding a briefcase, knee bent as if taking a step forward. I noticed an odd thing about the picture. The whole image was slightly tilted. "Work," and "unstable" were the thoughts that came to my mind.

God showed me that I feared what people might think of me, so *I worked hard to measure up*—but I always fell short. He was drawing me back into the foundation of His Love and grace! Jesus reminded me of *The Beautiful Dream* and how He wanted me to be seated in the Spirit where *God is Boss*. If we don't learn to dwell in the heavenly realms, we will live our lives from an *earthly plane*, trying to please Him and others by our own reasoning and strength.

God can speak to you through dreams and visions for your own benefit, or for the benefit of others. But just having a dream or an image pop-up in your mind doesn't mean God is speaking to you. Always ask the Lord if the dream or vision is from Him. The Bible tells us about many people who had visions from

God. Daniel was a man of God who devoted himself to prayer and did not compromise his relationship with God — even when he was threatened with death. Daniel experienced phenomenal visions. He saw Jesus presented before the Father!

"I kept looking in the night visions, and behold, with the clouds of heaven one like a son of man was coming, and He came up to the Ancient of Days and was presented before Him. And to Him was given dominion, honor, and a kingdom, so that all the peoples, nations, and populations of all languages might serve Him. His dominion is an everlasting dominion which will not pass away; and His kingdom is one which will not be destroyed.

Daniel 7:13-14 NASB

God is opening up dialog with you. He may give you a vision so you can pray for a situation or a person. It may or may not be meant to be shared. God may instruct you to share *part* of a dream or vision with others. Be sensitive and let God's Agape Love be your motivation for encountering Him!

If you really are an executive of a business, the Lord will give you the grace to be a blessing to your company without becoming overwhelmed. He has you positioned there for a wonderful purpose. Many lives will be blessed because of the platform God has given you. Live under His grace and Love!

Take off your suit-coat, loosen the tie, drop the heavy briefcase and *be seated at God's Conference Table*. Keep your eyes and ears open. God has amazing and important presentations just for you! He has things for you to do, but you won't be able to do them if you've decided to be *the boss* of your life. His Love and approval will give you the confidence you need. You were created to *succeed*, but only the God who created you can shape you and release you into your God-designed destiny. He may need to do a little *vision casting* from time to time. So have a seat and get ready! Life in the Spirit is going to be adventurous!

51

Fasting at the Table

In *The Beautiful Dream*, I craved being with Jesus and I wanted to know Him more intimately. The purpose of Biblical fasting is doing without food (and sometimes even drink) for a period of time in order to *draw closer to the Lord*. It's best if the Holy Spirit leads your fast, so ask Him. For instance, He may ask you to do without one full meal, or to eat only vegetables and fruit for a day. Follow the Spirit!

Once when John's disciples and the Pharisees were fasting, some people came to Jesus and asked, "Why don't your disciples fast like John's disciples and the Pharisees do?" Jesus replied, "Do wedding guests fast while celebrating with the groom? Of course not. They can't fast while the groom is with them. But someday the groom will be taken away from them, and then they will fast.

Besides, who would patch old clothing with new cloth? For the new patch would shrink and rip away from the old cloth, leaving an even bigger tear than before. And no one puts new wine into old wineskins. For the wine would burst the wineskins, and the wine and the skins would both be lost. New wine calls for new wineskins."

Mark 2:18-22 NLT

Jesus was *with* His disciples *in person*, so they didn't need to fast at that time. He was bringing them out of the old covenant of *the law* into the new covenant of *the Spirit*. Fasting is important *now* to bring us closer to Jesus through the Spirit. The

289

distractions of ordinary life, chaotic circumstances, lies from the devil and fleshly desires are some of the things that can keep us from greater intimacy with Jesus. We tend to become *satisfied* with our spiritual routine, ignoring the little foxes running through our vineyards, leaving our fruitless branches brittle and fragile.

The glory of Holy Spirit cannot *increase* in a heart that has grown lukewarm or cold. We need to exchange our old, worn out spiritual clothes for new ones, not just patch up the holes with new material. Regular fasting can help keep *the spirit of the law* dead so *Holy Spirit* can produce life!

New wine represents the Holy Spirit. A *wineskin* made of animal skin was used to store wine. Wineskins represent our hearts. A lifestyle of fasting for the Lord's increased light and glory can take a crusty old wineskin and make it elastic again. A heart that has withered and dried up cannot endure the power of God's presence in larger doses. But a Christian who humbles themselves by listening to the Spirit, reading God's Word, fasting, praying and obeying *because they want to know Jesus more intimately*, will be *transformed increasingly* from glory to glory.

Then Jesus was led by the Spirit into the wilderness to be tempted by the devil. After fasting forty days and forty nights, he was hungry. The tempter came to him and said, "If you are the Son of God, tell these stones to become bread." Jesus answered, "It is written: 'Man shall not live on bread alone, but on every word that comes from the mouth of God.
                                    Matthew 4:1-4 NIV

Wow! Jesus was *led by the Spirit to fast and to be tempted by the devil!* Our *flesh* needs to realize that we don't live on food alone but by the Word of God! Fasting food helps us!

For, as I have often told you before and now tell you again even with tears, many live as enemies of the cross of Christ. Their destiny is destruction, their god is their stomach, and their glory is in their shame. Their mind is set on earthly things.

Philippians 3:18-20 NIV

If our *stomach* becomes our god, we obsess about earthly things and it opens doors to the *flesh*. Fasting food is one of God's gifts to help us *crucify fleshly desires*.

Some think that if they *put in the hard work* of fasting, God will give them what they want. God's gifts are received by faith in His grace—*not by works*. The Lord cannot be *manipulated* by fasting. Fasting is for *our hearts* to change, not God's. Others fast to impress people, but God wants intimate relationship. We are seeking *Him* in the fast.

And when you fast, don't make it obvious, as the hypocrites do, for they try to look miserable and disheveled so people will admire them for their fasting. I tell you the truth, that is the only reward they will ever get. But when you fast, comb your hair and wash your face. Then no one will notice that you are fasting, except your Father, who knows what you do in private. And your Father, who sees everything, will reward you.
Matthew 6:16-18 NLT

When Jesus spent His lunch break talking to a woman at a well, He was so thrilled to pour His Father's Love and truth into her soul that He wasn't concerned about food.

Meanwhile his disciples urged him, "Rabbi, eat something." But he said to them, "I have food to eat that you know nothing about." Then his disciples said to each other, "Could someone have brought him food?" "My food," said Jesus, "is to do the will of him who sent me and to finish his work."
John 4:31-34 NIV

Following the Spirit and Loving people as He leads is like taking in food that nourishes your body!

God spoke to the people of Israel about *the heart behind the fast*. They were fasting for all the wrong reasons.

"'We have fasted before you!' they say. 'Why aren't you impressed? We have been very hard on ourselves, and you don't even notice it!'

I [God] will tell you why! I respond. It's because you are fasting to please yourselves. Even while you fast, you keep oppressing your workers. What good is fasting when you keep on fighting and quarreling? This kind of fasting will never get you anywhere with me. You humble yourselves by going through the motions of penance, bowing your heads like reeds bending in the wind. You dress in burlap and cover yourselves with ashes. Is this what you call fasting? Do you really think this will please the LORD?

No, this is the kind of fasting I want: Free those who are wrongly imprisoned; lighten the burden of those who work for you. Let the oppressed go free, and remove the chains that bind people. Share your food with the hungry, and give shelter to the homeless. Give clothes to those who need them, and do not hide from relatives who need your help. Then your salvation will come like the dawn, and your wounds will quickly heal. Your godliness will lead you forward, and the glory of the LORD will protect you from behind. Then when you call, the LORD will answer. 'Yes, I am here,' he will quickly reply.

Remove the heavy yoke of oppression. Stop pointing your finger and spreading vicious rumors! Feed the hungry, and help those in trouble. Then your light will shine out from the darkness, and the darkness around you will be as bright as noon. The LORD will guide you continually, giving you water when you are dry and restoring your strength. You will be like a well-watered garden, like an ever-flowing spring. Some of you will rebuild the deserted ruins of your cities. Then you will be known as a rebuilder of walls and a restorer of homes.

Keep the Sabbath day holy. Don't pursue your own interests on that day, but enjoy the Sabbath and speak of it with delight as the LORD's holy day. Honor the Sabbath in everything you do on that day, and don't follow your own desires or talk idly.

Then the LORD will be your delight. I will give you great honor and satisfy you with the inheritance I promised to your ancestor Jacob. I, the LORD, have spoken!"

Isaiah 58:3-14 NLT

The world falls apart and many Christians want God to change their nation — but they're not willing to change their own hearts. God wants to change the world *through* His children. No amount of fasting will drive out darkness unless His Church begins to fast for the right reason — to know God intimately and obey Him.

His commands are to *Love God* with all of our heart, soul, mind and strength, and to *Love people* as He has Loved us. In that place of intimate submission, our cities and nations will be changed because God's people have died to the flesh and come alive in Christ. God's light will shine and the Living Water will flow out from His true Church! If your desire is for your heart to become more like your Father's heart, you are fasting for the right reason!

When the early church fasted, worshiped and connected with God together, the Holy Spirit gave them guidance.

While they were worshiping the Lord and fasting, the Holy Spirit said, "Set apart for me Barnabas and Saul for the work to which I have called them."

Acts 13:2 NIV

If we fast in order to detach ourselves from our earthly desires and be seated with God in the heavenly realms, the gifts of the Spirit can increase in our lives. Daniel's desire to know God, hear from God and serve Him with a pure heart was his motivation for fasting and prayer. He had the great honor of seeing Jesus face to face on several occasions!

When this vision came to me, I, Daniel, had been in mourning for three whole weeks. All that time I had eaten no rich food. No meat or wine crossed my lips, and I used no fragrant lotions until those three weeks had passed. On April 23, as I was standing on the bank of the great Tigris River, I looked up and saw a man dressed in linen clothing, with a belt of pure gold around his waist. His body looked like a precious gem. His face flashed like lightning, and his eyes flamed like torches. His arms and feet shone like polished bronze, and his voice roared like a vast multitude of people.

Daniel 10:2-6 NLT

In scene three of *The Beautiful Dream*, there was no food on the Table. At God's Table of fasting, *the flesh has to die.* Fasting is an invitation to deny the earthly realm and meet with the Lord in the heavenly realms so you can *know Him more intimately.* The Spirit is inviting us now to be seated at God's Table of fasting. This is where our hearts become like His so *His will* can be done on earth.

See Notes: #10 Fasting Suggestions

Declaration

I FAST TO ENCOUNTER JESUS!

52

Be Seated in Persecution

"If the world hates you, keep in mind that it hated me first. If you belonged to the world, it would love you as its own. As it is, you do not belong to the world, but I have chosen you out of the world. That is why the world hates you. Remember what I told you: 'A servant is not greater than his master.' If they persecuted me, they will persecute you also. If they obeyed my teaching, they will obey yours also. They will treat you this way because of my name, for they do not know the one who sent me."

John 15:18-21 NIV

When I told Jesus I just wanted to be close to Him no matter the cost, He responded with *The Beautiful Dream*. Only a heart fully surrendered can draw close to Jesus. We no longer belong to this world. We belong to the Kingdom of God and live for our risen King—from the heavenly realms. We will be *despised* and *rejected* if we Love Jesus with all of our hearts.

Who has believed our message? To whom has the LORD revealed his powerful arm? My servant grew up in the LORD's presence like a tender green shoot, like a root in dry ground. There was nothing beautiful or majestic about his appearance, nothing to attract us to him.

He was despised and rejected— a man of sorrows, acquainted with deepest grief. We turned our backs on him and looked the other way. He was despised, and we did not care. Yet it was our weaknesses he carried; it was our sorrows that weighed him down. And we thought his troubles were a punishment from God, a punishment for his own sins!

But he was pierced for our rebellion, crushed for our sins. He was beaten so we could be whole. He was whipped so we could be healed. All of us, like sheep, have strayed away. We have left God's paths to follow our own. Yet the LORD laid on him the sins of us all. He was oppressed and treated harshly, yet he never said a word. He was led like a lamb to the slaughter. And as a sheep is silent before the shearers, he did not open his mouth.

Unjustly condemned, he was led away. No one cared that he died without descendants, that his life was cut short in midstream. But he was struck down for the rebellion of my people. He had done no wrong and had never deceived anyone. But he was buried like a criminal; he was put in a rich man's grave.

But it was the LORD's good plan to crush him and cause him grief. Yet when his life is made an offering for sin, he will have many descendants. He will enjoy a long life, and the LORD's good plan will prosper in his hands. When he sees all that is accomplished by his anguish, he will be satisfied. And because of his experience, my righteous servant will make it possible for many to be counted righteous, for he will bear all their sins. I will give him the honors of a victorious soldier, because he exposed himself to death. He was counted among the rebels. He bore the sins of many and interceded for rebels.

Isaiah 53:1-12 NLT

We who are *born again* are the spiritual descendants of Jesus. We will be mocked and slandered as He was.

God blesses you when people mock you and persecute you and lie about you and say all sorts of evil things against you because you are my followers. Be happy about it! Be very glad! For a great reward awaits you in heaven. And remember, the ancient prophets were persecuted in the same way.

Matthew 5:11-12 NLT

Even as Jesus was dying on the cross He forgave those who crucified Him. We also forgive! We don't share the Gospel to get recognition on earth or even in Heaven—though God does give *rewards*. We share the Gospel in the face of persecution because the Spirit placed *Agape Love* inside us for those who do not know Jesus.

Bless those who persecute you; bless and do not curse.
Romans 12:14 NASB

After the Holy Spirit baptized the believers with holy fire, the apostles were *overwhelmed*, caring for *everyone* in the churches. They realized they needed more time for praying and ministering the Word. They chose seven men *full of the Spirit and wisdom* to take care of feeding the poor. Stephen was one of them. He was full of faith, grace, power and performed great signs and wonders—like Jesus. Stephen shared the Gospel and was arrested—like Jesus. He was put on trial and spoke boldly—like Jesus.

None of them could stand against the wisdom and the Spirit with which Stephen spoke.
Acts 6:10 NLT

The religious leaders were determined to catch Stephen saying something wrong. But instead, he revealed truth through the scriptures and surprised them all. That's because he was full of the power of the Spirit. Stephen was so filled with Holy Spirit, his face shone!

And all who sat in the council, looking steadfastly at him, saw his face as the face of an angel.
Acts 6:15 NKJV

Stephen began his defense by sharing the history of God's glory, beginning with Abraham all the way to Jesus. The Sanhedrin knew the scriptures "backward and forward" but they lived as if they had not learned anything! Though they crucified Jesus who died, and three days later rose from the dead, *they still did not repent.* Stephen *was prompted by the Holy Spirit* to rebuke them and expose their religious pride, just as Jesus had done. He urged them to repent!

You stubborn people! You are heathen at heart and deaf to the truth. Must you forever resist the Holy Spirit? That's what your ancestors did, and so do you! Name one prophet your ancestors didn't persecute! They even killed the ones who predicted the coming of the Righteous One—the Messiah whom you betrayed and murdered. You deliberately disobeyed God's law, even though you received it from the hands of angels.

Acts 7:51-53 NLT

When the members of the Sanhedrin heard this, they were furious and gnashed their teeth at him. But Stephen, full of the Holy Spirit, looked up to heaven and saw the glory of God, and Jesus standing at the right hand of God. "Look," he said, "I see heaven open and the Son of Man standing at the right hand of God."

Acts 7:54-56 NIV

Stephen, who had Loved well, was then stoned to death for sharing the truth about Jesus. As they were pounding him with large rocks, he prayed, "Lord, do not hold this sin against them," just like Jesus did on the cross. Stephen went from the heavenly realms of the Spirit right into Heaven itself! He even got to see the Lord Jesus stand in honor as He waited for Stephen to arrive! Stephen brought light to a very dark world because he was full of the Spirit of Truth and Love—like His Lord! It's obvious that Stephen Loved Jesus and knew Him intimately. He acted just like Him!

Saul, a Pharisee partly responsible for Stephen's death, stood by watching. I believe Stephen's prayer of forgiveness was heard by God and made it possible for Saul to be saved. Before long, Saul met Jesus and became known later as Paul. Paul's encounter with Jesus was so dramatic that he understood why

298

Christians would not deny their faith! Paul Loved Jesus so much that he risked his life often just to be able to share the Good News of Jesus to anyone who would listen. He was persecuted for the rest of his life and eventually killed because of his faith in Jesus Christ! I believe many came to Jesus through Paul because Stephen was not ashamed of Jesus and knew how to forgive as Jesus did!

Look, I am sending you out as sheep among wolves. So be as shrewd as snakes and harmless as doves. But beware! For you will be handed over to the courts and will be flogged with whips in the synagogues. You will stand trial before governors and kings because you are my followers. But this will be your opportunity to tell the rulers and other unbelievers about me.

When you are arrested, don't worry about how to respond or what to say. God will give you the right words at the right time. For it is not you who will be speaking—it will be the Spirit of your Father speaking through you. A brother will betray his brother to death, a father will betray his own child, and children will rebel against their parents and cause them to be killed. And all nations will hate you because you are my followers. But everyone who endures to the end will be saved. When you are persecuted in one town, flee to the next. I tell you the truth, the Son of Man will return before you have reached all the towns of Israel.

Matthew 10:16-23 NLT

No matter how Loving we are, we will be persecuted in some way if we are *vocal* about Jesus. Jesus said it's okay to hide from your persecutors, but *it's never okay to deny Him.* Individuals, religious groups and governments around the world are already persecuting our Brothers and Sisters in Christ.

Persecution comes in many ways: Imprisonment, beatings, death, denying employment, denying education, seizing property, false accusation, denying the right to vote, not allowing Christians to meet together, not allowing people to talk about Christ, forcing private businesses to function in a way that contradicts their Biblical moral conscience, taxing people more heavily if they live by Christian morals, social media censorship, *and on and on and on...*

Be careful not to falsely accuse people of persecuting you. If your landlord evicts you because you haven't paid your rent, *that's not persecution.* If your child gets suspended from school for stealing, *that's not persecution either.* But if you are being accused falsely because of your faith in Jesus, *that's persecution.* And if your freedoms are being taken away because you live an *Agape* lifestyle and you share the Gospel, *that's persecution!*

Our Love-relationship with Jesus at His Table in the heavenly realms will make us bold like Stephen and Paul. Let's be seated with Jesus who suffered for us, and pray for our Brothers and Sisters who are being persecuted for their faith.

Dear Father,
Thank you for Loving us so faithfully. We praise you with all of our hearts! Jesus, we will not deny your wonderful name. So, we pray for our Brothers and Sisters and their sweet families who are being persecuted because they Love you. Lord, set captives free. Provide them with food, clothing and shelter. Give them Bibles. Surround them with your powerful protective arm and help them get where they need to go. Extend Your hand to release visions, dreams, signs, wonders, healings, miracles and resurrecting power. Release your angels to minister to them. Give them sweet sleep. Baptize them with your Agape Love! Give them courage and faith to share the Gospel when you prompt them to, and the courage to never deny you, Jesus! Bless and forgive those who persecute them. Reveal yourself to them as Savior so that they can receive your forgiveness and grace. We pray this in the name of Jesus, Amen!

Declaration

I WILL NOT DENY MY LOVE FOR JESUS!

53

Dance Courageously!

Joshua and Caleb tried to encourage Israel's tribes to go into the Promised Land but the other ten spies were *terrified* and *spread paralyzing fear* over the traveling nation! Finally after forty years in the wilderness, God instructed Joshua to take Moses' place and lead Israel into the land God had promised them. This is what God told Joshua:

No one will be able to stand against you as long as you live. For I will be with you as I was with Moses. I will not fail you or abandon you. Be strong and courageous, for you are the one who will lead these people to possess all the land I swore to their ancestors I would give them. Be strong and very courageous. Be careful to obey all the instructions Moses gave you. Do not deviate from them, turning either to the right or to the left. Then you will be successful in everything you do. Study this Book of Instruction continually. Meditate on it day and night so you will be sure to obey everything written in it. Only then will you prosper and succeed in all you do. This is my command—be strong and courageous! Do not be afraid or discouraged. For the LORD your God is with you wherever you go.

Joshua 1:5-9 NLT

Joshua's courage as a young spy for God was like a seed planted in his heart, in the desert. He stayed strong in the Lord and after forty years, that seed of courage had grown and produced seeds of faith for an entire nation. And yet, when the time came, God had to *command* Joshua to be strong and courageous! The Lord knew Joshua would need the *Word* of encouragement and that many years later *we* would need it too! That's why it was written down in God's Word. When these promises are *believed* and *declared* in unity at God's Table, the Church will see victory over the devil! You can declare these promises over your personal life, church, business, school, nation, etc!

- The enemy, Satan, will not be able to stand against me. (*...my family... our church... our nation...*)
- The Lord will be with me in miraculous power.
- The Lord will never leave me.
- I must be strong and courageous because I will help lead others into their destiny in Christ.
- *Again*, I must be strong and *very* courageous.
- I must obey the Word of God and never veer from it.
- I must recite and talk about the Word of God.
- I must meditate on the Word, day and night, so God can speak to me and guide me.
- If I do these things I will prosper and be successful.
- God commands me *the third time*, "Be strong and courageous."
- I must not be afraid or discouraged.
- The Lord will be with me wherever I go.

The Lord has a task for you to do! No matter how small or large it may seem *to you*, it will have a greater affect on people than you think, because the Lord will be the one empowering you. The people you encourage will change the course of your family, church, workplace, community and nation for God's glory. On the other hand, if you are *fearful* and *ignore* the Lord and His Word, the opposite will happen. But it's up to you, and people *need* what the Lord has planned for you to do in His Kingdom.

The Lord gave Joshua a key to prosperity and success — *God's Word!* If you *believe* God's Word, *speak* it, *meditate* on it and *obey* it, you will be *prosperous and successful!* Not only will you be blessed, but an entire company of people will be drawn into the flow of what Holy Spirit is doing through your life. You don't have to be a minister or own your own business to have Godly influence on others. You just have to listen to the Holy Spirit and remember that *He is with you wherever you go!* It is the Lord who is enabling you to do what He asks you to do! *Be strong and very courageous. Do not be afraid or discouraged. Believe the Lord is for you!*

When all the Amorite kings on the west side of the Jordan and all the Canaanite kings along the seacoast heard how the LORD had dried up the water of the Jordan before the Israelites while they crossed, they lost their courage and could not even breathe for fear of the Israelites.

Joshua 5:1 NET

This little passage of scripture is amazing because it shows us that when we courageously step out in faith and obey the Lord, *the devil is terrified!* At some point in your obedience, demons will melt in fear and will no longer have the courage to harass you. That's because the Lord is with you, you obey His commands, and you are choosing to be *strong and courageous in Him!*

As long as we stay in *fear* we will be nomads, complaining in the desert against the will of God. But if we take *courage* in *God's Word*, in *His Spirit*, and in *His Love* for His people, truly believing He is *with us and in us*, we will take possession of what God has promised!

Then Peter, filled with the Holy Spirit, said to them: "Rulers and elders of the people! If we are being called to account today for an act of kindness shown to a man who was lame and are being asked how he was healed, then know this, you and all the people of Israel: It is by the name of Jesus Christ of Nazareth, whom you crucified but whom God raised from the dead, that this man stands before you healed. Jesus is 'the stone you builders rejected, which has become the cornerstone.' Salvation is found in no one else, for there is no other name under heaven given to mankind by which we must be saved." When they saw the courage of Peter and John and realized that they were unschooled, ordinary men, they were astonished and they took note that these men had been with Jesus. But since they could see the man who had been healed standing there with them, there was nothing they could say.

Acts 4:8-14 NIV

Peter and John were *interrogated* because a man was healed! Instead of shrinking with fear, they seized the opportunity to *share the Gospel!* The rulers and elders saw Peter and John's *courage* and figured out that *they had been with Jesus!* We draw courage from *being with Jesus*, seated in the heavenly realms at God's Table!

Be on the alert, stand firm in the faith, act like men, be strong. All that you do must be done in love.

1 Corinthians 16:13-14 NASB

We are an army of Love, and that is why we do not shrink back in fear. We *know* that God is our Father and He controls the final outcome of this spiritual war. Those who remain in the Word will win in the end, and they will win many battles along the way!

And now, dear children, remain in fellowship with Christ so that when he returns, you will be full of courage and not shrink back from him in shame.

1 John 2:28 NLT

Stay in fellowship with Jesus! We are all in Christ, so that means stay in fellowship with one another as well. Even in times of persecution or war, we can be *courageous*. Jesus Loves you just as much today as the day He saved you, and He will *be with you* to the end! Do not fear!

For God has not given us a spirit of fear, but of power and of love and of a sound mind.

2 Timothy 1:7 NKJV

You have God's Spirit inside you so you lack nothing! *In Christ,* you are courageous, full of power, Love and you have a sound mind. The choice to be courageous and not fear is now ours to make. That is why the Lord tells us to do things we cannot do on our own.

I can do all things through Christ who strengthens me.
Philippians 4:13 NKJV

You can be *courageous* because you know Jesus! You can be *confident* because your Father Loves you beyond words! You can *accomplish* what God wants you to do today because *He is with you* and your motivation is His Love. You can, you can, you can! And even if you try and don't get the results you hoped for, Abba Loves you and is proud to call you His child. God will not leave you. Let Him help you and *en-courage* you so you can keep moving forward!

In scene one of *The Beautiful Dream*, Jesus placed His hands on my tummy and I was filled with perfect life and Love. That is the place where your spiritual heart is, and where the Holy Spirit dwells. When you are tempted to fear, close your eyes and spiritually look downward into your *heart*. Whisper aloud or speak God's truth silently to your heart, and the presence of the Lord will calm you. The Spirit's power will rise as the Word bathes your inner being.

For I am confident of this very thing, that He who began a good work among you will complete it by the day of Christ Jesus.
Philippians 1:6 NASB

The Israelites crossed into the Promised Land in one day, but it was years before they took possession of all of it. This was God's plan. They had to conquer one territory at a time and possess it before taking on another one.

I will not drive them out from before you in one year, lest the land become desolate and the beasts of the field become too

numerous for you. Little by little I will drive them out from before you, until you have increased, and you inherit the land.
Exodus 23:29-30 NKJV

It is the same way in our personal lives and in our hearts. We must not be discouraged when breakthrough seems to be coming one battle at a time. When you gain victory over one stronghold *through the Word*, let the Holy Spirit inhabit that area of your heart so the "wild beasts" can't come in and attack you. Then ask God where the next battle will be. Eventually, you will increase and inherit all the promises of God for your life. You will be rooted and established in God's Love!

"When an evil spirit goes out of a person, it travels over dry country looking for a place to rest. If it can't find one, it says to itself, 'I will go back to my house.' So it goes back and finds the house clean and all fixed up. Then it goes out and brings seven other spirits even worse than itself, and they come and live there. So when it is all over, that person is in worse shape than at the beginning." When Jesus had said this, a woman spoke up from the crowd and said to him, "How happy is the woman who bore you and nursed you!" But Jesus answered, "Rather, how happy are those who hear the word of God and obey it!"
Luke 11:24-28 GNT

So be strong and very courageous! God will not fail you or leave you. Obey His Word and don't veer from it. You will be successful in all He asks you to do. Don't fear or be discouraged. Be seated in unity with your Brothers and Sisters in Christ and together we will move the enemy out of the territories God has given us. By God's grace we will see victory in our own hearts, our families, our churches and in our nation!

Declaration

IN CHRIST I AM STRONG AND VERY COURAGEOUS!

54

Be Seated on the Stairway

In scene two of *The Beautiful Dream*, I was sitting on concrete bleachers that looked like giant stairs. I will take the liberty of assuming they can represent both bleachers and a very large stairway. What comes to my mind is the stairway Jacob saw in a dream God gave him.

Jacob left Beersheba and set out for Harran. When he reached a certain place, he stopped for the night because the sun had set. Taking one of the stones there, he put it under his head and lay down to sleep. He had a dream in which he saw a stairway resting on the earth, with its top reaching to heaven, and the angels of God were ascending and descending on it.

There above it stood the LORD, and he said: "I am the LORD, the God of your father Abraham and the God of Isaac. I will give you and your descendants the land on which you are lying. Your descendants will be like the dust of the earth, and you will spread out to the west and to the east, to the north and to the south. All peoples on earth will be blessed through you and your offspring. I am with you and will watch over you wherever you go, and I will bring you back to this land. I will not leave you until I have done what I have promised you."

Genesis 28:10-15 NIV

Jacob named that place Bethel, which means *House of God*, because he encountered the Lord there! God's angels traveled up and down the stairway bringing the promised blessings to Jacob and his descendants. We Gentile believers have been

307

adopted into God's promises through faith in Jesus. As we *encounter God* in His presence at His Table, His holy angels serve the Lord by blessing us as well!

If you say, "The LORD is my refuge," and you make the Most High your dwelling, no harm will overtake you, no disaster will come near your tent. For he will command his angels concerning you to guard you in all your ways; they will lift you up in their hands, so that you will not strike your foot against a stone. You will tread on the lion and the cobra; you will trample the great lion and the serpent.

Psalm 91:9-13 NIV

We don't pray to angels or worship them. *We worship the Lord and pray to Him only.* God knows who is seated with Him and gives His angels orders to help us.

See that you do not look down on one of these little ones; for I say to you that their angels in heaven continually see the face of My Father who is in heaven.

Matthew 18:10 NASB

God assigns angels to each one of us from the time we are conceived. They are continually reporting to the Lord and receiving assignments from Him regarding our lives and the lives of our children.

And to the angel of the church in Smyrna write...

Revelation 2:8a NKJV

God also assigns angels to churches. They are powerful beings who *obey God's Word without fail.* Where God's people are walking in the Spirit of Agape Love and Truth, I imagine their angels are busy using the stairway.

The LORD has established His throne in the heavens, and His sovereignty rules over all. Bless the LORD, you His angels, mighty in strength, who perform His word, obeying the voice of His word! Bless the LORD, all you His angels, you who serve

Him, doing His will. Bless the LORD, all you works of His, in all places of His dominion; bless the LORD, my soul!
Psalm 103:19-22 NASB

Angels praise the Lord and obey God's Word. They do what the Lord tells them to do. We don't tell angels what to do. But when the Word of God has become *alive and active in our hearts* by following the Spirit, we can declare the Word by the Spirit and the angels can respond on our behalf.

When the servant of the man of God got up and went out early the next morning, an army with horses and chariots had surrounded the city. "Oh no, my lord! What shall we do?" the servant asked. "Don't be afraid," the prophet answered. "Those who are with us are more than those who are with them."

And Elisha prayed, "Open his eyes, LORD, so that he may see." Then the LORD opened the servant's eyes, and he looked and saw the hills full of horses and chariots of fire all around Elisha. As the enemy came down toward him, Elisha prayed to the LORD, "Strike this army with blindness." So he struck them with blindness, as Elisha had asked.
2 Kings 6:15-18 NIV

Some believers, like Elisha, are able to *see* the angels of God around them! Whether you see them or not, you can know they are present because God's Word tells us so!

We know from scripture that Satan, whose name was *Lucifer,* was created as a beautiful, high-ranking holy being in Heaven. Lucifer and all the angelic beings lived in the pure glory of God's Loving presence. But instead of remaining humble and grateful for the honor of serving the Lord in an elevated position, he became prideful. Lucifer gathered a following of angels to help him overthrow God. Immediately Lucifer and his angel followers were ejected from Heaven by God's lightening power. We know them now as Satan (the devil) and his demons.

Two-thirds of the angels remained faithful to God and are serving Him to this day. Satan's troops are *outnumbered* by God's angelic army! Hallelujah! Holy angels do not ever sin. They always adore the Lord and follow His commands. They don't make mistakes. We can count on it!

But about the angels God said, "God makes his angels winds, and his servants flames of fire."

Hebrews 1:7 GNT

Angels and various heavenly beings have differing ranks and responsibilities and carry God's Holy presence of fire. Some carry out the judgments of God. Others are stationed in Heaven to lead worship and praise. Another receives the prayers of God's people. These are a few of the angelic roles mentioned in the Bible. Angels are spirit beings. God has given them heavenly bodies of different types. Some of the heavenly beings are *extremely unusual!*

God stripped the fallen angels of their bodies. The devil cannot create a body, although sometimes demons present themselves to people as translucent figures. Demons want to latch on to human beings so they can frighten them or perform their devilish work through them. But as believers, we can *submit to God, resist the devil and he will flee!*

Some of God's holy angels have appeared as *very large strong men in brilliant white robes* with golden sashes, swords or other heavenly attire. Other angels appear to us *as ordinary men.*

Do not neglect hospitality to strangers, for by this some have entertained angels without knowing it.

Hebrews 13:2 NASB

Angels were created to be angels for eternity, and humans were created to be children of God for eternity. Humans don't become angels and angels don't become humans. But God sometimes has an angel appear in a human-like body dressed like us so they can minister to a person who might otherwise become terrified. You may have seen someone who looked like an ordinary human being, who was actually an angel. That's another good reason to be kind to everyone!

Are not all angels ministering spirits sent to serve those who will inherit salvation?

Hebrews 1:14 NIV

How amazed the angels must have been when the Father announced that His Son would be leaving Heaven and coming to earth to redeem mankind!

But we do see Jesus, who was made lower than the angels for a little while, now crowned with glory and honor because he suffered death, so that by the grace of God he might taste death for everyone.

Hebrews 2:9 NIV

An angel appeared to both *Joseph and Mary* to help them understand that Mary would give birth to the Messiah. Angels appeared to *shepherds* announcing the birth of Jesus and inviting them to go visit their new King. Angels came *to serve Jesus* when He finished His forty day fast. And a mighty angel rolled away the stone from *the empty tomb* where Jesus' body had been laid.

There was a violent earthquake, for an angel of the Lord came down from heaven and, going to the tomb, rolled back the stone and sat on it.

Matthew 28:2 NIV

An angel of the Lord appeared to the women who were looking for Jesus' body and told them that He was alive! *God's angel* opened the doors of a jail and released the apostles. *An angel of the Lord* told Philip to walk down a certain road where he met an Ethiopian and brought him to faith in Jesus. *An angel* appeared to Cornelius instructing him to send for Peter, who obeyed, and a room full of guests received the Gospel and were baptized in the Spirit and water. King Herod, who allowed his people to praise him as a god, was struck down by *an angel of God*, was eaten by worms and died. *An angel* appeared beside Paul in a storm-tossed ship and assured him that everyone on board would survive and make it to shore, though the ship would be lost. It happened exactly as the angel had said! There are many more stories in the Bible about God's angels and many scriptures instructing us about them.

Angels are just as active today as they were in Bible days! There is at least one an angel assigned to you who is ready to assist you as you live by the Spirit! We are on the same Team as God's holy angels, worshiping and serving the same wonderful God for His glory! But let us all focus our gaze at the top of the stairway—on Jesus, our Lord and King! We are receiving help from angels on earth, but God is asking us to *be seated with Jesus* in the heavenly realms!

Declaration

ANGELS ARE OBEYING
THE WORD OF THE LORD!

55

Dancing with Love Himself

*For this is what the Lord GOD, the Holy One of Israel, has said:
"In repentance and rest you will be saved, in quietness and trust
is your strength." But you were not willing,*

Isaiah 30:15 NASB

God wants us to come to Him and *rest in His presence*, seated at
His Table. There we stop striving to earn His Love. We accept
His Love in confidence, sitting quietly, doing nothing and
planning nothing. He is blessed when we approach Him calmly
in awe of His goodness, because it is an *act of faith in His
unearned grace.*

Many people have a warped sense of who God is so they don't
spend time with Him. Some think they can only worship Him
from far away. Others just *talk at Him* without stopping to listen.
Jesus longs to have a genuine and unique relationship with each
of us. *He is not holding back His Love.* We can come to Him
confidently and rest in His salvation. He really Loves us.

*"For I know the plans I have for you," declares the LORD,
"plans to prosper you and not to harm you, plans to give you
hope and a future. Then you will call on me and come and pray
to me, and I will listen to you. You will seek me and find me
when you seek me with all your heart. I will be found by you,"
declares the Lord,*

Jeremiah 29:11-14a NIV

The sentences in the scripture above build upon one another.

Once you are convinced that God is for you, you can approach Him *with the right mindset.* Then you can seek Him with your whole heart and you will find Him!

Can anything ever separate us from Christ's love? Does it mean he no longer loves us if we have trouble or calamity, or are persecuted, or hungry, or destitute, or in danger, or threatened with death? No, despite all these things, overwhelming victory is ours through Christ, who loved us.

And I am convinced that nothing can ever separate us from God's love. Neither death nor life, neither angels nor demons, neither our fears for today nor our worries about tomorrow— not even the powers of hell can separate us from God's love. No power in the sky above or in the earth below—indeed, nothing in all creation will ever be able to separate us from the love of God that is revealed in Christ Jesus our Lord.

Romans 8:35, 37-39 NLT

The person who says *yes* to Jesus is *not exempt* from difficulty on this earth. Satan, your enemy, hates all of humanity and has plans to harm us all. But sometimes people create their own chaos for themselves and others. God Loves you no matter where your chaos came from. He wants to help you with every problem you face and has plans to give you overwhelming victory!

So you will dance through the trials of your life, *but not alone!* Jesus will lead. Some days will be simple—like a slow side-step. But when the unexpected *dips* come, the Spirit knows what's ahead and will hold you steady. If you are confident in His Agape Love, He will lead you through to the very end of your song!

Many Christians begin *fighting against the Lord* during trying times instead of dancing *with* Him. They don't rely on God's Word to guide them, and they don't know the power of joy and praise in the valley. That's because they are not *convinced* of His Love. Instead, they create their own solo dance routine. It feels easier to follow their own way for a while—*but that solo dance will never end well.* If the Holy Spirit corrects you for not trusting Him, it's because *He Loves you* and wants to rescue you. Take His hand and get back in the dance with Jesus!

The LORD your God is in your midst; he is a warrior who can deliver. He takes great delight in you; he renews you by his love; he shouts for joy over you.

Zephaniah 3:17 NET

The night Jesus was betrayed, He told His disciples that they would abandon Him in His most difficult hour. Peter, one of Jesus' most loyal disciples, insisted that he would *never* deny Him. But Jesus told Peter that before the rooster crowed in the early morning hours, he would have denied Jesus three times. And that's what happened—in a most heartbreaking and agonizing way.

Peter felt so horrible—like a traitor and a failure. He even wondered if Jesus really was the Messiah. How could He be? He just got killed! Peter was devastated, confused and heartbroken. He had lost his best friend and mentor. I believe Peter must have wondered how Jesus healed the sick and raised the dead but couldn't save Himself. His mind must have been swirling with so many confusing thoughts! And though he tried to remember all the things Jesus had said to prepare them for His death, it just didn't make any sense. Peter had healed the sick and had driven demons out of people *in Jesus' name*, but he thought the power was gone. He stopped fishing for souls and went back to his fishing boat, disillusioned and heartbroken.

But after Jesus rose from the dead, everything changed! He appeared to His disciples many times to encourage their faith, to give them instructions for their future, and to heal their broken hearts. Jesus knew Peter's heart was aching and that seeing Him risen again just caused him more *shame.*

So Jesus asked Peter two times if he *Agape* Loved Him, and both times Peter answered, "You know that I love you with a *friendship* love." But the third time, Jesus lowered His expectations and asked Peter if he loved Him as a friend. Peter *grieved* that Jesus would have to change the question. But in that moment, Jesus demonstrated the Agape Love of the Father and accepted Peter just as he was! Peter had denied Jesus three times, but that day, Jesus gave Peter three chances to affirm his devotion for Him. All three times, Jesus affirmed Peter's calling to minister to the beautiful Jewish people! Later, the Holy Spirit baptized Peter in Agape Love and he never again denied the Lord. In fact, Peter was persecuted and killed for sharing the Gospel. He danced with Agape Love to the very end!

But you, O Lord, are a God of compassion and mercy, slow to get angry and filled with unfailing love and faithfulness.

Psalm 86:15 NLT

In *The Beautiful Dream,* right before the dance, I felt self-conscious. I thought I might disappoint Him. But when Jesus touched me I was filled with Love and confidence *that came from Him.* His Love changed everything and gave me what I needed to live in joy and victory! There may be moments in our *dance* that we slump into confusion or lose focus. The music may grow faint, but do not fear or give up. *Hold on to Jesus* and trust in His unfailing Love!

So then, since we have a great High Priest who has entered heaven, Jesus the Son of God, let us hold firmly to what we believe. This High Priest of ours understands our weaknesses, for he faced all of the same testings we do, yet he did not sin. So let us come boldly to the throne of our gracious God. There we will receive his mercy, and we will find grace to help us when we need it most.

Hebrews 4:14-16 NLT

If you know Jesus, His blood has qualified you to approach God. You don't have to go through an earthly priest or minister because the Spirit is in you. Your High Priest, Jesus, understands and He will minister to you personally!

And you also were included in Christ when you heard the message of truth, the gospel of your salvation. When you believed, you were marked in him with a seal, the promised Holy Spirit, who is a deposit guaranteeing our inheritance until the redemption of those who are God's possession—to the praise of his glory.

Ephesians 1:13-14 NIV

When you said *yes* to Jesus, you were *born again* instantly. God deposited His Spirit inside you marking you as His child. His Spirit gave you Agape Love. Your lifestyle of Love and grace shows that Holy Spirit lives in you!

If you love Me, keep My commandments. And I will pray the Father, and He will give you another Helper, that He may abide with you forever—the Spirit of truth, whom the world cannot receive, because it neither sees Him nor knows Him; but you know Him, for He dwells with you and will be in you. I will not leave you orphans; I will come to you.

John 14:15-18 NKJV

So, what are those commands again? There are lots of them, but they all rest upon two commands of Love and the Spirit in us makes it possible for us to keep them.

Jesus said to him, "'You shall love the LORD your God with all your heart, with all your soul, and with all your mind.' This is the first and great commandment. And the second is like it: 'You shall love your neighbor as yourself.' On these two commandments hang all the Law and the Prophets."

Matthew 22: 37-40 NKJV

The Kingdom is filled with Agape Love! In *The Beautiful Dream* I was permeated with Love the moment Jesus touched me until the moment I felt ashamed for not being seated. God is trying to tell us to focus on His Love and not on our faults and imperfections! God wants us to be *impressed with His grace* instead of trying to impress God with our ability to be perfect. Relax. *Let God's Love set the atmosphere for your life and dance free of shame!* Abba has placed His Seal of authenticity in us and we are His own!

Place me like a seal over your heart, like a seal on your arm; for love is as strong as death, its jealousy unyielding as the grave. It burns like blazing fire, like a mighty flame.

Song of Solomon 8:6 NIV

Declaration

GOD SHOUTS FOR JOY OVER ME!

56

Treasures in Heaven

And my God will liberally supply (fill until full) your every need according to His riches in glory in Christ Jesus.
Philippians 4:19 AMP

Jesus knows what we need. He lived on the earth in flesh and blood just like us. Jesus felt the biting cold winter wind and the burning summer sun. He allowed Himself to go hungry so He would understand what an empty stomach felt like. Jesus created the earth and was the King of kings, but He chose to live a humble life in human form.

A teacher of the Law came to him. "Teacher," he said, "I am ready to go with you wherever you go." Jesus answered him, "Foxes have holes, and birds have nests, but the Son of Man has no place to lie down and rest."
Matthew 8:19-20 GNT

God knows that we need food, clothing and shelter. He wants to provide for us, and He will, if we *seek His Kingdom and His righteousness* alone. He'll give us what we need.

"So don't worry about these things, saying, 'What will we eat? What will we drink? What will we wear?' These things dominate the thoughts of unbelievers, but your heavenly Father already knows all your needs.

Seek the Kingdom of God above all else, and live righteously, and he will give you everything you need. "So don't worry

about tomorrow, for tomorrow will bring its own worries. Today's trouble is enough for today.
Matthew 6:31-34 NLT

Seeking the Lord and *what He wants* should be number one in every area of our lives. Having lots of money is not necessarily evil, but *the love of money* is like an evil weed that takes over and chokes out our Love for God.

But godliness with contentment is great gain. For we brought nothing into the world, and we can take nothing out of it. But if we have food and clothing, we will be content with that. Those who want to get rich fall into temptation and a trap and into many foolish and harmful desires that plunge people into ruin and destruction. For the love of money is a root of all kinds of evil. Some people, eager for money, have wandered from the faith and pierced themselves with many griefs.
1 Timothy 6:6-10 NIV

The ways of God's Kingdom are so different from the ways of this world! Many in the world find their pleasure, identity and self-esteem from fancy food, nice clothing, beautiful homes and their body's appearance. *God's children* find their pleasure, identity and self-esteem in the Agape Love of their Father. There is nothing wrong with having nice things if the Spirit has led you to have them. But if those *things*, or the lack of them *define* you or keep you from spending time with God, your faith is at risk. You are not what you have or look like on the outside. What's on the inside is who you truly are!

If you are suffering financially right now, do not feel *ashamed* and *compare* yourself to others. You are already rich in God! You are seated at the same royal Table in the heavenly realms as your Brothers and Sisters in Christ. What God is looking for are *hearts of humility and Love.* It's important that your needs are met, so be humble enough to accept help if you need it. But do not let this difficult season you are in cause you to *obsessively desire* what another person has. Rich or poor—don't let your heart become angry, jealous or prideful. Keep your spirit "poor" by investing your heart of Love in the Kingdom of Heaven!

Blessed [spiritually prosperous, happy, to be admired] are the poor in spirit [those devoid of spiritual arrogance, those who regard themselves as insignificant], for theirs is the kingdom of heaven [both now and forever].

Matthew 5:3 AMP

God calls some of His children to be financially wealthy because of their great humility and generosity toward God's Kingdom and the poor. Jesus cautions us to let His Love be our desire for financial prosperity. Getting out of debt can free us to be able to be generous with our money.

Pay your taxes, too, for these same reasons. For government workers need to be paid. They are serving God in what they do. Give to everyone what you owe them: Pay your taxes and government fees to those who collect them, and give respect and honor to those who are in authority.

Owe nothing to anyone — except for your obligation to love one another. If you love your neighbor, you will fulfill the requirements of God's law. For the commandments say, "You must not commit adultery. You must not murder. You must not steal. You must not covet." These — and other such commandments — are summed up in this one commandment: "Love your neighbor as yourself." Love does no wrong to others, so love fulfills the requirements of God's law.

Romans 13:6-10 NLT

It is not God's will for anyone to be lacking and poor. So God requires the financially blessed to *voluntarily* open their hearts and hands generously with a cheerful attitude!

But if there are any poor Israelites in your towns when you arrive in the land the LORD your God is giving you, do not be hard-hearted or tightfisted toward them. Instead, be generous and lend them whatever they need. Give generously to the poor, not grudgingly, for the LORD *your God will bless you in everything you do. There will always be some in the land who are poor. That is why I am commanding you to share freely with the poor and with other Israelites in need.*

Deuteronomy 15:7-8, 10-11 NLT

If you lose everything in this life but know Jesus and His Love, you still have everything. But if you choose the treasures of this world over the treasure of God's Love—you've lost everything.

A certain ruler asked him, "Good teacher, what must I do to inherit eternal life?" "Why do you call me good?" Jesus answered. "No one is good—except God alone. You know the commandments: 'You shall not commit adultery, you shall not murder, you shall not steal, you shall not give false testimony, honor your father and mother.'" "All these I have kept since I was a boy," he said.

When Jesus heard this, he said to him, "You still lack one thing. Sell everything you have and give to the poor, and you will have treasure in heaven. Then come, follow me." When he heard this, he became very sad, because he was very wealthy. Jesus looked at him and said, "How hard it is for the rich to enter the kingdom of God! Indeed, it is easier for a camel to go through the eye of a needle than for someone who is rich to enter the kingdom of God." Those who heard this asked, "Who then can be saved?" Jesus replied, "What is impossible with man is possible with God."

Peter said to him, "We have left all we had to follow you!" "Truly I tell you," Jesus said to them, "no one who has left home or wife or brothers or sisters or parents or children for the sake of the kingdom of God will fail to receive many times as much in this age, and in the age to come eternal life."

Luke 18:18-30 NIV

The Spirit must be *Lord over our will*. He doesn't require every person to sell everything and give it to the poor, but He does ask *some* to do so. God requires all of us *to be willing* to give up

322

everything to follow Jesus. It is from that place of *complete surrender of the will* that the Father's generosity can lead us into the plans He has for us in the Kingdom. His heart of generosity will never disappoint us!

"Ever since the days of your ancestors, you have scorned my decrees and failed to obey them. Now return to me, and I will return to you," says the LORD of Heaven's Armies. "But you ask, 'How can we return when we have never gone away?' Should people cheat God? Yet you have cheated me! But you ask, 'What do you mean? When did we ever cheat you?' You have cheated me of the tithes and offerings due to me. You are under a curse, for your whole nation has been cheating me."

"Bring all the tithes into the storehouse so there will be enough food in my Temple. If you do," says the LORD of Heaven's Armies, "I will open the windows of heaven for you. I will pour out a blessing so great you won't have enough room to take it in! Try it! Put me to the test! Your crops will be abundant, for I will guard them from insects and disease. Your grapes will not fall from the vine before they are ripe," says the LORD of Heaven's Armies. "Then all nations will call you blessed, for your land will be such a delight," says the LORD of Heaven's Armies.

Malachi 3:7-12 NLT

Entire nations can suffer when God's people decide to love their money. God has *commanded* that we give 10% of our income to Him. This is called the *tithe*. Giving above 10% is an *offering* and is also required. The Spirit will guide you and tell you which Kingdom ministry to give your tithes and offerings to. Investing in God's Kingdom from a heart filled with *Agape Love* is storing up *treasures in Heaven!*

In *The Beautiful Dream*, my husband and I were sitting on concrete bleachers. The empty bleachers can represent the stadiums of people who have not heard about Jesus. As the Body of Christ, we can find them and tell them the Good News!

Do not lay up for yourselves treasures on earth, where moth and rust destroy and where thieves break in and steal, but lay up for yourselves treasures in heaven, where neither moth nor rust destroys and where thieves do not break in and steal. For where your treasure is, there your heart will be also.

Matthew 6:19-21 NKJV

God has called us to invest in His treasures—*people!* His ways are *higher* than ours and so full of Love! God's children can *rise above the gravity of earthly wealth* to be seated in the heavenly realms. That's where we can see the Father's extravagant and generous Love from a different perspective! His riches are lavishly multiplied from His Table to bless those in need *financially, physically, spiritually and in every way!* And He has chosen *us* to distribute His limitless expressions of supernatural Agape Love!

Declaration

I'M STORING UP TREASURES IN HEAVEN!

57

House of Prayer for All Nations

And foreigners who bind themselves to the LORD to minister to him, to love the name of the LORD, and to be his servants, all who keep the Sabbath without desecrating it and who hold fast to my covenant—these I will bring to my holy mountain and give them joy in my house of prayer. Their burnt offerings and sacrifices will be accepted on my altar; for my house will be called a house of prayer for all nations.

Isaiah 56:6-7 NIV

I believe the *House of Prayer* is the place Jesus took me to in the third scene of *The Beautiful Dream!* It is positioned *high up on God's Holy Mountain,* where His presence dwells. All of God's children from every nation who follow Jesus wholeheartedly, are invited to this House of Prayer by *resting in the Sabbath grace of Jesus Christ!*

On reaching Jerusalem, Jesus entered the temple courts and began driving out those who were buying and selling there. He overturned the tables of the money changers and the benches of those selling doves, and would not allow anyone to carry merchandise through the temple courts. And as he taught them, he said, "Is it not written: 'My house will be called a house of prayer for all nations'? But you have made it 'a den of robbers.'" The chief priests and the teachers of the law heard this and began looking for a way to kill him, for they feared him, because the whole crowd was amazed at his teaching.

Mark 11:15-18 NIV

Jesus was *passionate* about God's *House of Prayer* where God's presence was intended to dwell. But the priests were unmoved by God's presence and had allowed the temple to become commonplace and unholy. Now *we* are the temple of the Holy Spirit. We live righteously by the power of the Spirit of grace, not by our own strength. What did Jesus mean by "a den of thieves?"

The LORD gave another message to Jeremiah. He said, "Go to the entrance of the LORD's Temple, and give this message to the people: 'O Judah, listen to this message from the LORD! Listen to it, all of you who worship here! This is what the LORD of Heaven's Armies, the God of Israel, says:

"'Even now, if you quit your evil ways, I will let you stay in your own land. But don't be fooled by those who promise you safety simply because the LORD's Temple is here. They chant, "The LORD's Temple is here! The LORD's Temple is here!" But I will be merciful only if you stop your evil thoughts and deeds and start treating each other with justice; only if you stop exploiting foreigners, orphans, and widows; only if you stop your murdering; and only if you stop harming yourselves by worshiping idols. Then I will let you stay in this land that I gave to your ancestors to keep forever.

"'Don't be fooled into thinking that you will never suffer because the Temple is here. It's a lie! Do you really think you can steal, murder, commit adultery, lie, and burn incense to Baal and all those other new gods of yours, and then come here and stand before me in my Temple and chant, "We are safe!" — only to go right back to all those evils again? Don't you yourselves admit that this Temple, which bears my name, has become a den of thieves? Surely I see all the evil going on there. I, the LORD, have spoken!

Jeremiah 7:1-11 NLT

When Jesus was driving out the buyers and sellers in the temple, he was *painting a picture so we could understand*. *Compromise* has no place in the hearts of believers. The world will turn to fleshly entertainment, love of money, philosophy, fame, religion and sin of all kinds. But our faith rests on Jesus.

Can we *claim grace* and also *oppress* the helpless and needy? Can we enjoy sin and draw near to the Most Holy God? Can we *change* the Word of God to blend with culture and then also expect the Word Himself to back us up? Can we *close our eyes* to the wicked laws of our land when we have the power to change them and also call on God to bless our land?

The light of God's House drives out darkness. Those who sit at God's Table will have God's Love and righteousness at the core of their values and the courage to stand up and make a difference. If we don't overturn the tables of our own hearts, the Lord will have to do it for us *to wake us up.*

Don't team up with those who are unbelievers. How can righteousness be a partner with wickedness? How can light live with darkness? What harmony can there be between Christ and the devil? How can a believer be a partner with an unbeliever? And what union can there be between God's temple and idols?

For we are the temple of the living God. As God said: "I will live in them and walk among them. I will be their God, and they will be my people. Therefore, come out from among unbelievers, and separate yourselves from them, says the LORD. *Don't touch their filthy things, and I will welcome you. And I will be your Father, and you will be my sons and daughters, says the* LORD *Almighty."*

2 Corinthians 6:14-18 NLT

We do not earn our salvation by living a good lifestyle, but *we live good lifestyles because we are in Christ.* When we trusted Jesus, He took us to be seated in God's presence *where there is no sin,* so we could have the power to live victoriously against sin on earth. We Love all people with our Father's Agape Love, therefore, we don't participate with others in sin. His Love has no sin in it. We live and Love from a Kingdom that is not earthly. Our bodies, souls and spirits belong to Jesus now and we live by His Spirit, seated at His Table in *The House of Prayer for All Nations!*

God has never been *confined* to a building. But while Israel was in the wilderness with Moses, God came in tangible power and dwelled with them in a special *portable tabernacle* that looked like a big tent. They carried the tabernacle into the Promised Land with Joshua as their leader. *Eventually,* King Solomon, built a beautiful temple on Jerusalem's mountain to replace the tabernacle. Solomon prayed a *humble and powerful prayer* on the day they dedicated the temple to the Lord.

When Solomon finished praying, fire came down from heaven and consumed the burnt offering and the sacrifices, and the glory of the LORD filled the temple. The priests could not enter the temple of the LORD because the glory of the LORD filled it. When all the Israelites saw the fire coming down and the glory of the LORD above the temple, they knelt on the pavement with their faces to the ground, and they worshiped and gave thanks to the LORD, saying, "He is good; his love endures forever."

2 Chronicles 7:1-3 NIV

Even though the Spirit did not dwell in their *bodies*, the people of Israel *experienced the presence and glory of the Lord* on the day the temple was dedicated! God's fire came from Heaven into the Temple and they were awestruck by the Lord just by being near His glory! They worshiped and thanked Him because *they felt God's power, goodness and Love in a tangible way!* This fire from Heaven was the same Holy fire of the Spirit that came upon the heads of Jesus' disciples in Jerusalem at Pentecost!

When the day of Pentecost came, they were all together in one place. Suddenly a sound like the blowing of a violent wind came from heaven and filled the whole house where they were sitting. They saw what seemed to be tongues of fire that separated and came to rest on each of them. All of them were filled with the Holy Spirit and began to speak in other tongues as the Spirit enabled them.

Acts 2:1-4 NIV

They too were awestruck and worshiped the Lord with joy when the Holy Spirit baptized them in holy fire! They went out on the street, and by the power of Holy Spirit, they declared the wonders of God in foreign languages they did not know. About 3,000 people from different countries came to faith in Jesus that day as the new Temple of the Lord, the hearts of those believers, became *The House of Prayer for All Nations!*

So Solomon finished the Temple of the LORD, as well as the royal palace. He completed everything he had planned to do in the construction of the Temple and the palace. Then one night the LORD appeared to Solomon and said,

"I have heard your prayer and have chosen this Temple as the place for making sacrifices. At times I might shut up the heavens so that no rain falls, or command grasshoppers to devour your crops, or send plagues among you. Then if my people who are called by my name will humble themselves and pray and seek my face and turn from their wicked ways, I will hear from heaven and will forgive their sins and restore their land. My eyes will be open and my ears attentive to every prayer made in this place. For I have chosen this Temple and set it apart to be holy—a place where my name will be honored forever. I will always watch over it, for it is dear to my heart.
2 Chronicles 7:11-16 NLT

The Lord allows trials to bring us to our knees in prayer. Jesus wants us to *seek His face*. He has plans to *restore the land* and He will do it through His children who are seated at His Table in *The House of Prayer for All Nations!*

In the first scene of *The Beautiful Dream*, Jesus danced with me and dipped me to the left, symbolizing the baptism that puts to death the old self. I followed His lead as He showed me how to turn over the tables in my heart. He dipped me to the right, symbolic of the Spirit's fire baptism. This is the Baptism of the Holy Spirit who empowers us to live supernaturally on this earth for God's Kingdom and glory. Jesus wants us to be seated in both baptisms. We can't start setting up our own tables in our hearts. There is only one Table in the temple of our hearts now and it is empowered by the wonderful Holy Spirit!

Just as the Holy Spirit filled the tabernacle in the wilderness, the temple in Jerusalem and the disciples at Pentecost, His fire falls powerfully on believers all over the world today! God is calling the Body of Christ to *overturn any worldly tables in their hearts* so that they can become a holy temple for God's purpose in these end times. With great anticipation, joy, submission and Love, believers everywhere are seated together with God at His Table. God's children all over the world are gathered together in one place where they can boldly bring their requests to God: *The House of Prayer for All Nations!*

Declaration

**I'M SEATED IN THE
HOUSE OF PRAYER FOR ALL NATIONS!**

58

The Most Holy Place

In *The Beautiful Dream*, Jesus escorted me into a Room. It is obvious that I had not gone to Heaven itself because I was *not paying attention*. In Heaven, we will be fully aware! The only thing I saw vividly was the pink dress—representing the Holy Spirit. Everything else in the Room was seen *in the Spirit*. I knew where things were and who was in specific places *without seeing them*. All these things indicate that this Room is the *spiritual place* where we are seated with God now in the heavenly realms. There were no shadows in this Room. *This Room was full of light!*

This is the message we have heard from him and declare to you: God is light; in him there is no darkness at all.

1 John 1:5 NIV

The room in the dream had no doors. The only opening was wide and curved at the top edges. The moment Jesus died on the cross, *the curtain* that covered the entrance to the Most Holy Place in the temple in Jerusalem was torn in two by God. The *Most Holy Place* was the room in the Jewish temple where the presence of God was *seated*, or *rested*, on the Ark of the Covenant.

The Ark of the Covenant was a beautiful chest containing the 10 Commandments written on stone, a jar of manna and Aaron's staff. Only the high priest could enter the Most Holy Place one special day each year to intercede for the sins of Israel. He could only do that after a specific animal had been sacrificed

331

and its blood was sprinkled as God had instructed. The other priests could worship and pray on the other side of the curtain or in the special courtyard, but never in the Most Holy Place. Other Israelites worshiped from afar.

When Jesus died, His blood made *atonement* for the sin of the whole world, *once for all,* and the actual curtain to the Most Holy Place ripped in two pieces from top to bottom! When Jesus was raised from the dead, *He* became our High Priest, ushering us directly into the Most Holy Place!

The Spirit no longer rests on the Ark behind a curtain in Jerusalem's temple, but in the bodies of those who have been spiritually sprinkled with Jesus' Blood by faith! We have the *laws of God* written on our hearts, we eat the *Bread of Life* and Jesus has given us *His staff of authority*—all because the Holy Spirit lives in us and we are in Christ! We have been invited to *be seated* in the *Most Holy Place!*

And so, dear brothers and sisters, we can boldly enter heaven's Most Holy Place because of the blood of Jesus. By his death Jesus opened a new and life-giving way through the curtain ["the curtain, that is, his body" NIV, "the veil, that is, his flesh" NKJV], into the Most Holy Place. And since we have a great High Priest who rules over God's house, let us go right into the presence of God with sincere hearts fully trusting him. For our guilty consciences have been sprinkled with Christ's blood to make us clean, and our bodies have been washed with pure water. Let us hold tightly without wavering to the hope we affirm, for God can be trusted to keep his promise.
Hebrews 10:19-23 NLT

The body of Jesus was the curtain that was torn! Through Him our guilty consciences have been made clean and even our bodies have been washed and purified! Thank You, Jesus!

First of all, then, I urge that requests, prayers, intercessions, and thanks be offered on behalf of all people, even for kings and all who are in authority, that we may lead a peaceful and quiet life in all godliness and dignity. Such prayer for all is good and welcomed before God our Savior, since he wants all people to be saved and to come to a knowledge of the truth. For there is one God and one intermediary between God and humanity, Christ Jesus, himself human, who gave himself as a ransom for all, revealing God's purpose at his appointed time.

1 Timothy 2:1-6 NET

Jesus was *the only escort* in the dream, and the entrance was located right behind *His chair.* Jesus is the Door — the only way to come to God!

I am the door. If anyone enters by Me, he will be saved, and will go in and out and find pasture.

John 10:9 NKJV

Jesus is the door to our freedom! He is the way out of every bondage of the enemy! And *Jesus, the Door,* has control of the entrance to the heavenly realms. No demon can come into this holy place where God brings Heaven to earth.

Therefore, since we are surrounded by such a huge crowd of witnesses to the life of faith, let us strip off every weight that slows us down, especially the sin that so easily trips us up. And let us run with endurance the race God has set before us. We do this by keeping our eyes on Jesus, the champion who initiates and perfects our faith. Because of the joy awaiting him, he endured the cross, disregarding its shame. Now he is seated in the place of honor beside God's throne. Think of all the hostility he endured from sinful people; then you won't become weary and give up.

Hebrews 12:1-3 NLT

Jesus is seated in *the highest place of honor* at God's Table! If you are following Jesus, He is seated directly across from you so that you can keep your eyes on Him!

I am with you always, to the end of the age.

Matthew 28:20b NASB

You will be walking around in your body on earth, but at the same time, seated with God in the heavenly realms. You don't have to worry because God is *not going to leave the Most Holy Place* to do something else. You're safe!

See how great a love the Father has given us, that we would be called children of God; and in fact we are.
1 John 3:1a NASB

Jesus has brought you to the Father, the One who Loves you so much that He sent His Son to die in your place. The Father has chosen to seat you next to His heart!

Jesus replied, "I assure you, no one can enter the Kingdom of God without being born of water and the Spirit. Humans can reproduce only human life, but the Holy Spirit gives birth to spiritual life. So don't be surprised when I say, 'You must be born again.' The wind blows wherever it wants. Just as you can hear the wind but can't tell where it comes from or where it is going, so you can't explain how people are born of the Spirit.
John 3:5-8 NLT

We really have a hard time understanding how we can be born again by the Holy Spirit. That's because we can't *see* what's going on when we say *yes* to Jesus. What God does for us through the Holy Spirit is more powerful than we realize! I can tell you from *The Beautiful Dream* God gave me that when Jesus touched me I became a different person and I felt like I was in Heaven—literally. When Jesus took me to His Table in the heavenly realms the atmosphere was the same!

The Holy Spirit is the presence of God—the atmosphere of Heaven. He brings the glory of God to us when we are born again. In the dream, I was saturated with the fruit of the Spirit and I felt so free! That's the power of the Holy Spirit within us. But we have to be that tree that keeps growing in the presence of God to spiritually feel the effects of His wind blowing through the leaves of our lives. My unbelief was exposed when

I felt fear and shame. But the veil (Jesus' body) was torn so I could come into the Most Holy Place free of guilt! Sometimes we have to go back to *the dance* and remember what Jesus has done for us!

I pray not only for them, but also for those who believe in me because of their message. I pray that they may all be one. Father! May they be in us, just as you are in me and I am in you. May they be one, so that the world will believe that you sent me. I gave them the same glory you gave me, so that they may be one, just as you and I are one: I in them and you in me, so that they may be completely one, in order that the world may know that you sent me and that you love them as you love me.

John 17:20-23 GNT

We are now *one with God*. Hallelujah! Male and female, we all live in unity with Him. Holy means *set apart*. When we were *born again* we were cleansed by the Blood of Jesus and made righteous *in Christ*. That is why Jesus has taken us to the *Most Holy Place* where we are *set apart* from the world. We live on the earth, but *we aren't of the world* anymore.

As the world gets darker and darker, it will not be possible for a person to *pretend* they are a Christian anymore. They will either live from the Holy of Holies and stand out like a bright light, or they will live from the earthly realm and blend in with the darkness of the world. It's time to *wake up and be seated* in the *Most Holy Place*. We have to live from a higher place, separated from the evil of the world for our own sake, for the sake of the lost and for the sake of future generations.

Jesus met with His disciples in an *upstairs room* for the Last Supper the night before His crucifixion. And after He rose again, the believers also met in an *upstairs room*. Jesus was preparing them to live from a higher spiritual place!

Then they returned to Jerusalem from the mountain called Olivet, which is near Jerusalem, a Sabbath day's journey away.

When they had entered the city, they went up to the upstairs room where they were staying, that is, Peter, John, James, and Andrew, Philip and Thomas, Bartholomew and Matthew, James the son of Alphaeus, Simon the Zealot, and Judas the son of James. All these were continually devoting themselves with one mind to prayer, along with the women, and Mary the mother of Jesus, and with His brothers.

Acts 1:12-14 NASB

I believe God chose *mountains* and *upper rooms* because they were *symbolic* of the heavenly realms!

At this point I had another vision and saw an open door in heaven. And the voice that sounded like a trumpet, which I had heard speaking to me before, said, "Come up here, and I will show you what must happen after this."

Revelation 4:1 GNT

We don't have to live *underneath* the harassment of the devil. Satan's air space has been restricted. The *Most Holy Place* is a "no-fly zone" where only those who have been sprinkled by the Blood and are *set apart for God* can dwell! It is *in Christ* that we are *set apart* from the world. We are different from those who don't know Jesus, but we're not ashamed of it! *We're amazed!* We will experience troubles on the earth, but we face them from God's perspective as we follow the Holy Spirit. Jesus has taken us *higher* to the *Upper Room!* There is no middle ground. If we want to live victoriously in Christ, we need to wake up, pay attention to the Spirit and *be seated with God in the Most Holy Place!*

Declaration

**JESUS' FLESH WAS TORN
SO I COULD BE SEATED IN THE MOST HOLY PLACE!**

59

The Gifts of the Spirit

God has created each one of us unique, with different personalities, abilities, desires and strengths. His plan is so complex and fluid that He can change it continuously depending on whether or not we are *paying attention* to Him. God can take even our mistakes and flip them for good *if we will wake up and follow the Spirit!* Jesus' plan is to assign each of us to a useful purpose in His Body where we become a blessing to one another and His creation.

God has blended together the body, giving greater honor to the lesser member, so that there may be no division in the body, but the members may have mutual concern for one another. If one member suffers, everyone suffers with it. If a member is honored, all rejoice with it.

1 Corinthians 12:24b-26 NET

Every service in the Kingdom is *equally important,* whether visible or not, and is maximized when we sincerely care about and honor one another. Your obedience to serve Jesus by blessing anyone who is weak is always noticed by the King, and He will reward you in His Kingdom! Holy Spirit wants to empower you supernaturally for His glory.

Therefore you do not lack any spiritual gift as you eagerly wait for our Lord Jesus Christ to be revealed.

1 Corinthians 1:7 NIV

These gifts aren't talents we develop, though God uses them as well. The Spirit equips us with *supernatural unearned gifts* to minister to believers and non-believers.

There are different kinds of spiritual gifts, but the same Spirit is the source of them all. There are different kinds of service, but we serve the same Lord. God works in different ways, but it is the same God who does the work in all of us. A spiritual gift is given to each of us so we can help each other. To one person the Spirit gives the ability to give wise advice; to another the same Spirit gives a message of special knowledge. The same Spirit gives great faith to another, and to someone else the one Spirit gives the gift of healing. He gives one person the power to perform miracles, and another the ability to prophesy. He gives someone else the ability to discern whether a message is from the Spirit of God or from another spirit. Still another person is given the ability to speak in unknown languages, while another is given the ability to interpret what is being said. It is the one and only Spirit who distributes all these gifts. He alone decides which gift each person should have.

1 Corinthians 12:4-11 NLT

The gifts of the Spirit are amazing. The Spirit will give someone a *word of wisdom* for someone else and it will be exactly what they needed to hear from God. Jesus gave the woman at the well a *word of knowledge* when He told her things about her life that a stranger should not have known. There are many gifts of the Spirit and *God* gives them to His children to build up the Body of Christ.

For you are all children of God through faith in Christ Jesus. And all who have been united with Christ in baptism have put on Christ, like putting on new clothes. There is no longer Jew or Gentile, slave or free, male and female. For you are all one in Christ Jesus. And now that you belong to Christ, you are the true children of Abraham. You are his heirs, and God's promise to Abraham belongs to you.

Galatians 3:26-29 NLT

We are still biologically male or female on earth. But our *flesh* died when we died with Christ in baptism and we were raised to the heavenly realms with Him. Male or female, rich or poor, and whatever you might look like here on earth—we are all given the same grace, the same Holy Spirit and gifts from the same source. God makes the plans and God gives the power. We must be seated, trust and obey Him.

"Again, the Kingdom of Heaven can be illustrated by the story of a man going on a long trip. He called together his servants and entrusted his money to them while he was gone. He gave five bags of silver to one, two bags of silver to another, and one bag of silver to the last—dividing it in proportion to their abilities. He then left on his trip.

The servant who received the five bags of silver began to invest the money and earned five more. The servant with two bags of silver also went to work and earned two more. But the servant who received the one bag of silver dug a hole in the ground and hid the master's money.

After a long time their master returned from his trip and called them to give an account of how they had used his money. The servant to whom he had entrusted the five bags of silver came forward with five more and said, 'Master, you gave me five bags of silver to invest, and I have earned five more.'

The master was full of praise. 'Well done, my good and faithful servant. You have been faithful in handling this small amount, so now I will give you many more responsibilities. Let's celebrate together!'

The servant who had received the two bags of silver came forward and said, 'Master, you gave me two bags of silver to invest, and I have earned two more.'

The master said, 'Well done, my good and faithful servant. You have been faithful in handling this small amount, so now I will give you many more responsibilities. Let's celebrate together!'

Then the servant with the one bag of silver came and said, 'Master, I knew you were a harsh man, harvesting crops you didn't plant and gathering crops you didn't cultivate. I was afraid I would lose your money, so I hid it in the earth. Look, here is your money back.'

But the master replied, 'You wicked and lazy servant! If you knew I harvested crops I didn't plant and gathered crops I didn't cultivate, why didn't you deposit my money in the bank? At least I could have gotten some interest on it.'

Then he ordered, 'Take the money from this servant, and give it to the one with the ten bags of silver. To those who use well what they are given, even more will be given, and they will have an abundance. But from those who do nothing, even what little they have will be taken away. Now throw this useless servant into outer darkness, where there will be weeping and gnashing of teeth.'"

Matthew 25:14-30 NLT

The Love gifts of the Spirit are like *investments* He gives us that will *increase* if we use them. Fear will cause you to disobey and be fruitless. So be strong and very courageous! Allow the Spirit to begin to use you even if you feel what God has given you is small.

For instance: If you are raising a family, which is one of the most powerful callings, do it in the power of the Spirit. If someone in your family is sick, lay hands on them and pray for their healing. If your child has nightmares, command them to leave in the name of Jesus as your child sleeps, and softly declare scripture over them. Ask the Spirit if there is anything external causing the nightmares that you have control over. Ask Holy Spirit how you can express God's Love to your neighbors. The gifts will *multiply* as you use them in the power of Agape Love and with a heart surrendered to Him.

Jesus told the guy with one bag of gold that *he should have deposited it with the bankers.* Perhaps the *bankers* are those who are *already investing and producing interest* in the Kingdom by caring for the poor, spreading the Gospel, etc. Investing *financially* into the Kingdom of God will multiply the resources God has given us. Whatever you do for the Lord, do it because the Spirit prompted you to. Invest out of *Love for God and genuine Love for people.* Don't do it because you're afraid God will punish you. When *Love* is invested by faith, it will bring great eternal returns!

So we are to use our different gifts in accordance with the grace that God has given us. If our gift is to speak God's message, we should do it according to the faith that we have; if it is to serve, we should serve; if it is to teach, we should teach; if it is to encourage others, we should do so. Whoever shares with others should do it generously; whoever has authority should work hard; whoever shows kindness to others should do it cheerfully.

Love must be completely sincere. Hate what is evil, hold on to what is good. Love one another warmly as Christians, and be eager to show respect for one another. Work hard and do not be lazy. Serve the Lord with a heart full of devotion.
Romans 12:6-11 GNT

The Holy Spirit *wants* His gifts to flow through us. It's not prideful for God to use you supernaturally unless you take the glory for yourself, and we can't because we didn't earn them! The Spirit can work through you with supernatural gifts and change someone's life *because you Love.*

Beware of the false prophets, who come to you in sheep's clothing, but inwardly are ravenous wolves. You will know them by their fruits. Grapes are not gathered from thorn bushes, nor figs from thistles, are they? So every good tree bears good fruit, but the bad tree bears bad fruit. A good tree cannot bear bad fruit, nor can a bad tree bear good fruit. Every tree that does not bear good fruit is cut down and thrown into the fire. So then, you will know them by their fruits [character, words, actions, etc.]
Matthew 7:15-20 NASB

In every truly Spirit-led body of believers God appoints mature leaders. They help equip believers to live by the Spirit and they minister to them through the *gifts God has given them.* Don't let your "ministry" be to criticize your leaders. Pray for them and seek to be a blessing!

It will come about after this that I will pour out My Spirit on all mankind; and your sons and your daughters will prophesy, your old men will have dreams, your young men will see visions. And even on the male and female servants I will pour out My Spirit in those days.

Joel 2:28-32 NASB

What I experienced in *The Beautiful Dream* assures me that we are fully equipped by God to accomplish His will. We just have to be seated in the heavenly realms with God and pay careful attention. Holy Spirit wants to empower *all of His children* with supernatural gifts for His glory! Let us not limit how the Spirit wants to work. Humbly *be seated* in the gifts of the Spirit, and *expect* God's Love and power to flow and increase through you in amazing ways for His glory!

Declaration

**THE SPIRIT HAS EMPOWERED US
WITH AGAPE LOVE GIFTS!**

60

Stand Up!

In *The Beautiful Dream*, I had been daydreaming about Jesus when the Holy Spirit asked the Body of Christ to *be seated.* After I came back to my senses and realized everyone had sat down but me, *I felt so ashamed!* Then God and my Brothers and Sisters in Christ stood up. The Holy Spirit said a second time, "Be seated."

In the dream, I was in Love with Jesus, *but I was not paying attention* to the Holy Spirit. This can represent all that can go wrong in a Christian's life when they are caught up in the joy of serving their Savior, but they aren't following His Spirit. *It happens a lot* and can get in the way of a person's spiritual growth. But the Lord is *patient* and *forgiving* as we grow up in Him! Those who follow the Holy Spirit will be *patient* and *forgiving,* just like the Spirit they are following!

Therefore, as God's chosen people, holy and dearly loved, clothe yourselves with compassion, kindness, humility, gentleness and patience. Bear with each other and forgive one another if any of you has a grievance against someone. Forgive as the Lord forgave you. And over all these virtues put on love, which binds them all together in perfect unity.

Let the peace of Christ rule in your hearts, since as members of one body you were called to peace. And be thankful.
Colossians 3:12-15 NIV

The moment we believed in Jesus we became guilt-free. He

clothed us in His righteousness and forgave us. *We must keep that robe on so we can see our Brothers and Sisters in Christ the same way.* Their sins have been atoned for and they have been *redeemed!* Sometimes their spiritual immaturity may show, and you might be tempted to gossip about them. But by *criticizing instead of nurturing,* you are judging from the law and living by the flesh, not by the Spirit of grace.

And above all things have fervent love for one another, for "love will cover a multitude of sins."

1 Peter 4:8 NKJV

We must clothe one another in God's grace and *point each other toward the face of Jesus,* not toward a spirit of shame.

Do not judge others, and you will not be judged. For you will be treated as you treat others. The standard you use in judging is the standard by which you will be judged.

And why worry about a speck in your friend's eye when you have a log in your own? How can you think of saying to your friend, 'Let me help you get rid of that speck in your eye,' when you can't see past the log in your own eye? Hypocrite! First get rid of the log in your own eye; then you will see well enough to deal with the speck in your friend's eye.

Matthew 7:1-5 NLT

Evil religious, jealous and prideful spirits tempt believers to throw darts of guilt, shame, accusation and condemnation at their Brothers and Sisters. Then the devil turns around and brings shame upon them for *misjudging* Christ's Body. So walk in the Spirit of grace. *Jesus made you holy* so you can be seated with God in *His righteousness,* not your own.

Or do you despise the riches of His goodness, forbearance, and longsuffering, not knowing that the goodness of God leads you to repentance?

Romans 2:4 NKJV

Yes, there may be times when Holy Spirit may lead you to talk with someone about their sin.   Just as God's *kindness* led you to repentance, your kindness can do the same.

Dear friends, let us love one another, because love is from God, and everyone who loves has been fathered by God and knows God. The person who does not love does not know God, because God is love. By this the love of God is revealed in us: that God has sent his one and only Son into the world so that we may live through him. In this is love: not that we have loved God, but that he loved us and sent his Son to be the atoning sacrifice for our sins.

Dear friends, if God so loved us, then we also ought to love one another. No one has seen God at any time. If we love one another, God resides in us, and his love is perfected in us. By this we know that we reside in God and he in us: in that he has given us of his Spirit. And we have seen and testify that the Father has sent the Son to be the Savior of the world.

If anyone confesses that Jesus is the Son of God, God resides in him and he in God.

1 John 4:7-15 NET

The Lord has *commanded us* to Love one another because *we are in Jesus* and He is Love. The Lord created us to *need one another* and to *bless one another* in many different ways—led by the Spirit. When you have *thoughts* that would shame a Brother or Sister, it is either your *flesh* that needs to die, or a *whisper* from a demon. Either way, submit to the Lord of Agape Love and resist the thought! It's not who you are in Christ!

As it is, there are many parts, but one body. The eye cannot say to the hand, "I don't need you!" And the head cannot say to the feet, "I don't need you!"

1 Corinthians 12:20-21 NIV

We need each other!   Many Christians think of their local church as a "club" they have joined. They want their club to be the best, so they look for things to criticize about other churches. We have got to *rejoice* when we see our Family doing the works the Father has for them to do! *We are on the same team!* And if we want to see victory in the Kingdom, we have to start *building one another up* instead of tearing each other down. No good ball team can play their best if they hate each other. Our "fighting spirit" should be aimed *against the enemy*, not against the Body of Christ!

"Teacher," said John, "we saw someone driving out demons in your name and we told him to stop, because he was not one of us." "Do not stop him," Jesus said. "For no one who does a miracle in my name can in the next moment say anything bad about me, for whoever is not against us is for us. Truly I tell you, anyone who gives you a cup of water in my name because you belong to the Messiah will certainly not lose their reward.
Mark 9:38-41 NIV

How are we going to see a great move of God's glory if churches or believers within churches are *angry, jealous, competitive* or *gossiping* against one another? Living like that is living from an earthly demonic realm.

Be kindly affectionate to one another with brotherly love, in honor giving preference to one another;
Romans 12:10 NKJV

We know we are supposed to *stand up for believers*, but how do we treat those who don't know the Lord?

Therefore, as we have opportunity, let us do good to all, especially to those who are of the household of faith.
Galatians 6:10 NKJV

God loves everybody and sent Jesus to die for the sins of the world. From a heavenly realms perspective we must remember that everyone's sin has been atoned for, even the ones who have not said *yes* to Jesus. They are precious in God's sight, so they are precious in our sight too. There are some in this world who have *rejected* Jesus and have become filled with evil, seeking ways to hurt others. Of course, we cannot respect them for their evil ways, but we must not give in to the spirit of hatred. Unfortunately, some people need to be put in jail to keep them from hurting others. But we must *forgive them* and pray that they will hear about Jesus and be *saved!* If we want people to come to Jesus, we must *be seated* in prayer and ask God to fill us with the *supernatural power of Agape Love* for one another and for the lost! Otherwise, we open a door of hatred that does not exist in the heavenly realms.

By this all will know that you are My disciples, if you have love for one another.

John 13:35 NKJV

Sometimes we need to *stand up* for our Brothers and Sisters when they make mistakes. We do not tear one another down with our *thoughts, words or actions.* But if we do, we ask God's forgiveness and make things right *from the heart.*

Is there any encouragement from belonging to Christ? Any comfort from his love? Any fellowship together in the Spirit? Are your hearts tender and compassionate? Then make me truly happy by agreeing wholeheartedly with each other, loving one another, and working together with one mind and purpose. Don't be selfish; don't try to impress others. Be humble, thinking of others as better than yourselves. Don't look out only for your own interests, but take an interest in others, too.

Philippians 2:1-4 NLT

Here are some questions we can ask ourselves: "What realm am I living from, the earthly realm of the flesh, or the Loving realm of the Spirit? Who am I dancing with? Who am I seated with? Whose voice do I long to follow and am I listening carefully to the voice of Love, the Holy Spirit? Do I see myself as a saint or a sinner? Am I still carrying fear and shame? Do I see my Brothers and Sisters as redeemed by Jesus' Blood?"

Everything is pure to those whose hearts are pure. But nothing is pure to those who are corrupt and unbelieving, because their minds and consciences are corrupted. Such people claim they know God, but they deny him by the way they live. They are detestable and disobedient, worthless for doing anything good.

Titus 1:15-16 NLT

We cannot stand up for our Brothers and Sisters if we're not yet seated. So be seated in the Agape Love and grace of God! We are no longer impure and unloving. We have been forgiven and filled with the riches of grace! Just as *God stood up for us* we also must *stand up* for one another. So, be seated with God and listen to the Spirit. You might need to stand and sit—*a lot!*

Declaration

**I AM READY TO STAND UP
AND GIVE MY BROTHER'S AND SISTERS
ANOTHER CHANCE TO BE SEATED!**

61

TABLE TALK: *Color Vision*

In this Table Talk, I will share with you the most unusual vision I had up until writing this book. It has been a great encouragement to me. Almost six years after God gave me *The Beautiful Dream*, I began to ask Jesus if I could see Him again in some way. My faith was anchored in Jesus but I *felt* a bit discouraged and weak at that time.

One morning I woke up and still laying in bed, I asked the Lord what He would like to say to me or show me. I closed my eyes and waited to *hear* or *see* from Him. Suddenly I began to see what looked like "paint-by-number" leaves of various vibrant shades of green blowing in the wind on both sides of a gray paved road. I was flying about 15 or 20 feet above the road.

The road seemed to be heading in one direction even though sometimes it slightly twisted and turned. I glided swiftly and effortlessly over it, not knowing what might be ahead. I was being carried along in the air somehow. The unusual leaves were oval-like kidney shapes constantly changing in shape. They were continually moving and being exchanged, making the scene alive, joyful and interesting. I noticed that they arched over me and the road like a thick living canopy.

Way in the distance ahead of me as I flew, an opening to the sky like a light at the end of a tunnel came into my view. Then as the road turned, the foliage would seem to close in and block the sky for a moment. I was captivated by everything going on!

When the sky appeared again, the *profile* of Jesus' face was in the left side of the opening. His face was looking toward the right side of the opening. He had dark brown wavy hair, a beard and I could see the top part of His white robe. If I remember correctly, I saw a bit of His red sash as well. I was still a long distance from Him, flying in His direction.

I kept my eyes on Him in the vision, but then I said, "Jesus," aloud. Immediately His face disappeared, but the rest of the scene continued happening in full motion. My heart sank. I longed to see His face appear again, so I just kept quiet, looking intently and waiting.

I was still flying above the road, and the green leaves were still interchanging as if they were ecstatically cheering me on. But my eyes were fixed on the sky, longing to see Jesus again! Soon, His face appeared again! I kept quiet, with my eyes fixed on Jesus as I continued to fly along toward Him. After a while, the vision just faded away.

This vision encouraged me so much! The Lord wanted me to know that though it seemed at the time that I was getting nowhere in my pursuit of Jesus, I truly was. There was growth happening all around me. I was flying in the power of the Spirit and getting closer to the place He wanted me to be. I was *moving toward* Jesus.

There would be turns ahead and times that I wouldn't see Him. I wouldn't even see the sky at times. But I could be sure that as I kept following the Spirit, He would lead me to my destination—close to Jesus! When I say "close to Him," it doesn't mean that He has left me. Through the Holy Spirit, Jesus and the Father are always with us and in us. But this is a closeness we can pray for that is at another level. It is like coming closer to His light and the revelation of His glory.

But the path of the righteous is like the light of dawn that shines brighter and brighter until the full day.
Proverbs 4:18 NASB

The light dawning is an increase in the presence of God. The Bible says to come near to God, and He will come near to you. Because I was yielding to the Spirit, the Spirit was carrying me closer to Jesus in the heavenly realms.

When I opened my physical mouth and spoke His name, I interrupted the flow of the Spirit in the vision. This is how easily we can disrupt what God is showing us in the *heavenly realms* if we begin *reacting* from the *earthly realm* while He is ministering to us at His Table.

I believe there is a wonderful *change of direction* ahead for all believers who are seeking to follow the Spirit. This vision happened in January of 2019. God's children have had many twists and turns along the road, and many have sought Jesus like never before. There will be more twists and turns ahead.

But I believe there is a great awakening happening in the Body of Christ right now. And if you are pursuing Jesus, you will soon *collide with Him — in a good way!* His power will overtake us, and though the earth may be reeling in chaos, when we are walking hand in hand with Jesus, we will experience phenomenal *spiritual* blue skies in the heavenly realms! In that place of glory, God's Agape Love will draw many into the arms of Jesus!

So keep your *eyes fixed on Jesus* and the ears of your heart *listening attentively to the Spirit* who is carrying you along. Do not live from the earthly realm even though you are living in it. Live seated in the heavenly realms where Jesus is right across the Table from you!

Whatever lies ahead, God's Spirit will be with you and will lead you *toward victory!* Watch expectantly for visions by the Spirit and ask the Lord for revelation and interpretation. Everything He shows you is intended for your good! So lean into His heart of Love and learn from Him. Your light will become brighter and the Holy Spirit will keep you on the path of righteousness.

And best of all, you will get *close* to Jesus. There will be a change in direction and together you will walk out the plans He has for your life in the power of His glory!

"Indeed, my plans are not like your plans, and my deeds are not like your deeds," says the LORD. *"for just as the sky is higher than the earth, so my deeds are superior to your deeds and my plans superior to your plans."*

"The rain and snow fall from the sky and do not return, but instead water the earth and make it produce and yield crops, and provide seed for the planter and food for those who must eat."

"In the same way, the promise that I make does not return to me, having accomplished nothing. No, it is realized as I desire and is fulfilled as I intend."

"Indeed you will go out with joy; you will be led along in peace; the mountains and hills will give a joyful shout before you, and all the trees in the field will clap their hands."

"Evergreens will grow in place of thorn bushes, firs will grow in place of nettles; they will be a monument to the LORD, *a permanent reminder that will remain."*
Isaiah 55:8-13 **NET**

62

Prepare for War!

So the LORD *God said to the serpent, "Because you have done this, [deceived Adam and Eve] cursed are you above all livestock and all wild animals! You will crawl on your belly and you will eat dust all the days of your life. And I will put enmity [fighting] between you and the woman, and between your offspring and hers; he [Jesus] will crush your head, and you will strike his heel."*

Genesis 3:14-15 NIV

God was pronouncing judgment on Satan and his demons. Jesus is the offspring of the woman because Mary gave birth to Jesus in the natural realm. Satan thought he had triumphed over Abba's precious Son when Jesus was *crushed for our sins* on the cross. But really, Satan only *bruised his heel!* Jesus gave Satan a *deadly blow to the head* and then rose from the dead! Our enemy is *already defeated* by the Blood of Jesus and will be locked up forever at the end of time! The Bride of Christ is *the spiritual woman* that Satan and his demons are targeting now, *so prepare for war!*

Loving God means keeping his commandments, and his commandments are not burdensome. For every child of God defeats this evil world, and we achieve this victory through our faith. And who can win this battle against the world? Only those who believe that Jesus is the Son of God.

1 John 5:3-5 NLT

We are victorious *with Jesus as our Commander!* But choosing to disobey God opens doors for the devil to make a mess of our personal lives, family, community, nation, etc.

Adam and Eve's first sons were Cain and Abel. Cain was a farmer and Abel was a shepherd. They brought offerings to God and God rejected Cain's offering.

By faith Abel offered to God a better sacrifice than Cain,
Hebrews 11:4a NASB

I believe Abel had *faith* in God as a *Loving Shepherd* but Cain lived by *works and achievement*. So Cain *turned his anger against Abel* and began to sulk. The Lord Loved Cain and came to warn him and help him. He gave Cain a Word that would save his life and the life of his brother, Abel.

"Why are you so angry?" the LORD *asked Cain. "Why do you look so dejected? You will be accepted if you do what is right. But if you refuse to do what is right, then watch out! Sin is crouching at the door, eager to control you. But you must subdue it and be its master."*
Genesis 4:6-7 NLT

In the beginning, God told Adam and Eve that they were to *subdue, rule* and *manage* the earth under God's direction. They lost their first battle when they didn't *rule over the serpent.* Then later their son, Cain, was Lovingly warned by the Lord but he *rejected the Word of the Lord* and killed his precious brother, Abel.

Rule! God has given us His Word to follow. Lock the door to the temptation to despise others, because by despising them you would be *despising the Savior* who Loves them and died for them on the cross. Stepping through the door of offense is walking from light into darkness. *Prepare for war! Lock the door!*

Gideon was chosen by the Lord to lead the people of Israel in war against a very wicked nation. Israel was enslaved by the Midianites because Israel had *adopted the idols of the world* and worshiped other gods. That opened doors to the kingdom of darkness. Gideon, an Israelite farmer, had trouble believing that God had sent an angel to ask *him* to lead the army. But then he encountered Jesus *face to face* and everything changed!

"It is all right," the LORD replied. "Do not be afraid. You will not die." And Gideon built an altar to the LORD there and named it Yahweh-Shalom (which means "the LORD is peace").

That night the LORD said to Gideon, "Take the second bull from your father's herd, the one that is seven years old. Pull down your father's altar to Baal, and cut down the Asherah pole standing beside it. Then build an altar to the LORD your God here on this hilltop sanctuary, laying the stones carefully. Sacrifice the bull as a burnt offering on the altar, using as fuel the wood of the Asherah pole you cut down."

So Gideon took ten of his servants and did as the LORD had commanded.

Judges 6:23, 24a, 25-27a NLT

Jesus spoke to Gideon and gave Him supernatural *shalom* peace! But *before* the Lord could teach him to *rule*, Gideon had to tear down his father's gods. He faced ridicule and threats for doing it, but because of Gideon's *obedience* the Lord's grace was on him.

The Lord then built up Gideon's faith and helped him with supernatural signs, wonders and powerful angelic troops! Together, they led 300 Israelites against a huge army of terrorists and won!

But sadly, after the battle, Gideon traded his relationship with the Lord of Shalom Peace for a pagan lifestyle of fame, riches, ease, and fleshly desires. *Gideon worshiped himself.* After he died, *Gideon's children suffered* the horrific consequences of his rebellion against God. His story didn't have to end that way!

If you don't want to ask God about something it may be a god in your life, right? Jesus cannot build your faith for *war against darkness* until the idols are torn down. Are you drinking from the fountains of this world or from the Living Water in the heavenly realms?

The world's fruit is rooted in lust, witchcraft, jealousy, lies, fame, greed, hatred, anger and all forms of sin. It is served to us on platters like entertainment, education, politics, social media, new age practices, friends, family traditions and on many other platforms. *We don't owe the world anything, but we owe Jesus everything!*

I'm not saying that you can *avoid* being around sin in this world or that you should be afraid because evil is lurking everywhere. Not at all. You are covered by the Blood of Jesus and nothing will harm you if you're seated with God. However, choosing to eat the world's fruit will make you sick — spiritually. Following the Spirit and eating from Him will give you life. When you're seated with God in the heavenly realms, His Living Water will cleanse you from undesired exposure to the world's sin. It is impossible to make a list of *do's and don'ts* for you to follow. You must follow the conviction of the Holy Spirit for yourself.

The Lord isn't calling us *away* from the earth. He is calling us *into* the earth to fulfill His great plan. God chose Daniel and Joseph to serve under pagan rulers, but they fulfilled God's purpose *without compromising* their faith or morals. Through many trials, *they kept meeting with God*, prayed, obeyed and kept their hearts pure. They saw God work in supernatural ways! God will never ask you to sin in order to do His will. But if He asks you to be around people who don't know the Lord, He will give you the grace to stay true to His Word. You are in the world but not of it!

Accept the one whose faith is weak, without quarreling over disputable matters.

Romans 14:1 NIV

The Lord works in mysterious ways. So don't argue with believers about *debatable issues*. Trust that your Brothers and

Sisters can hear from God and follow the Lord into their destiny. They may be the next *Daniel* or *Joseph!*

Now the Spirit expressly says that in latter times some will depart from the faith, giving heed to deceiving spirits and doctrines of demons, speaking lies in hypocrisy, having their own conscience seared with a hot iron,

1 Timothy 4:1-2 NKJV

Following your own ideas and ignoring the Spirit can *sear your conscience* so that you are led into a demonic trap.

My people are being destroyed because they don't know me. Since you priests refuse to know me, I refuse to recognize you as my priests.

Hosea 4:6 NLT

Like *The Beautiful Dream*, our High Priest, Jesus, takes us to the heavenly realms to be seated. That is where we can know God's heart and live in victory on this earth.

I know all the things you do. I have seen your love, your faith, your service, and your patient endurance. And I can see your constant improvement in all these things.

But I have this complaint against you. You are permitting that woman—that Jezebel who calls herself a prophet—to lead my servants astray. She teaches them to commit sexual sin and to eat food offered to idols. I gave her time to repent, but she does not want to turn away from her immorality.

Therefore, I will throw her on a bed of suffering, and those who commit adultery with her will suffer greatly unless they repent and turn away from her evil deeds. I will strike her children dead. Then all the churches will know that I am the one who searches out the thoughts and intentions of every person. And I will give to each of you whatever you deserve.

Revelation 2:19-23 NLT

Jesus spoke this for believers in the end times. "Jezebel" is a demon or demonic system that *seduces, intimidates, deceives and controls.* It tempts believers to shrink back in unbelief and not fulfill their destiny! The world will entice you to be seated with her. *Guard* your heart and the hearts of your children with God's Love, grace and righteousness!

But I also have a message for the rest of you in Thyatira who have not followed this false teaching ('deeper truths,' as they call them—depths of Satan, actually). I will ask nothing more of you except that you hold tightly to what you have until I come. To all who are victorious, who obey me to the very end,

To them I will give authority over all the nations. They will rule the nations with an iron rod and smash them like clay pots.

They will have the same authority I received from my Father, and I will also give them the morning star! Anyone with ears to hear must listen to the Spirit and understand what he is saying to the churches.
                              Revelation 2:24-29 NLT

Be courageous and set apart, holy in the Lord! Remember that Jesus has given us authority over all the power of the enemy and in Christ we have *already* won the war! There is a battle for the souls of *many* who have not met Jesus, and Abba is sending us out to bring them in. We just have to stay seated in the heavenly realms, receive our orders and fulfill our destiny on earth for His glory! And *we can do this* by staying close to Jesus and following the Holy Spirit! Stay in His Love!

Declaration

**IN CHRIST
THE WAR HAS ALREADY BEEN WON!**

63

Be Seated in the Armor of God

But let all who take refuge in you be glad; let them ever sing for joy. Spread your protection over them, that those who love your name may rejoice in you.

Psalm 5:11 NIV

We are protected when we take refuge in the presence of the Lord. We can remain joyful even when we are under attack from the enemy because we know we are safe in Christ! We are seated in God's presence, resting in His grace and submitting to His orders. God Himself is our supernatural armor!

Be sober, be vigilant; because your adversary the devil walks about like a roaring lion, seeking whom he may devour.

1 Peter 5:8 NKJV

Satan is out to steal, kill and destroy everybody. But God has equipped His children to be *warriors* against the kingdom of darkness! We fight and win battles from the heavenly realms where we are seated with God and dressed *in His armor!*

Finally, build up your strength in union with the Lord and by means of his mighty power. Put on all the armor that God gives you, so that you will be able to stand up against the Devil's evil tricks. For we are not fighting against human beings but against the wicked spiritual forces in the heavenly world, the rulers, authorities, and cosmic powers of this dark age.

So put on God's armor now! Then when the evil day comes, you will be able to resist the enemy's attacks; and after fighting to the end, you will still hold your ground.

So stand ready, with truth as a belt tight around your waist, with righteousness as your breastplate, and as your shoes the readiness to announce the Good News of peace. At all times carry faith as a shield; for with it you will be able to put out all the burning arrows shot by the Evil One. And accept salvation as a helmet, and the word of God as the sword which the Spirit gives you.

Ephesians 6:10-17 GNT

We are not fighting people, *the devil is*. God Loves people, so He has equipped us to resist the kingdom of darkness and win. The devil will try to get us to fight our fellow warriors. Peace must first be established within God's ranks for us to be victorious! We Love like God Loves!

So then we pursue the things which make for peace and the building up of one another.

Romans 14:19 NASB

We are seated at *the War Table* with our full attention upon the voice of the Holy Spirit. We don't make the rules or strategies — our Commanding Officer does. As soldiers we trust Him to *train* us and *empower* us. Then in unity we can advance *as a mighty army* for the Kingdom of God.

Soldiers don't get tied up in the affairs of civilian life, for then they cannot please the officer who enlisted them. And athletes cannot win the prize unless they follow the rules.

2 Timothy 2:4-5 NLT

Learning to wear your spiritual armor usually takes time. The devil sneaks around looking for someone who has taken their armor off, so keep it on! It is both *defensive* and *offensive* armor. Every part of the armor is God Himself, through the Spirit. So, put on Christ!

THE BELT OF TRUTH

Jesus said to him, "I am the way, the truth, and the life. No one comes to the Father except through Me."

John 14:6 NKJV

Jesus is the Truth! The Spirit of Truth stabilizes our spiritual core by revealing the Word, Jesus, to us. Jesus exposes the enemy's lies and gives us power against them. Jesus, the Truth, allows us to stand tall in confidence and courage against the enemy's constant false accusations!

THE BREASTPLATE OF RIGHTEOUSNESS

This righteousness is given through faith in Jesus Christ to all who believe.

Romans 3:22a NIV

Our hearts are protected when we are convinced that it is Jesus who makes us righteous. When we think we have to *do something* to be righteous we are a target for the enemy. We can't become righteous by our own works! But if our faith is in the righteousness of Jesus Christ, we become one with Him. His Love makes us want to stay out of darkness and sin! *Our hearts belong to Him* and He guards our hearts for us!

THE SHOES OF THE GOSPEL OF PEACE

The God of peace will soon crush Satan under your feet. The grace of our Lord Jesus be with you.

Romans 16:20 NIV

When we dress our feet with the Prince of Peace, He will stomp on Satan for us. One of the best ways to stomp on the enemy is to share the Gospel of Jesus! The Bible says that the feet of those who bring *the Good News of Jesus* are beautiful! With Jesus on our feet, we always stand ready to introduce others to Him!

THE SHIELD OF FAITH

But you, LORD, are a shield around me, my glory, the One who lifts my head high. I call out to the LORD, and he answers me from his holy mountain.

Psalm 3:3-4 NIV

Our faith is in the Lord our Shield! We're now seated with Him on His holy Mountain in the heavenly realms. *God surrounds us like a force field,* and by faith there is no reason to fear the fiery darts of the enemy! Hold on to your faith in God!

THE HELMET OF SALVATION

For, "Who can know the LORD's thoughts? Who knows enough to teach him?" But we understand these things, for we have the mind of Christ.

1 Corinthians 2:16 NLT

What we allow into our minds affects our faith in Christ. It will either build our faith or weaken it. We cannot trust earthly reasoning. We trust in the One who saves us. We must *guard our relationship with the Head of the Body of Christ,* who is Jesus! He is our Salvation—our helmet! His Spirit gives us a *sound mind* and the power to live in victory! *We have the mind of Christ!*

THE SWORD OF THE SPIRIT — THE WORD

Coming out of his [Jesus'] mouth is a sharp sword with which to strike down the nations. "He will rule them with an iron scepter." He treads the winepress of the fury of the wrath of God Almighty. On his robe and on his thigh he has this name written: KING OF KINGS AND LORD OF LORDS.

Revelation 19:15-16 NIV

The Lord is our Mighty Warrior. He fights with the Words coming from His mouth! We have been bombarded by the words of this dark world, but the Spirit has written God's Word *on our hearts.* When we make the Word *our only belief system,* the

Lord fights for us! It is not the will of God that we merely survive *defensively*. Jesus has commissioned us to advance against the enemy *offensively* and that requires wielding the sword from Jesus' mouth—the Word! When we are *one with Jesus* and speak His Word of Truth, Holy Spirit speaks through us destroying the works of the devil!

The armor of God is the powerful presence, authority and power of Jesus our King! Take a blank piece of paper and personalize each piece of armor with scriptures that speak to protect and strengthen your vulnerability. Ask God to help you understand the scriptures from your heart. Meditate on them with God and declare them often. The devil will not be able to lie to you anymore!

In Christ's full armor, we are ready for any battle, *defensively* and *offensively* against the enemy! The devil and his demons cannot go through the Door where we are seated in the heavenly realms with God! We are surrounded and protected by the Lord Himself!

"For I," says the Lord, "will be a wall of fire all around her, and I will be the glory in her midst."
Zechariah 2:5 NKJV

The Bride of Christ can dwell in the holy fire of the presence of God. His fire is our protection against the enemy. We are strong *in the armor of God* against the powers of darkness and we are safe. With the Sword of the Spirit we fight for our Brothers and Sisters in Christ. The Gospel *spoken* fights for lost souls. We fight for the salvation of our country and God's light to be revealed to the nations. In the armor of God our battle is powerfully effective and we advance against the enemy!

And He said to them, "I saw Satan fall like lightning from heaven. Behold, I give you the authority to trample on serpents and scorpions, and over all the power of the enemy, and nothing shall by any means hurt you.
Luke 10:18-19 NKJV

So be seated in God's armor! Don't believe the devil's lies. Always believe *the Truth* and Jesus will set you free. Cover your heart in *the righteousness of Christ*. Walk in *God's Peace* and share the Good News of Jesus. Put your *faith* in Jesus, your Shield, and *do not doubt* God's Love and grace. Wield the Word like a *sword* against every work of the enemy! In Jesus name, declare the Word of God into the atmosphere to demolish strongholds! We are victorious *in Christ* when we are seated at God's Table, fully suited up in *His armor!*

In *The Beautiful Dream* I was at peace until I looked off—away from God and started making my own plans *for* Jesus! Whenever you are tempted to fear, *take your thoughts captive* and look back to God's Table. God has not left you! The atmosphere is still filled with Agape Love! Be seated with God and with the Body of Christ. Pray and trust the Lord, your armor, because you are safe in Him!

The LORD will fight for you; you need only to be still.
Exodus 14:14 NIV

Declaration

THE LORD IS A WALL OF FIRE AROUND ME!

64

Thankful

As Jesus continued on toward Jerusalem, he reached the border between Galilee and Samaria. As he entered a village there, ten men with leprosy stood at a distance, crying out, "Jesus, Master, have mercy on us!"

He looked at them and said, "Go show yourselves to the priests." And as they went, they were cleansed of their leprosy.

One of them, when he saw that he was healed, came back to Jesus, shouting, "Praise God!" He fell to the ground at Jesus' feet, thanking him for what he had done. This man was a Samaritan.

Jesus asked, "Didn't I heal ten men? Where are the other nine? Has no one returned to give glory to God except this foreigner?" And Jesus said to the man, "Stand up and go. Your faith has healed you."

Luke 17:11-19 NLT

What happened here!? All ten men were *healed of leprosy* on the way to the priest, but *only one* was overwhelmed with thanksgiving—and he was not of Jewish faith. He came back praising God loudly! The man knew he had been healed by God and *had* to give Jesus the praise! Everything else could wait. He had met the Messiah!

I'm sure the man had *no* answer for Jesus when asked where the others were. Perhaps he was even shocked and heartbroken.

This man was free of painful sores, and his toes, fingers and nose had miraculously been restored. He stayed on his knees thanking the Lord until Jesus said, "Rise and go; *your faith* has made you well." What a beautiful heart this man had!

The *religious* heart can become so callous and selfish that it is not *thankful* for the Lord's wonderful blessings. It is an unthankful religious heart that only *hears orders and carries them out*. Yes, all the men were *doing what Jesus had asked them to do* and all of them were healed. But the thankful man saw with his heart what *the others could not see*. His heart was tender and sensitive to the powerful Love that Jesus had for him. This man knew *Jesus was the source of His healing!* He *had* to be in His presence again! This is the man that Jesus said *was healed because of his faith* — the man with a thankful heart! He had come to *know* the Lord!   When we know Jesus intimately, true faith is overwhelmed and thankful to God for all of His unending blessings.

Come, let us sing for joy to the LORD. *Let us shout out praises to our Protector who delivers us. Let us enter his presence with thanksgiving. Let us shout out to him in celebration.*
Psalm 95:1-2 NET

Giving thanks to God is a portal that opens us up to the Holy Spirit in the heavenly realms.   In *The Beautiful Dream*, Jesus touched me, I was permeated with His Love and all evil and pain left.   I was so thankful that I wanted to be with Jesus forever!   If we are attentive in the heavenly realms *we will continue to experience Jesus personally* and our hearts will remain thankful!

Since you have accepted Christ Jesus as Lord, live in union with him. Keep your roots deep in him, build your lives on him, and become stronger in your faith, as you were taught. And be filled with thanksgiving.
Colossians 2:6-7 GNT

The soil in the heavenly realms is very rich! That is where our roots grow down deep *into Jesus Himself* so that His Word gives us supernatural life. If we keep growing strong in God's Spirit, our hearts will always produce the fruit of thanksgiving. Knowing Jesus more intimately in the Spirit and being thankful for His grace keeps us from becoming *prideful* and *religious.*

...in every situation [no matter what the circumstances] be thankful and continually give thanks to God; for this is the will of God for you in Christ Jesus..

1 Thessalonians 5:18 AMP

It is *God's will* for us to be thankful in the seasons of blessings as well as the seasons of great trial. We get to live this life *with Jesus* and He has blessed us with the incomparable riches of His grace! Not being thankful in the middle of our trials can be a sign that we think God is withholding something from us that Jesus already paid for on the cross. Thanking the Lord in tough times is a *deep expression of faith,* believing that all He has provided for us is ours even if we haven't seen it come to pass yet.

Let there be no sexual immorality, impurity, or greed among you. Such sins have no place among God's people. Obscene stories, foolish talk, and coarse jokes—these are not for you. Instead, let there be thankfulness to God. You can be sure that no immoral, impure, or greedy person will inherit the Kingdom of Christ and of God. For a greedy person is an idolater, worshiping the things of this world.

Ephesians 5:3-5 NLT

The believer who takes God's grace for granted will begin to cater to the desires of the world and become satisfied with religious Christianity. Their twisted relationship with God becomes a *transaction:* "I'll do something for God and He'll do something for me when I need it."

And whatever you do in word or deed, do all in the name of the Lord Jesus, giving thanks to God the Father through Him.

Colossians 3:17 NKJV

I believe this verse is giving us keys to powerful ministry. For instance, when we pray over a person's need, *thanking the Father for His Love* connects us to Abba in the heavenly realms. And when we command their sickness, depression, etc. to leave, it is the *authority of the name of Jesus*, His Son, that brings Heaven to earth, allowing us to see healing, deliverance and miracles. When we do warfare from the heavenly realms, we are seated in our Father's Love but *commanding* and releasing the Word of God in the mighty name of Jesus. It is the humility of *a thankful heart* that connects us to the Father's presence and enables us to be a blessing to others.

The *thankful* believer knows that every good opportunity they have in life was given to them by God—parenting, work, study, play, eating, hobbies, ministry, travel, generosity, etc., etc., etc. *Everything* we do is *from Him* and *for His glory*. Many are even thankful for the honor of suffering for the sake of the Gospel. We are so blessed and grateful to carry the Holy Spirit's power and grace everywhere we go.

We can express our thankfulness by being vocal about our faith—just like the man Jesus healed of leprosy. Allow your thankfulness to *overflow* in your conversations with neighbors, family, friends and coworkers—not plastic, religious statements, but from your heart, prompted by the Spirit. If you really are thankful to God, just be real about it! You might say, "I am so thankful to God that you're okay..." Simple words can open a door to share your faith and be a blessing to others.

I will praise you, LORD, with all my heart; I will tell of all the marvelous things you have done.

Psalm 9:1 NLT

Jesus was not ashamed of His Father God. He knew His Abba well because He spent much time alone in prayer at night, even after a long hard day of doing everything His Father had asked Him to do. In the Spirit, Jesus worshiped His Father, learning from Him and submitting to Him. Even the Son of God, who left His throne in Heaven to give His life as a living sacrifice for us *was thankful!* He cherished His Father's presence and knew His heart. The thanksgiving that flowed from Jesus' heart *multiplied resources* for the work Father God had for Him to do.

About this time another large crowd had gathered, and the people ran out of food again. Jesus called his disciples and told them, "I feel sorry for these people. They have been here with me for three days, and they have nothing left to eat. If I send them home hungry, they will faint along the way. For some of them have come a long distance."

His disciples replied, "How are we supposed to find enough food to feed them out here in the wilderness?" Jesus asked, "How much bread do you have?" Seven loaves," they replied.

So Jesus told all the people to sit down on the ground. Then he took the seven loaves, thanked God for them, and broke them into pieces. He gave them to his disciples, who distributed the bread to the crowd. A few small fish were found, too, so Jesus also blessed these and told the disciples to distribute them.

They ate as much as they wanted. Afterward, the disciples picked up seven large baskets of leftover food. There were about 4,000 men in the crowd that day, and Jesus sent them home after they had eaten.

Mark 8:1-9 NLT

Jesus was *compassionate* because He was God *in a human body* and lived by the Holy Spirit. He knew what it meant to be hungry. Jesus was also *full of gratitude toward the Father,* knowing Abba desired to feed the hungry crowd. Jesus *gave thanks* for seven loaves of bread and a few fish and about four thousand men were fed! Miracles like this take place today when we *live from Abba Father's Love* and are *thankful* for His generous heart!

All the angels were standing around the throne and around the elders and the four living creatures. They fell down on their faces before the throne and worshiped God, saying: "Amen! Praise and glory and wisdom and thanks and honor and power and strength be to our God for ever and ever. Amen!"

Revelation 7:11-12 NIV

Angels in Heaven continually give God praise and thanks! How much more should we, the ones Jesus died for!

Thanks be to God for His indescribable gift!

2 Corinthians 9:15 NASB

When you are given a gift, you say, "Thank you!" It shows that you joyfully and humbly received the gift as an expression of love. Salvation is a priceless and precious eternal gift from God because He Loves us!

We are thankful because we know God intimately. Being seated with Him helps us not take His blessings and answered prayers for granted. They are Love-gifts from God so we say, "Thank You!" God the Father, Son and Holy Spirit are *continually* giving us Love, life, opportunities, good friends, peace and many wonderful things that some people might credit to their own good nature or hard work. But even the good things that we sow and reap in life started as seeds from God. Our talents and abilities are given to us by God. The Lord deserves *all* the glory for *all* good things! So let's be seated in His bountiful Agape Love and give Him thanks! A thankful heart is a heart full of faith in His Love!

Give thanks to the LORD, for he is good. His love endures forever.

Psalm 136:1 NIV

Declaration

THANK YOU FATHER! YOU ARE SO GOOD!

65

Be Seated – Immoveable!

Jacob was born holding on to his twin brother's heel so his mother and father named him Jacob, which means *deceiver*. When Jacob was a young man, he *deceived* his elderly father and stole his brother Esau's blessing. Jacob was sent on a journey to look for a wife. On the way, he camped under the stars. God gave him the dream about angels going up and down on a staircase to Heaven. He named the place Bethel, which means house of God. Jacob finally arrived at the place where he was to find his wife, and quickly spotted her.

Jacob became engaged to Rachel, but his father-in-law, Laban, began deceiving him and taking advantage of him. It was as if the deception Jacob had sown in his youth was now bearing bitter fruit. He was manipulated by Laban to work for the family for around 20 years! Finally, by the grace of God, Jacob and his large family broke free and headed home to *make things right with his brother*. On the way, God sent two angels to encourage him! Jacob was extremely nervous about encountering his brother, Esau. He sent his family, possessions and livestock across the ford of the Jabbok River. But Jacob lingered behind and spent the night alone.

So Jacob was left alone, and a man wrestled with him till daybreak. When the man saw that he could not overpower him, he touched the socket of Jacob's hip so that his hip was wrenched as he wrestled with the man. Then the man said, "Let me go, for it is daybreak." But Jacob replied, "I will not let you go unless you bless me." The man asked him, "What is your name?" "Jacob," he answered. Then the man said, "Your name will no longer be Jacob, but Israel, because you have struggled with God and with humans and have overcome." Jacob said, "Please tell me your name." But he replied, "Why do you ask my name?" Then he blessed him there. So Jacob called the place Peniel, saying, "It is because I saw God face to face, and yet my life was spared."*

Genesis 32:24-30 NIV

Jacob humbled himself to go home and make things right with Esau, even at the risk of losing everything. He was financially prosperous, but his pride had brought him to his knees. Jacob wrestled with Jesus! I believe he came face to face with his own *stronghold of deception* as he struggled face to face with Jesus. And that night Jacob did receive God's blessing. He was delivered and set free. The Lord changed his name from *Jacob*, the deceiver, to *Israel*, the one who wrestles with God — or the one who turns God's face toward himself.

Jacob had an *unquenchable thirst for God's blessing* and wouldn't quit wrestling with God until he received what he knew God had for him! It took him a while to get there, but when Jacob finally *humbled himself*, he was ready to *encounter Jesus!* Not only was Jacob's *name* changed, *he* was changed and received God's promise because he would not give up! *Jacob was immoveable!*

Once you have encountered Jesus, nothing but His blessing will do! His blessing is full of Agape Love, the kind that is not jealous of the blessings of your Brothers and Sisters. And when your faith in His mercy, grace and favor are *immoveable*, you will be inwardly changed, for you will be seated at the Kingdom Table face to face with Jesus!

I keep my eyes always on the LORD. With him at my right hand, I will not be shaken.

Psalm 16:8 NIV

In *The Beautiful Dream*, Father God was at my right hand.

Sitting next to Abba is the only place I want to be! I won't fall if I stay seated next to my Papa and my eyes on Jesus!

If you need wisdom, ask our generous God, and he will give it to you. He will not rebuke you for asking. But when you ask him, be sure that your faith is in God alone. Do not waver, for a person with divided loyalty is as unsettled as a wave of the sea that is blown and tossed by the wind. Such people should not expect to receive anything from the Lord. Their loyalty is divided between God and the world, and they are unstable in everything they do.

James 1:5-8 NLT

Holy Spirit freely gives us wisdom so we can become *single-minded,* only bowing to our King. The person whose faith is partly in God and partly in the world is *spiritually unstable.* We can't *serve* two kingdoms at the same time.

If you think you are standing strong, be careful not to fall. The temptations in your life are no different from what others experience. And God is faithful. He will not allow the temptation to be more than you can stand. When you are tempted, he will show you a way out so that you can endure.

1 Corinthians 10:12-13 NLT

You will be able to *remain strong in the Lord* even when you are tempted, if you humble yourself and tune your ear to the Holy Spirit. The Lord taught us to pray that He would *"lead us not into temptation but deliver us from evil."* In other words, pray in advance that God will help you submit to Him so that you are victorious whenever the enemy comes to tempt you. The closer you get to the Light, the less power the kingdom of darkness will have over your life. We must stay ahead of the enemy's plans!

So, my dear brothers and sisters, be strong and immovable. Always work enthusiastically for the Lord, for you know that nothing you do for the Lord is ever useless.

1 Corinthians 15:58 NLT

You see, whether God calls you to ministry, a secular job, home, or elsewhere, *it's all God's work* when you are motivated by God's Love. He fills you to overflowing in the secret place and then goes with you to bless others. You are *consistently* honest, patient and caring at work and home. You do your job to the best of your ability with a good attitude. You are quick to make things right when you fail.

The people around you will *taste the fruit of the Spirit*. Eventually someone will ask for your help because they sense that *you will give them good advice*. Some may hate you for it, but God will bless you for it. The seeds you sow will in time reap a harvest for God. Because you have been *immoveable*, seated only with God, your place of service is the Spirit's stage to shine through you!

And although you were previously alienated and hostile in attitude, engaged in evil deeds, yet He has now reconciled you in His body of flesh through death, in order to present you before Him holy and blameless and beyond reproach—if indeed you continue in the faith firmly established and steadfast, and not shifting from the hope of the gospel that you have heard, which was proclaimed in all creation under heaven, and of which I, Paul, was made a minister.
Colossians 1:21-23 NASB

You are holy and blameless in Christ, *but you must continue to believe this* and live in His presence!

But blessed is the one who trusts in the LORD, whose confidence is in him. They will be like a tree planted by the water that sends out its roots by the stream. It does not fear when heat comes; its leaves are always green. It has no worries in a year of drought and never fails to bear fruit.
Jeremiah 17:7-8 NIV

When others are in a season of spiritual drought, you will be able to encourage them. Success and prosperity *in God's*

Kingdom will be yours as you drink from *the Living Water*. You are seated with God at the center of His Kingdom — *His Throne Room*. This is His boardroom for the Body of Christ where He discusses His plans for our lives. If you build your life on your relationship with God, you will be *secure, immoveable and established*. But if you build your life upon anything else, *even the machine of ministry*, you will not be safe. Jesus is our *Rock and Foundation*.

"Not everyone who calls out to me, 'Lord! Lord!' will enter the Kingdom of Heaven. Only those who actually do the will of my Father in heaven will enter. On judgment day many will say to me, 'Lord! Lord! We prophesied in your name and cast out demons in your name and performed many miracles in your name.' But I will reply, 'I never knew you. Get away from me, you who break God's laws.'

"Anyone who listens to my teaching and follows it is wise, like a person who builds a house on solid rock. Though the rain comes in torrents and the floodwaters rise and the winds beat against that house, it won't collapse because it is built on bedrock. But anyone who hears my teaching and doesn't obey it is foolish, like a person who builds a house on sand. When the rains and floods come and the winds beat against that house, it will collapse with a mighty crash."

Matthew 7:21-27 NLT

We are not saved by our own efforts or even through operating in the supernatural gifts of the Spirit. We are saved by the *Love and grace* brought to us by Jesus. We didn't do anything except say *yes* to Him and agree to follow His lead. Our faith is always in the cross of Jesus and God's Love for us!

Let God be the architect of your life. Sit down at His Table and follow the blueprint of *His Word*. Talk *with* God and *know Him*. Let Him walk into every room of your heart. If you don't know His big purpose for your life yet, it's okay. Follow His lead by Loving God and others from the heart! *God's Love* and grace is the *stability* of your life and destiny. With Jesus as the foundation, your house will endure the storms of this life!

So God has given both his promise and his oath. These two things are unchangeable because it is impossible for God to lie. Therefore, we who have fled to him for refuge can have great confidence as we hold to the hope that lies before us. This hope is a strong and trustworthy anchor for our souls. It leads us through the curtain into God's inner sanctuary. Jesus has already gone in there for us. He has become our eternal High Priest in the order of Melchizedek.

Hebrews 6:18-20 NLT

The promises of God are *already ours in Christ* and delivered to us through the Spirit. We can be *confident and immoveable* through every storm that *Jesus* is the anchor of our ship. He is the foundation of our lives and we will not be shaken!

Don't stop wrestling until you get your breakthrough! Rejoice and be *confident* in Abba's promises! Your ship may dip and sway in the wind and waves of this world's chaos. But if you'll *stay seated,* face to face with Jesus, your anchor will keep you stable and immoveable! Jesus *will not* let you drown!

Declaration

MY FAITH IN JESUS IS IMMOVEABLE!

66

When Will I See You Again?

In *The Beautiful Dream*, scene one, Jesus asked if He could see me again. He was asking if we could *meet together* again. I said *yes*, and later He came and took me to the heavenly realms. I also asked Jesus when I would see Him again. I am going to use *my question to Him* as an opportunity to write about our hope of *Heaven* itself, the beautiful place He has prepared for us!

And just as each person is destined to die once and after that comes judgment, so also Christ was offered once for all time as a sacrifice to take away the sins of many people. He will come again, not to deal with our sins, but to bring salvation to all who are eagerly waiting for him.

Hebrews 9:27-28 NLT

All of us are going to *die physically* and meet the Lord at that time unless He comes back to lift us out of the earth first. We aren't twiddling our thumbs doing nothing. *We are on assignment* and our King expects each of us to fulfill what He has called us to do—*in His great Love!* The anticipation is building for those in Love with Jesus!

So you, too, must keep watch! For you don't know what day your Lord is coming. Understand this: If a homeowner knew exactly when a burglar was coming, he would keep watch and not permit his house to be broken into. You also must be ready all the time, for the Son of Man will come when least expected.

A faithful, sensible servant is one to whom the master can give

*the responsibility of managing his other household servants
and feeding them. If the master returns and finds that the
servant has done a good job, there will be a reward. I tell you
the truth, the master will put that servant in charge of all he
owns. But what if the servant is evil and thinks, 'My master
won't be back for a while,' and he begins beating the other
servants, partying, and getting drunk? The master will return
unannounced and unexpected and he will cut the servant to
pieces and assign him a place with the hypocrites. In that place
there will be weeping and gnashing of teeth.*

Matthew 24:42-51 NLT

The Lord is the owner of His House. We are the "servants" and
have all the riches of Love and grace in Christ Jesus to carry out
the tasks He has given us to do. In this parable, treating one
another with care and compassion is of utmost importance. We
do that by *yielding to the Spirit's power* of Love, joy, peace,
patience, kindness, goodness, faithfulness, gentleness and self-
control. These are within us supernaturally, but we still must
choose to *follow the Spirit* instead of following the *flesh*.

We are supposed to always be about our Father's business and
our hearts need to be burning with God's light. We can shine
His light in dark places if His Light is filling us up from the
inside out like a lamp.

*"At that time the kingdom of heaven will be like ten virgins
who took their lamps and went out to meet the bridegroom.
Five of the virgins were foolish, and five were wise. When the
foolish ones took their lamps, they did not take extra olive oil
with them. But the wise ones took flasks of olive oil with their
lamps. When the bridegroom was delayed a long time, they all
became drowsy and fell asleep. But at midnight there was a
shout, 'Look, the bridegroom is here! Come out to meet him.'
Then all the virgins woke up and trimmed their lamps. The
foolish ones said to the wise, 'Give us some of your oil, because
our lamps are going out.' 'No,' they replied. There won't be
enough for you and for us. Go instead to those who sell oil and
buy some for yourselves.' But while they had gone to buy it, the*

WHEN WILL I SEE YOU AGAIN?

bridegroom arrived, and those who were ready went inside with him to the wedding banquet. Then the door was shut. Later, the other virgins came too, saying, 'Lord, lord! Let us in!' But he replied, 'I tell you the truth, I do not know you!' Therefore stay alert, because you do not know the day or the hour."

Matthew 25:1-13 NET

In scene three of *The Beautiful Dream*, I was daydreaming. I might as well have been *asleep* because I was *not paying attention* to what God was saying to me in the Spirit realm. The only way for our hearts to be filled with His oil is to *wake up* and be seated in His presence while we have the opportunity.

God wants to touch the places that need deliverance and the healing light of His Love. He wants us to draw closer to Him so we can know His Love. Sometimes we doze off or let our minds wander. The Lord is not angry with us when that happens. But if it becomes a habit, our oil will run out and our light will disappear. That's why He is concerned. God wants us seated next to our Father's heart, listening to the Holy Spirit and looking straight into the Son's Loving face. Only in this position can we receive the oil from the Table of the Lord that keeps us filled with His light.

Jesus is not going to marry a bride He doesn't know! We have to want to be one with Him. It's time for the Bride to *know Jesus intimately*, to be filled with the oil of His Spirit and the fire of God's presence. One day we're going to see Him again in all of His glory! If we are faithful to keep replenishing our oil from His storehouse in the heavenly realms and to burn brightly for Him in this dark world, we will be ready when He comes!

God Loves you so much! He wants to fill your lantern daily with Agape Love because His Love is filled with salvation! His Love is infinitely better than earthly love! Let His Word shine into every chamber of your heart! You will strive less and Love more. Jesus will be your first Love again and you will be filled with His light, freedom and Love. You will only do what He says and serving will become a joy, not a chore. Just stay close to your source of oil and keep filling your reserve!

Now may the God of peace make you holy in every way, and may your whole spirit and soul and body be kept blameless until our Lord Jesus Christ comes again. God will make this happen, for he who calls you is faithful.
1 Thessalonians 5:23-24 NLT

Only God can make us holy and only He can keep us holy. That's why we have to know Him and yield to His Spirit until the day we finally see Him face to face.

Be patient, then, my friends, until the Lord comes. See how patient farmers are as they wait for their land to produce precious crops. They wait patiently for the autumn and spring rains. You also must be patient. Keep your hopes high, for the day of the Lord's coming is near.

Do not complain against one another, my friends, so that God will not judge you. The Judge is near, ready to appear. My friends, remember the prophets who spoke in the name of the Lord. Take them as examples of patient endurance under suffering. We call them happy because they endured. You have heard of Job's patience, and you know how the Lord provided for him in the end. For the Lord is full of mercy and compassion.
James 5:7-11 GNT

Heaven is going to be awesome and knowing that can make us a little impatient! But if we can bring one more soul into God's Kingdom it will be worth the wait!

As you *look forward to* the day Jesus takes you to Heaven, stay close to Him. Let His Love become more real to you—even in difficult times. Jesus told us that only the Father knows when Jesus will return to take us home. He said wars and bad weather are not necessarily signs of His coming. These things will always occur, but *perhaps more intensely* toward the end.

For I consider that our present sufferings cannot even be

380

compared to the coming glory that will be revealed to us. For the creation eagerly waits for the revelation of the sons of God. For the creation was subjected to futility—not willingly but because of God who subjected it—in hope that the creation itself will also be set free from the bondage of decay into the glorious freedom of God's children. For we know that the whole creation groans and suffers together until now. Not only this, but we ourselves also, who have the firstfruits of the Spirit, groan inwardly as we eagerly await our adoption, the redemption of our bodies.

Romans 8:18-23 NET

The Bible says that in the end times we are living in now, there will be false messiahs and prophets causing an *increase in wickedness* and *great deception*. When the end is near, Jesus tells us that strange and frightening things will take place in the sky, on the earth and the sea, but *we must not fear*. If we are following our dance partner, our Prince will keep us in perfect peace. Those seated with God will not fall!

And there will be strange signs in the sun, moon, and stars. And here on earth the nations will be in turmoil, perplexed by the roaring seas and strange tides. People will be terrified at what they see coming upon the earth, for the powers in the heavens will be shaken. Then everyone will see the Son of Man coming on a cloud with power and great glory. So when all these things begin to happen, stand and look up, for your salvation is near!

Luke 21:25-28 NLT

I won't attempt to explain the different doctrines about the rapture, the millennium and the second coming of Jesus. *Only God knows* when the great events of the end times will occur. What is perfectly clear from scripture is that we must stay alert and ready for Jesus to call us home!

If the world begins to fall apart, you can trust in Jesus and confidently lift up your head. That's because you are seated in the heavenly realms, listening to God, believing His Word and acting on what He says. He doesn't require perfection but He does require that we keep growing in His perfect Love. He Loves you even if you are afraid, so don't become condemned by your feelings. Though you may feel anxious, there is nothing to fear because His Spirit lives in you and His perfect Love drives out fear. Worship God alone. Trust that Jesus Loves you and shine for Him. He's coming soon!

I felt Heaven in *The Beautiful Dream* and nothing in this world compares to being in the arms of Jesus! The truth is that *we are in His arms right now* through the Holy Spirit. He is worth pursuing with all of your heart! In Heaven there will be no more *seeking* the Lord because God's presence will saturate the atmosphere! We will *never again* have fear, sickness, disappointments, pain, sadness, tears or evil of any kind. There will be *no more fighting the devil* because Satan and his demons will be locked up in hell for eternity! Hallelujah! And those who eagerly waited for Jesus will finally see Him in person *in all of His glory!*

Jesus will escort us to all the beautiful breathtaking sights of the New World called Heaven He has prepared for us! Our perfect senses will be *saturated with bliss.* There will be rivers, trees and streets of gold! Every aroma and taste will be indescribably wonderful. Every face will be lit up with joy! We will worship continually and experience in person the infinite goodness, holiness and Love of our Awesome God! We will be with Abba and Holy Spirit, and we will *finally be with Jesus in person for eternity!* Heaven will be our eternal reward for dancing with Jesus and being seated with the magnificent God of Agape Love and grace!

Declaration

JESUS IS COMING BACK FOR US!

67

The Glory of the Lord

The Word became flesh and made his dwelling among us. We have seen his glory, the glory of the one and only Son, who came from the Father, full of grace and truth.

John 1:14 NIV

In *The Beautiful Dream*, I experienced the glory of the Lord in the awesome, indescribable immersion of His Majesty, Perfection and Love! It is my prayer that I will continue to experience His glory, not only in dreams and visions, but *fully awake* — not just through the testimonies of others, but for myself in increasing measure here on earth! That is also my prayer for the beautiful Bride of Christ! Jesus' disciples experienced His glory as they lived with Him for three years. Peter, James and John even *saw* Jesus' body shine in supernatural glory!

Six days later Jesus took Peter and the two brothers, James and John, and led them up a high mountain to be alone. As the men watched, Jesus' appearance was transformed so that his face shone like the sun, and his clothes became as white as light.

Matthew 17:1-2 NLT

I don't believe it was a coincidence that Jesus took them up a high mountain. The mountain was symbolic of *the heavenly realms* where we are seated with God. But even after this transfiguration, the disciples struggled spiritually, until after Jesus was raised from the dead and ascended into Heaven. They waited *in Jerusalem* for the power of the Holy Spirit to come on them, just like Jesus had instructed.

This is what Isaiah son of Amoz saw concerning Judah and Jerusalem: In the last days the mountain of the LORD's temple will be established as the highest of the mountains; it will be exalted above the hills, and all nations will stream to it.

Isaiah 2:1-2 NIV

Let's review again what happened on the day of Pentecost when the Spirit came in extraordinary power:

When the day of Pentecost came, they were all together in one place. Suddenly a sound like the blowing of a violent wind came from heaven and filled the whole house where they were sitting. They saw what seemed to be tongues of fire that separated and came to rest on each of them. All of them were filled with the Holy Spirit and began to speak in other tongues as the Spirit enabled them.

Acts 2:1-4 NIV

They were not sitting in Jerusalem's temple. They were in an ordinary house. But they were seated *in unity at God's Table in the heavenly realms, the highest of the mountains!* People had crowded into Jerusalem from other countries for the Jewish Pentecost festival. When the disciples received the fire of the Spirit, *foreigners* heard them speaking in their own language! Peter preached the Gospel and 3,000 came to faith in Jesus! Peter assured the people that this power from the Spirit had been foretold by the prophet Joel, and that Jesus truly was the Messiah!

"These people are not drunk, as some of you are assuming. Nine o'clock in the morning is much too early for that. No, what you see was predicted long ago by the prophet Joel: 'In the last days,' God says, 'I will pour out my Spirit upon all people. Your sons and daughters will prophesy. Your young men will see visions, and your old men will dream dreams. In those days I will pour out my Spirit even on my servants — men and women alike — and they will prophesy. And I will cause wonders in the heavens above and signs on the earth below — blood and fire

and clouds of smoke. The sun will become dark, and the moon will turn blood red before that great and glorious day of the LORD arrives. But everyone who calls on the name of the LORD will be saved.'"

Acts 2:15-21 NLT

Men and women alike are filled with the same power, producing the same *good fruit of Agape Love* and operating in *the same supernatural gifts*. They can do this because they are not seated in the fleshly earthly realm but *in the Spirit!*

I, the LORD, have called you in righteousness; I will take hold of your hand. I will keep you and will make you to be a covenant for the people and a light for the Gentiles, to open eyes that are blind, to free captives from prison and to release from the dungeon those who sit in darkness. I am the LORD; that is my name! I will not yield my glory to another or my praise to idols. See, the former things have taken place, and new things I declare; before they spring into being I announce them to you.

Isaiah 42:6-9 NIV

In the last days there will be extremely difficult times all over the world and people will suddenly either grow more evil *or* seek the Lord more intensely. *A great polarization* will take place—a clear divide separating those in the Kingdom of God from those in the kingdom of darkness. It will be nearly impossible to remain lukewarm. God is purifying His people right now. He will not share His glory and praise with other gods!

In the west, people will respect the name of the LORD; in the east, they will glorify him. For he will come like a raging flood tide driven by the breath of the LORD.

Isaiah 59:19 NLT

I believe a great outpouring of God's glory is coming like a tidal wave over the earth in these end times. We must ask Holy Spirit to cleanse us and fill us with His Love *now* so our hearts will be able to carry the glory of the Lord! The Gospel will be shared in the power of God's glory and *many* all over the earth will come to Jesus! The Gospel is not a message of working hard to be holy. It is the Good News of the extravagant Love, mercy and grace of God through Jesus Christ!

One of the criminals hanging beside him scoffed, "So you're the Messiah, are you? Prove it by saving yourself—and us, too, while you're at it" But the other criminal protested, "Don't you fear God even when you have been sentenced to die? We deserve to die for our crimes, but this man hasn't done anything wrong." Then he said, "Jesus, remember me when you come into your Kingdom." And Jesus replied, "I assure you, today you will be with me in paradise."

Luke 23:39-43 NLT

It's that simple? Really? Yes. That's it. God just wants us to realize that we are in big trouble because of our sin, believe that Jesus is the Savior and asks to have a relationship with Him — forever. The criminal on the cross who recognized Jesus as the Messiah declared his faith in Jesus and went straight to Heaven that day when he died! He didn't have to *do any good works* to receive the gift of eternal life and begin his relationship with God. He received and followed Jesus for the very short time he had left to live on earth. His testimony is still sowing seeds of faith to this day! Hallelujah!

Most of us are blessed to be able to follow Jesus for days, months or years! In His Agape Love, Jesus escorts us to the *heavenly realms* where we are seated with God at His Table. It is from that place in the Holy Spirit that we live our lives on earth *victoriously* for His Kingdom's glory! We have the joy of living in the atmosphere of Love and Truth, even in this fallen world, because we are surrounded and filled with Love Himself. But many Christians do not choose to be nurtured by God.

Then he told this parable: "A man had a fig tree growing in his vineyard, and he went to look for fruit on it but did not find any. So he said to the man who took care of the vineyard, 'For three years now I've been coming to look for fruit on this fig tree and haven't found any. Cut it down! Why should it use up the soil?' 'Sir,' the man replied, 'leave it alone for one more year, and I'll dig around it and fertilize it. If it bears fruit next year, fine! If not, then cut it down.'"

Luke 13:6-9 NIV

The fig tree may represent the beautiful Jewish people who were given the glorious honor of bringing the Messiah, Jesus, into the world. They still have time to acknowledge their Messiah and many are doing so today!

Or perhaps the fig tree is the person planted in God's vineyard but has not responded to the Vine Dresser. Grape vines produce grapes and each grape has many seeds for planting. Fig trees produce figs with many more seeds to plant new fig trees. Sheep produce more sheep. Creation is God's picture of His Kingdom. There is always *reproduction* and *multiplication* of His glory or something has gone wrong.

Usually, when that happens, like the fig tree, we have forgotten who we are. We haven't planted ourselves firmly in our chair in the *heavenly realms* and we haven't been drinking Living Water. But apparently, it's not too late. The Vine Dresser believes He can work on our root system and make us fruitful again, that is, if we respond to His Love! Our Vine Dresser has come through the Spirit and His glory is rising upon us!

Arise, shine, for your light has come, and the glory of the LORD rises upon you. See darkness covers the earth and thick darkness is over the peoples, but the LORD rises upon you and his glory appears over you. Nations will come to your light, and kings to the brightness of your dawn.

Isaiah 60:1-3 NIV

What brings the glory of the Lord? It's when we want to be close to Jesus no matter the cost! We don't care if our flesh is embarrassed because it needs to die anyway. He came to us and we've fallen in Love. We know Him and have to be close!

In *The Beautiful Dream*, I kept thinking that I wanted to be alone with Jesus. That sounds sweet, but *He has much higher plans* for us and His Kingdom! Jesus is our King, and the only way to find out what He wants is to *be seated at God's Table* and experience Him together with the Body of Christ. It is the place of God's glory.

If we don't drink of the Living Water now, it will drown us when God's glory is poured out on the earth. Our old dry wineskins need to be renewed in order to carry the *new wine!* The criminal who gave His heart to Jesus was instantly filled with God's light and Love, even as he took his last few breaths on this earth. This man was in a very dark place but his lamp was shining bright because he was close to Jesus.

We are the temple of the Holy Spirit on this earth. God intended for us to carry His glory into all the world. It doesn't happen automatically, and it doesn't happen through our own efforts to be good. We have to be close to God's glory in order to be filled with His glory. He gives us oil in the heavenly realms and fills us with the light of His Word. We are the light of the world, carrying His glory in the end times! Hallelujah!

The Spirit of the Sovereign LORD is upon me, for the LORD has anointed me to bring good news to the poor. He has sent me to comfort the brokenhearted and to proclaim that captives will be released and prisoners will be freed. He has sent me to tell those who mourn that the time of the LORD's favor has come, and with it, the day of God's anger against their enemies. To all who mourn in Israel, he will give a crown of beauty for ashes, a joyous blessing instead of mourning, festive praise instead of despair. In their righteousness, they will be like great oaks that the LORD has planted for his own glory.

They will rebuild the ancient ruins, repairing cities destroyed long ago. They will revive them, though they have been deserted for many generations. Foreigners will be your servants. They will feed your flocks and plow your fields and tend your vineyards. You will be called priests of the LORD, ministers of our God. You will feed on the treasures of the nations and boast in their riches. Instead of shame and dishonor, you will enjoy a double share of honor. You will possess a double portion of prosperity in your land, and everlasting joy will be yours.

For I, the LORD, love justice. I hate robbery and wrongdoing. I will faithfully reward my people for their suffering and make an everlasting covenant with them. Their descendants will be recognized and honored among the nations. Everyone will realize that they are a people the LORD has blessed.

I am overwhelmed with joy in the LORD my God! For he has dressed me with the clothing of salvation and draped me in a robe of righteousness. I am like a bridegroom dressed for his wedding or a bride with her jewels. The Sovereign LORD will show his justice to the nations of the world. Everyone will praise him! His righteousness will be like a garden in early spring, with plants springing up everywhere.

Isaiah 61:1-11 NLT

The Spirit of the Lord is in us and on us and has anointed us to minister His Love! Through us, Jesus will bring beauty for ashes, joy for mourning, and praise for despair!

The earth is the LORD's, and everything in it, the world, and all who live in it; for he founded it on the seas and established it on the waters.

Who may ascend the mountain of the LORD? Who may stand in his holy place? The one who has clean hands and a pure heart, who does not trust in an idol or swear by a false god.

They will receive blessing from the LORD and vindication from God their Savior. Such is the generation of those who seek him, who seek your face, God of Jacob.

Lift up your heads, you gates; be lifted up, you ancient doors, that the King of glory may come in. Who is this King of glory? The LORD strong and mighty, the LORD mighty in battle. Lift up your heads, you gates; lift them up, you ancient doors, that the King of glory may come in. Who is he, this King of glory? The LORD *Almighty— he is the King of glory.*

Psalm 24:1-10 NIV

Jesus is the King of glory! Who will be able to *ascend to the Mountain of the Lord* and receive His blessing? The one who stays in the dance, following His lead no matter the cost—the one who *listens* to Holy Spirit and *cherishes the honor* that they have been *seated next to their Abba's heart!*

They are the *unified* and *Loving* Body of Christ—the ministering priests of the temple of the Holy Spirit—the courageously uncompromised Warriors of the Kingdom—the royal sons and daughters dearly Loved by the Father—and the stunningly beautiful Bride of Christ, dressed in brilliant robes of white, who are and forever will be *in Love with Jesus*, the King of Glory!

Declaration

THE GLORY OF THE LORD IS RISING UPON US!

NOTES

1. The Bakery

My early memories of visiting the old bakery with my mother are like snapshots because I was so young. So, I used a little "writer's privilege" to "fill in the frames" and add dialog.

2. Saying Yes to Jesus

If at any point in reading *The Beautiful Dream* you're ready to follow Jesus, *just talk to Him.* Jesus wants to forgive you and make you a child of God. He is inviting you to receive Him by faith. Be yourself when you talk with Him. He likes it when we come to Him like a child, humble and authentic. Jesus Loves you *very* much!

3. Resisting the Devil

The Bible tells us that the devil, Satan, is an *evil spirit*, the enemy and the father of all lies. Satan accuses the children of God even after they have been forgiven by God. The devil seeks to steal, kill and destroy. Satan does these things through his demon subjects because he has no love or sympathy at all, only hate. The dark demonic kingdom is not a myth or a fairytale. It's real, and its leader doesn't play. He deceives with deadly intentions in mind. If you have ever been involved in deliverance ministry you will never play with the demonic. But if you have submitted your life to the Lordship of Jesus Christ, you don't have to fear its power either. There are many names in the Bible for the devil and the fallen angels including names of earthly creatures such as snakes, scorpions, lions, etc. But what we must know is that the Holy Spirit within us is greater than any demon, so no matter what lie or plan he devises against you, you can live in victory over the demonic realm! If you choose the Blood of Jesus over the law that condemns, faith in God's grace over fear, God's light over darkness, God's Kingdom over Satan's kingdom, God's Agape Love over the devil's hateful ways, the Word of God over the lies that Satan whispers, life over death, and blessings over curses, you will overcome the enemy and will be able to help others overcome as well! If that seems like a lot—I simply mean *choose Jesus!* Desire to draw close to

Jesus, your Savior, no matter the cost. James chapter 4 talks about inward and outward temptations. In order to resist the devil and cause his demons to leave, you must *humble yourself and draw near to God*. Admit where you have not been submitting to God. Be sincerely remorseful, confessing your sin to Him. Ask Him to cleanse your heart so you aren't double-minded. You don't want to resist God, you want to resist the devil. Your goal is to *wholeheartedly* follow the Holy Spirit. Where you have wrong thoughts about yourself or others, go to God, get to the root of it, admit it to the Lord, forgive anyone who wronged you, let go of the offense and receive the healing Love of God. Then *renounce* the work of the devil (the addiction, the fear, the accusation, the shame or whatever it is) that is stealing your victory and *command it to leave in Jesus' name*. Make it a habit to quote scripture against those dark feelings or thoughts, declaring who you truly are in Christ. If it's too much for you to do by yourself, find someone who can agree with you in prayer and deliverance until you are free enough to resist the devil on your own. *The most important part of resisting the devil is drawing near to God.* You may experience freedom as you are worshiping Him, reading the Word or ministering to someone else. *Do not dwell on the demonic!* Keep your eyes fixed on the joy of your Salvation, Jesus Himself!

4. Declarations and Decrees
When you know something is God's will because scripture has already said so, you can declare or decree it over yourself, your family, your child's school, your church, your nation, etc. A decree is a legal statement from God's Word. God's decrees demolish the lies, plans, and strongholds of the devil when they are made by faith in the power of Holy Spirit. Declaring the decree means saying it, preferably aloud—but *you can* say it in the spirit realm if for some reason you can't say it aloud. They can be done by quoting scripture or simply declaring Truth that you know is from God's Word.

5. The Church
I have capitalized the word *Church* in this book to mean those who are seated with God in the heavenly realms *following the Spirit*. I haven't capitalized the word *church* when referring to a group of people whose organization claims Christianity and meets together here on earth. Not every person who attends a church is part of *The Church*. A church's goal should be to encourage everyone in their congregation to be seated with God and follow the Spirit. *The Church, The Body of Christ* and *The Bride of Christ* are terms for those seated in the heavenly realms. God is trying to show us that His authority, power and Love are being delegated to each one of us so that His will on earth can be accomplished through us, His Church.

6. Old Covenant – New Covenant

The Bible is divided into two sections, The Old Testament (old covenant) and the New Testament (new covenant). Jesus' birth and life begin with the NT books because it is Jesus who gave us the new covenant of grace. I will try to explain the two covenants *very* briefly: Very early in history God made a covenant with an imperfect but God-fearing couple, Abraham and Sarah. God's plan was that Abraham's descendants, the Jewish people, would become a nation that would carry God's Truth, Presence and Love. The Lord was clear that anyone in the world could join the Jewish faith and be forgiven of their sin, as long as they Loved and obeyed God. Abraham and Sarah were spiritually saved because of their *faith in God's mercy and grace*, and they obeyed God. The world continued to be very wicked, and the Jewish people needed guidance, so when Moses brought them out of Egypt, God gave them laws. The laws were a glaring reminder that they needed to always depend on God's mercy and forgiveness. God required that the Jewish people make certain animal sacrifices and other beautiful faith expressions. The blood sacrifices would *paint a picture of the Lamb of God, Jesus,* who would one day die to take the sins of the world upon Himself. If they would have faith in the mercy of the God who gave them the laws, and do what He commanded them, they would be saved. The prophets of the OT foretold the Messiah who would come from the Jewish bloodline to save the world. Jesus is the Messiah who came, died and was raised to life again. His Blood has given us the new covenant of grace! In the new covenant, our faith is in *Jesus* whose sacrifice on the cross takes away our guilt and gives us life. Whoever believes in Jesus and chooses to follow Him is born again *by the Holy Spirit* and becomes a child of God. The first four books of the NT are about the life of Jesus. Most of the other NT books and letters are about the early church or letters to them. John, one of Jesus' disciples wrote down the Revelation God gave him about the end times we are beginning to experience right now.

7. Renewing Your Mind

Jesus said that if you take to heart what He has said then you will believe the truth and the truth will set you free from the bondages of the enemy. The opposite is true as well. If we are more interested in what the world is telling us, it will take root in our minds and we can easily become ensnared by the devil. Renewing your mind is wanting to know Jesus so much that you spend time with Him allowing Him to explain His Words to you so you can receive them into your heart. You are not desiring information so much as you are desiring Jesus! Your mind is *changed* and *renewed* as He unwraps the Word to you and you believe it with your heart. His Word is Light, so as you receive His Word in His presence, darkness is driven out and His Light increases. You can see spiritually from a Kingdom perspective more and more. Reading and memorizing scripture is important in renewing your mind. Jesus told some prideful religious leaders that it wasn't in *searching* the scriptures that they have eternal life, but in coming to Jesus (who is the Word). So when you renew your mind through scripture you *must* come to Jesus and *He* will give you life through His Word. Your mind, will, and emotions will change and you won't be the same as you were!

8. The Written Word

God has given us His Words of life, written down by men, in a book of books we call the Bible. We also call it the Word. *The Bible* begins with the book of Genesis and ends with the Book of Revelation. *The Old Testament* begins with Genesis and ends with Malachi. *The New Testament* begins with Matthew and ends with Revelation. The Old Testament events happened before the New Testament. But the OT and NT sections in themselves are not always in chronological order. All the words in these books were inspired by God. They can be trusted and obeyed as Truth.

Beware! Some groups have published versions of "the Bible" that are *not* God's Word. They have changed the wording to suit their own sinful desires. A true <u>translation</u> will take the early manuscripts in Hebrew, Aramaic and Greek and translate them *accurately* so that the Biblical message is *correctly conveyed* in your own language. There are 66 books of the Bible beginning with Genesis and ending with Revelation. Any "Bible" that adds or subtracts from these books is false.

There are so many good translations available. Some are word-for-word translations and are more difficult for the average reader to understand but excellent for deep study. Others translate the thought or the meaning, are easier to read and still accurately portray the original text. And then there are some versions of the Bible called paraphrases that are great for devotional inspiration and encouragement. A paraphrase can give you a true message and can be anointed by the Spirit, but it isn't the closest translation from the earliest manuscripts. A good online Bible app has lots of different translations and paraphrases to choose from, and some of them allow you to *listen* to the Word.

9. Forgiveness Questions & Answers

Do you have to contact the people who wronged you in order to forgive them?
Not always. You must forgive them—between you and God. If they are a Brother or Sister in Christ and you know for a fact that they are holding something against you, it is likely that the Spirit will ask you to go and try to make things right. But if they don't know that you were offended by them it is *unlikely* that the Spirit will tell you to go to them. In every case, always ask Holy Spirit.

Do you have to contact all the people you may have offended or sinned against in your past and ask for forgiveness? I don't know if that's possible. But if you are sure you sinned against them, ask the Holy Spirit if you should contact them. If He says yes, wait in the peace and patience of the Holy Spirit for His timing and method. When you ask forgiveness, do it in a way that doesn't add another burden upon the person you "hurt." Don't talk deeply about it so as to raise emotions. Be sincere and very brief. Make it easy for them to accept your apology in their own way and then let it go. If they don't want to forgive you, just say from the bottom of your heart, "I hope some day you will be able to." And leave it at that. In this process, you must remain in the Spirit of grace so that you don't start taking on condemnation again. You have been forgiven by God, but God sometimes requires us to go ask someone to forgive us. Just follow the Spirit and stay in a state of rejoicing.

What if there is a restraining order against you? If there is a restraining order against you, do not break that order to ask someone for forgiveness. You will just have to ask God for forgiveness, pray for them and place the person in God's hands.

Do I ever have to forgive God? God doesn't sin, so the simple answer is no. You may have to come to grips with the fact that there are many things we will not understand on this earth. But we can be sure of this—that God is Love and He has always Loved you with a perfect and holy Love. He is so compassionate that He stores every tear you cry in a bottle in Heaven. God is deeply moved by your grief and loss and wants to comfort you and heal your broken heart.

10. Fasting Suggestions

I strongly suggest that if you have never fasted, do not set out to do an extreme fast the first several times. Just like any spiritual discipline we must *humble ourselves* like a child and grow up into it. The best way to do a fast is to hear from Holy Spirit Himself. But if you are having trouble hearing from Him, start slow by skipping one meal of your choice. Or you could fast by making a list of foods you crave the most and don't eat those over a certain period of time.

ABOUT THE AUTHOR

I was born and raised in Asuncion, Paraguay because my parents were missionaries. Paraguay was very closed to the Gospel when my parents first arrived. I was honored to watch them bring *the light of Jesus* to that beautiful country.

I met my wonderful husband, Mark, at Samford University in Birmingham, Alabama. We were married in 1978. After about five years of youth ministry, Mark served as lead pastor at a small church in Missouri while he was in graduate school. We returned to Alabama where he has served as an associate pastor for many years.

Mark and I have two wonderful daughters and sons-in-law who love God with all of their hearts. One of our greatest joys is being able to watch our precious grandchildren growing up. God has been so gracious to our family and we are eternally grateful!

As a child, I saw the land of my birth and childhood, Paraguay, come out of spiritual darkness into a place of greater freedom and light. Now I am watching a spiritual battle growing in intensity in the nation of my earthly citizenship, the USA. My passion is to learn to hear God's voice more clearly so that I don't miss His purpose and calling for my life. I am pressing in to know Jesus like never before. I believe very soon we will witness the greatest spiritual awakening our nation and our world has ever experienced and many will come to faith in Jesus! I desire to be fully awake, dressed, shining and seated at God's Table when He comes back for His Bride!

"Arise, shine, for your light has come,
and the glory of the Lord rises upon you."

Isaiah 60:1 NIV